Colección Támesis

SERIE A: MONOGRAFÍAS, 276

# A COMPANION TO
# GABRIEL GARCÍA MÁRQUEZ

RAYMOND LESLIE WILLIAMS

# A COMPANION TO
# GABRIEL GARCÍA MÁRQUEZ

TAMESIS

First published 2010
Tamesis, Woodbridge

Transferred to digital printing

ISBN 978–1–85566–191–2

Tamesis is an imprint of Boydell & Brewer Ltd
PO Box 9, Woodbridge, Suffolk IP12 3DF, UK
and of Boydell & Brewer Inc.
668 Mount Hope Ave, Rochester, NY 14604, USA
website: www.boydellandbrewer.com

The publisher has no responsibility for the continued existence or accuracy of
URLs for external or third-party internet websites referred to in this book,
and does not guarantee that any content on such websites is,
or will remain, accurate or appropriate.

A CIP catalogue record for this book is available
from the British Library

This publication is printed on acid-free paper

In memory of César Negrete, Germán Vargas
and Professor John S. Brushwood

# CONTENTS

# ABBREVIATIONS

| | |
|---|---|
| *Relato de un náufrago* | *Relato de un náufrago que estuvo diez días a la deriva en una balsa sin comer ni beber, que fue proclamado héroe de la patria, besado por las reinas de la belleza hecho rico por la publicidad, y luego aborrecido por el govierno olvidado para siempre. (The Story of a Shipwrecked Sailor)* |
| *El coronel* | *El coronel no tiene quien le escriba. (No One Writes to the Colonel)* |
| *Los funerales* | *Los funerales de la mamá grande. (Big Mama's Funeral)* |
| *Cien años* | *Cien años de soledad. (One Hundred Years of Solitude)* |
| *La increíble* | *La increíble y triste historia de la cándida Eréndira y de su abuela desalmada. (The Incredible and Sad Tale of Candid Erendira and her Heartless Grandmother)* |
| *El otoño* | *El otoño del patriarca. (The Autumn of the Patriarch)* |
| *Crónica* | *Crónica de una muerte anunciada. (Chronicle of a Death Foretold)* |
| *El amor* | *El amor en los tiempos del cólera. (Love in the Time of Cholera)* |
| *El general* | *El general en su laberinto. (The General in his Labyrinth)* |
| *Noticia* | *Noticia de un secuestro. (News of a Kidnapping)* |
| *Doce cuentos* | *Doce cuentos peregrinos. (Strange Pilgrims: Twelve Stories)* |
| *Del amor* | *Del amor y otros demonios. (Of Love and Other Demons)* |
| *Memoria* | *Memoria de mis putas tristes. (Memories of My Melancholy Whores)* |

# FOREWORD

Nobel Laureate Gabriel García Márquez has been one of the major novelists of the twentieth century in Latin America and has remained a writer
of continuing interest well into the twenty-first. From an early age, he was
interested in modernizing the traditional literature of his native Colombia,
and participating in the Western tradition of modernism that fascinated
an entire generation of writers across Latin America. An ardent reader of
William Faulkner, Ernest Hemingway, Franz Kafka, and Jorge Luis Borges
from an early age, he began writing his own version of Faulknerian fiction in
the 1950s, his 'cycle of Macondo' (a set of fictions centered on the invented
town of Macondo) culminating in the novel *Cien años de soledad* (1967).
That work has made his name virtually synonymous with 'magic realism'
throughout the world.

   García Márquez is also known as a public intellectual and political voice
and has been committed from an early age to social, economic, and political
change in Latin America. He stated in his Nobel Address that 'the interpretation of our reality through patterns not our own serves only to make us
ever more unknown, ever less free, ever more solitary'.[1] In his lifetime, his
understanding of these patterns has been shaped by his having experienced
the violence of the civil war in Colombia known as 'La Violencia': the dictatorships in Colombia of Gustavo Rojas Pinilla and in Venezuela of Marcos
Pérez Jiménez. Some of this political experience, as well as the presence of
the United Fruit Company in the coastal region of Colombia in the early
twentieth century, has, as we shall see, informed his writing.

   This book is intended to be the most complete study to date of the fiction
of García Márquez. It offers discussion and analysis of many facets of
his writing: as a traditionalist who draws from classic Western texts, as a

---

[1]   García Márquez, 'The Solitude of Latin America', tr. Marina Castañeda, in *Gabriel
García Márquez and the Powers of Fiction*, ed. Julio Ortega and Claudia Elliott (Austin TX
& London: University of Texas Press, 1988), 88–91 (89).

modernist committed to modernizing the conservative literary tradition of Colombia and Latin America, as an internationally recognized major writer of the 1960s Boom, as the key figure in popularizing what has been called 'magic realism', and, finally, as a modernist who has occasionally found uses for some of the strategies of the postmodern. In discussing the multiplicity of facets of his writing and career, my intention is to demonstrate how García Márquez is above all a highly accomplished modernist fiction writer who has successfully synthesized his political vision in his writing and drawn upon a vast array of cultural and literary traditions. In my discussion of his major themes, reference will be made to his progressive social vision and to the political interests implicit and explicit in his work.

We already have many critical studies on the work of García Márquez and many biographical accounts of his life. Early studies of the fiction that appeared in the late 1960s and early 1970s were published by Germán Carrillo, Biruté Ciplijauskaité, Carlos Fuentes, Ricardo Gullón, René Jara, Suzanne Jill Levine, Wolfgang Luchting, Josefina Ludmer, Jaime Mejía Duque, Klaus Muller-Bergh, Julio Ortega, Ángel Rama, Emir Rodríguez Monegal, and Mario Vargas Llosa. Vargas Llosa befriended García Márquez in Caracas in 1968, soon after the publication of *Cien años de soledad*, and not long after wrote the first in-depth biographical and critical study of the Colombian author. Early readings by Fuentes, Ludmer, Rama, and Rodríguez Monegal provided many initial insights. Later work in English that introduced García Márquez to a broader readership included studies by Jean Franco, George McMurray, and Harley Oberhelman. Since then, such accomplished scholars as Alicia Borinsky, Aníbal González, Roberto González Echevarría, and José Miguel Oviedo have published important essays. The most complete biography available in English is Gerald Martin's *Gabriel García Márquez: A Life*.

Having read and written about García Márquez for over three decades, I am aware how frequently I find myself (and other critics) noting, almost in passing, how he evokes 'medieval' codes of honor, 'medieval' religious practices, 'medieval' social interactions among characters, 'medieval' hierarchies, and so on. These passing remarks, however, are infrequently developed into a broader discussion of medieval attitudes in García Márquez's work. One noteworthy exception to this generalization is Christopher Little's article '*Eréndira* in the Middle Ages'. It is not my intention here to demonstrate the influence of medieval writing on the work of García Márquez. Rather, I shall consider how García Márquez exposes, in a critical way, the remnants of a medieval and feudal society that was exported to Latin America from the Iberian Peninsula and has survived in Latin America for over five centuries, being closely tied with the colonial legacy of the Americas. I am particularly interested in the presence of medieval Iberian and African cultures in the fiction of García Márquez.

Chapter 1 offers an overview of García Márquez's work in the context of his literary formation, as well as the social and political contexts that were important at each key moment of his life. Chapter 2 offers an analysis of the 'Macondo cycle' of his fiction, with special focus on his masterpiece *Cien años de soledad*. Chapter 3 analyzes his most politically oriented writings, in particular *El otoño del patriarca* (*The Autumn of the Patriarch*). The main focus of Chapter 4 is the novel *El amor en los tiempos del cólera* (*Love in the Time of Cholera*), while Chapter 5 discusses his most recent writing, including *Del amor y otros demonios* (*Of Love and Other Demons*) and *Memoria de mis putas tristes* (*Memories of my Melancholy Whores*).

This book does not have a formal conclusion because it does not have a formal 'thesis' to prove. Chapter 6 is an epilogue in which I offer a series of reflections on the previous five chapters and on issues that arise from those chapters, from the work of García Márquez, and from the critical work that has been published on him. As a part of these reflections, I reflect on some of the conversations García Márquez has had with other critics, with journalists, and with me, particularly as these conversations relate to the main topics of this book.

This study also explores the importance of some aspects of the non-literary in García Márquez's fiction, especially the oral tradition and the visual arts. In earlier publications, I began this discussion with some analysis of the oral tradition in *Cien años de soledad* and have interviewed García Márquez about the visual arts in his work.[2] The presence of the oral tradition and the visual arts in this work runs counter, in certain ways, to a purely 'literary' understanding of fiction and provides a more complete insight into both his strategies as a modernist with heterogeneous aesthetic interests and his social and political interests.

This study suggests critical revisionism in at least two general areas. With respect to literary history, it offers a broader context for García Márquez's formative years and for the already well documented Group of Barranquilla; I have reviewed recent research concerning the young writer's experience in Cartagena, taking into account personal interviews with intellectuals in Cartagena, and offer relatively new insights into the importance for the

---

2   Raymond L. Williams, 'The Visual Arts, the Poetization of Space and Writing: An Interview with Gabriel García Márquez', *Publications of the Modern Language Association of America*, 104/ii (1989), 131–40.

young writer of the Cartagena experience. With respect to the ubiquitous references to García Márquez as a 'magic realist', I attempt to offer a more precise analysis of facets often considered as 'magic realism' in the light of the writer's development as a committed modernist reared in a region identified as a 'primary oral culture'.[3]

I have attempted to avoid the use of specialized terminology. I do use key terms developed by Walter Ong, and their exact meaning deserves some explanation. Ong demonstrates that writing is not just a kind of complement to oral speech but a transformer of verbalization. In chapter 3 of his *Orality and Literacy*, entitled 'Some psychodynamics of orality', he outlines in detail the characteristics of primary oral cultures. Following Ong's model, I use the terms 'primary oral culture' and 'oral culture' interchangeably.

I have chosen to use the Spanish 'Costa' for the Caribbean coastal region of Colombia. In English, 'coastal region' could give the false impression that it included only the coastal area itself. In fact, the departments of the Costa are numerous and cover much territory inland from Barranquilla and Cartagena. García Márquez is considered a *costeño* in Colombia, but his native Aracataca is actually inland.

My work on García Márquez over the years has been supported by numerous institutions and individuals. Fulbright Grants in Colombia gave me the opportunity to do research on Colombian literature, and during two of my Fulbright-supported residencies I met with García Márquez. Research funds and a teaching release provided by the Executive Vice-Chancellor of the University of California Riverside, Ellen Wartella, were important for the early stages of this book. A sabbatical granted by the Dean of the College of Humanities Arts and Social Sciences, Stephen Cullenberg, and the Chair of the Department of Hispanic Studies, David Herzberger, allowed me to complete the writing. I am grateful for the efficient work of research assistants Filiberto Mares, Lila McDowell, and George Carlsen, as well as the reading of the manuscript by Darline Miller, Rachel Neff, Amanda Parker, and Pamela Williams. I am grateful for the support, exceptional patience, and professionalism of Elspeth Ferguson of Tamesis. This book is written in memory of César Negrete, a *compañero* in the Cabina 11 of the University of Concepción, a brilliant intellectual and exceptionally generous person, as well as committed socialist, who was my first intellectual interlocutor in the Spanish language when I studied there in 1970. César's first employment was with the government of Salvador Allende, and he disappeared immediately

---

[3]   See Walter Ong, *Orality and Literacy: The Technologizing of the Word,* New Accents (London: Methuen, 1982).

after the military coup by Augusto Pinochet in 1973. I also write this book in memory of Germán Vargas and Professor John S. Brushwood, whose generosity, goodwill, and mentorship in the 1980s and 1990s made it possible. A special thanks also to Nigel Griffin, whose suggestions and contributions have vastly improved this book.

# 1

## García Márquez, the Modernists
## and the Boom

Gabriel García Márquez is one of the major modernist writers of the West in the twentieth century. He belongs to a generation of Latin American novelists who were devotees of William Faulkner and other modernists; excited by reading the modernists of North America and Europe, these Latin American writers conceived the bold ambition of modernizing Latin American literature. Along with the Cuban Alejo Carpentier, the Guatemalan Miguel Angel Asturias, the Mexican Carlos Fuentes, the Peruvian Mario Vargas Llosa, the Argentine Julio Cortázar, and others, García Márquez has committed a lifetime to this project.

In addition to the desire to be modern, García Márquez has consistently pursued other interests. First, he has been concerned with the social, economic, and political realities of his homeland of Colombia and of Latin America as a whole. Second, he was reared in an oral culture and has often explored ways of incorporating the oral tradition into his writing. Third, he has been drawn to the visual arts and has found innovative ways of utilizing them in his fiction, all of which is structured around central visual images. Finally, he has been consistently engaged in exploring, questioning, and satirizing the remnants of medieval and feudal societies that still survive in Latin America some five centuries after the arrival of the Spanish and Portuguese colonizers. A noteworthy aspect of the medieval in Latin America that has interested García Márquez is its hybrid nature, with the presence of African, Arabic, and indigenous cultures in this region.

Gabriel José García Márquez was born in Aracataca, Colombia, in 1927.[1] The son of telegraphist Gabriel Eligio García and Luisa Santiaga Márquez, he was reared from an early age by his grandparents, Colonel Nicolás

---

[1]   In the early stages of his career, García Márquez claimed to have been born in 1928 and this date has appeared in many scholarly studies, including some of my own early publications on the writer. In recent years, I have seen written documentation and spoken with the writer's mother; both confirm the correct year of his birth as 1927.

Márquez and Tranquilina Iguarán, in Aracataca after his parents left him in their care when his father took a job elsewhere. Both grandparents were essential contributors to García Márquez's later writing. His grandfather had been a hero in Colombia's civil wars and was a prominent member of the Liberal Party.

From the beginning of his career to today, García Márquez has often noted the importance of his grandmother and his aunts in his formation as a story-teller, claiming that he had learned everything that was important to him by the time he was eight years old. He has reiterated the importance of his grandmother's and aunts' stories, from the early *Cien años de soledad* (*One Hundred Years of Solitude*) to the later novel *Del amor y otros demonios* (*Of Love and Other Demons*). In addition, the Caribbean region of Colombia was still rich with a lively and vital oral tradition inherited from Africa, Spain, and indigenous groups in Colombia.

After his childhood years in Aracataca, García Márquez went inland with a scholarship for secondary school at the Colegio Nacional de Internos de Zipaquirá, some thirty miles from Bogotá; his fiction is replete with the knowledge he gained about the Catholic church, both from this experi-ence and by virtue of having attended Catholic mass as a child. In 1946 he completed his secondary-school studies and enrolled in the law school of the Universidad Nacional in Bogotá in January of 1948. Having little interest in the study of law compared to his passion for literature, he pursued this discipline primarily to please his parents.

During these adolescent years, García Márquez became an enthusiastic and ambitious reader of classic and modern literature written in Europe, North America, Asia, Latin America in general, and Colombia in particular. He also began writing his first stories. Some of this amateurish fiction appeared in local newspapers. The Colombian writer Eduardo Zalamea Borda had written an editorial in the nationally distributed newspaper, *El Espectador*, challenging the youth of García Márquez's generation to come forth and demonstrate that they did indeed possess some creative talent. García Márquez responded to the challenge, and the result was his first published story, 'La tercera resig-nación' ('The Third Resignation'), which appeared in that newspaper in 1947.

In this story, García Márquez begins to explore ways to write outside the limits of traditional realist fiction. He tells the story of a man who might be dead, but who lives in some gray area between life and death. The peculiarity of this 'living death' shows García Márquez's early attempt to write some-thing along the lines of what he had read in Kafka. García Márquez demon-strates an interest in escaping the limits of the rational, in creating universal human experience for his readers (rather than descriptions of local events), and in ignoring political boundaries. Unlike Kafka, however, he occasionally falls into directly stating his goals rather than creating a compelling story. The other stories written during this early period from 1947 to 1952 are similar both in their accomplishments and defects. In 'La otra costilla de la muerte' ('The Other Side of Death'), the young author experiments with narrative point of view. In these early stories, he further experiments with various kinds of narrative situations: the use of three blind narrators, a dead narrator, and a plural 'we' narrator representing three characters. He also employs innovative concepts of time and space. While he is clearly intrigued with the idea of making time stop, at this point he is not yet capable of actually creating this experience for the reader. In the story 'Eva está dentro de su gato' ('Eva is inside Her Cat'), the protagonist lives in a fictional world in which all 'dimensions' have been eliminated. She lives in a world of 'death' that is, simultaneously, somehow 'real'. After recalling that spirits can be reincarnated in other living bodies, she decides to be reborn in her cat. The next level of the inexplicable takes place when she discovers that neither her cat nor her house exists any longer. In the end, the narrator is as confused as the character about what has transpired, and offers no clarification for the reader. These early pieces are the work of a young writer searching for literary tools beyond the rational; though flawed, they do manage to portray an absurd and irrational world.

García Márquez's most overt exercises in practising the techniques of modernism are the stories 'Diálogo del espejo' ('Dialogue with a Mirror') and 'Tubal-Caín forja una estrella' ('Tubal-Cain Forges a Star'). In the first of the two, a businessman rises early in the morning and prepares for a boring day at the office. What appears at first to be merely a typical piece of *ennui* literature of the postwar period proves to be also an early experiment with a double figure explored by use of a mirror. In 'Tubal-Caín forja una estrella', García Márquez uses free association to create wild associations, even though the story does not actually reach any coherent conclusion.

García Márquez experiments with first-person narrators in the stories 'Ojos de perro azul' ('Eyes of a Blue Dog', which became the title of a volume of these early stories published years later, after the writer had become a celebrity) and 'Alguien desordena estas rosas' ('Someone Disorders these Roses'). The first of these involves a situation that is once again reminiscent of French existentialist literature of the 1950s: two characters are hopelessly isolated within the confines of a room. The male narrator observes a nude woman, and a minimalist description of their surroundings is accompanied by a cold and distant conversation between the two. The title of the story refers to the man's dream of a woman whose eyes are astonishing. The couple continue seeing each other, not in the 'real' world of the room in which they are isolated, but in their dreams. This story, like some of the others, crosses the line of thought-provoking ambiguity to be simply confusing and, in the end, is not of the quality that has characterized almost all the work García Márquez has produced throughout his professional career.

Not all of the stories of his late adolescent and amateur period are as weak as this one. In fact, in 'Alguien desordena estas rosas', he exhibits some of the talent that will surface in his professional career. As Machado de Assis had already done in Brazil, and as Juan Rulfo was to do several years later in Mexico in 1955, García Márquez here uses a first-person narrator who is dead. This is one of the few early stories to use the real empirical world, rather than the fantastic, as its point of departure. The narrator's statement in the first line of the story that he will carry flowers to a tomb is conveyed in the voice of a small boy who had died many years before. The house in which he lives has a small chapel and each Sunday a breeze places flowers on the altar. It is the spirit of the boy and not the wind that moves the flowers each Sunday. One can imagine a connection between this story and the oral tales García Márquez had heard as a child from his aunts and grandmother. Thus, this story can be seen as a transition between the early stories of the horror-fantasy mode and the later stories of the Macondo cycle. In fact, it was published in 1952 during the period when García Márquez was already advanced in his Macondo writing, and it has an identifiable Faulknerian tone.

Two very similar stories, 'Nabo el negro que hizo esperar a los ángeles' ('Nabo, the Black who Made the Angels Wait') and 'Amargura para tres sonámbulos' ('Bitterness for Three Sleepwalkers'), also function within empirical reality. 'Nabo' has many overtones of Faulkner; its ambience is similar to that of the Deep South of the United States, with a main character who is black and whose job it is to take care of the horses on the plantation and to play music to entertain a mentally retarded girl. The presence of several incredible details foreshadows the Macondo fiction and what will soon be identified by some critics as magic realism. 'Amargura para tres sonámbulos' is a similar case.

The lives of most Colombians, including García Márquez, changed dramatically in April 1948. The assassination of Jorge Eliécer Gaitán, the populist presidential candidate of the Liberal Party, led to an outburst of violence on the streets of Bogotá. These events set the stage for a civil war in Colombia that took place from 1948 to 1956. Identified as La Violencia, it was fundamentally an armed conflict between the Liberal Party and the Conservative Party.[2]

---

[2]  I use the dates 1948 to 1956 as an introductory simplification of the history of La Violencia. Numerous historical studies in recent years confirm that the armed conflict

The intensity of the conflict in Bogotá and the surrounding region, which resulted in the burning of his room in a boarding house, led García Márquez to move back to the more peaceful Caribbean coast. There he pursued his law studies on a part-time basis, his career as a journalist for economic survival, and his interest in becoming a fiction writer as his real passion and desired vocation. He first moved to the Caribbean colonial port city of Cartagena, then to the larger and more modern port city of Barranquilla. His residence in Cartagena (1947–48 and again in 1951) was a key stage in García Márquez's formation as a literary modernist; later, this city was the setting for a few passages of *El otoño de patriarca* (*The Autumn of the Patriarch*) and for the setting of most of *El amor en los tiempos del cólera* (*Love in the Time of Cholera*) and *Del amor y otros demonios* (*Of Love and Other Demons*). The importance of his apprenticeship in Cartagena has often been overlooked by scholars and critics.[3] Later, in Barranquilla (1949–50), he socialized regularly with Germán Vargas, Alvaro Cepeda Samudio, and Alfonso Fuenmayor, who would become lifelong friends and would appear as characters towards the end of *Cien años de soledad*.[4] These friends were of approximately the same age and had in common the fact that they were avid readers of the kind of writers soon to be recognized as García Márquez's modernist masters: William Faulkner, Franz Kafka, Jorge Luis Borges, Virginia Woolf, John Dos Passos, and the like. These four young intellectuals in Barranquilla shared books and spent endless hours at their main meeting places: a bookstore and a bar.

In this period on the Caribbean coast, the two most meaningful discoveries for García Márquez were the writings of Faulkner and Kafka. These two writers served as lifetime models, for entirely different reasons.[5] Faulkner

---

actually predated 9 April 1948 and continued after the peace agreements of 1956. In-depth analyses have found the roots of this conflict in the Colombian society of the 1930s and have demonstrated that the armed guerrilla warfare of the 1960s and 1970s was a continuation of many of the conflicts of La Violencia in the 1950s. See Vernon Lee Fluharty, *Dance of the Millions: Military Rule and the Social Revolution in Colombia, 1930–1956* (Pittsburgh PA: University of Pittsburgh Press, 1957).

3    The most informed and complete recent study on García Márquez's years in Cartagena is Jorge García Usta, *García Márquez en Cartagena: sus inicios literarios*, Los Tres Mundos (Bogotá: Planeta Colombiana, 2007).

4    See the interview by Ernesto González Bermejo, 'And Now, Two Hundred Years of Solitude', tr. Gene H. Bell-Villada, in *Conversations with Gabriel García Márquez*, ed. Gene H. Bell-Villada (Jackson MS: University of Mississippi Press, 2006), 3–30, That interview, originally published in *Triunfo* (Madrid), 25/cdxli (1971), 12–18, is also reprinted in *García Márquez habla de García Márquez*, ed. Alfonso Rentería Mantilla (Bogotá: Rentería, 1979), 49–64.

5    García Márquez has related in numerous interviews and writings that it was upon

was the model for the use of narrative point of view and structure, Kafka the model for uninhibited invention. As several critics have observed, García Márquez's first novel, *La hojarasca* (1955, *Leafstorm*), contained an organizational structure very similar to Faulkner's *As I Lay Dying*. In his Nobel Prize acceptance speech in 1982, García Márquez referred to Faulkner as his mentor and was acutely aware of following in the footsteps of his master, for Faulkner had received this recognition in 1949.

During these crucial formative years in Barranquilla in the late 1940s and early 1950s, García Márquez was engaged in an ongoing dialogue on modernity and literary modernism with his three friends and with two mentor figures who often joined them – the writer José Félix Fuenmayor and the Catalan intellectual Ramón Vinyes. Years later, this group (García Márquez, Vargas, Cepeda Samudio, and Alfonso Fuenmayor) became known as the Group of Barranquilla. In their respective adult lives, each of the members of this informal 'Group of Barranquilla' participated in the culture of modernity in his own way: García Márquez as a world-class modernist writer; Cepeda Samudio as an accomplished and greatly respected modernist writer and the author of one novel, *La casa grande* (1962);[6] Vargas as a journalist, promoter of modernist literature in Colombia, literary critic and lifetime mentor and friend of García Márquez; Fuenmayor as a journalist and well-known writer in Colombia.

German Vargas and the French scholar Jacques Gilard have been the main promoters of the idea of the Group of Barranquilla as the exclusive formative influence on García Márquez's work, and there is much merit to their claim.[7] Nevertheless, the young intellectual's readings in Cartagena, as well as his interaction with the journalist and editor Clemente Manuel Zabala, the writer and painter Héctor Rojas Herazo, and the poet and teacher Gustavo Ibarra Merlano were also significant for his early literary education. All three were older than García Márquez, and always more mentor figures than peers. Two months before García Márquez's arrival in Cartagena in 1947, a new news-

---

reading the first page of Kafka's *Metamorphosis* (upon seeing the transformation of the protagonist into an insect), that he decided to become a writer. Clearly, the writer's ability to invent was extremely attractive to him.

   [6]   Several studies have pointed to the fact that the rise of the modern novel in Colombia was signaled by the publication of three key modernist novels, all written in the Faulknerian mode: *La hojarasca* (1955) by García Márquez; *La casa grande* (1962) by Alvaro Cepeda Samudio; and *Respirando el verano* (1962) by Héctor Rojas Herazo. See especially Seymour Menton, *La novela colombiana: Planetas y satélites*, Crítica Literaria (Bogotá: Plaza & Janés, 1978).

   [7]   On the Group of Barranquilla, see especially Jacques Gilard, 'García Márquez, le Groupe de Barranquilla, et Faulkner', *Caravelle*, 27 (1976), 123–46.

paper of liberal tendencies, *El Universal*, had been founded. Its editor, Clemente Manuel Zabala, hired García Márquez and became the first editor of his journalistic writings; over his career, García Márquez has made numerous references to the red ink of Zabala's editorial pen on all the first drafts of the journalistic pieces he published in *El Universal*.

Zabala, Rojas Herazo, and Ibarra Merlano were also García Márquez's literary mentors during the key period in which he wrote much of the first draft for the book originally carrying the title of *La casa* and later rewritten and published under the title *La hojarasca* (*Leafstorm*).[8] In an interview published in 1971, García Márquez stated that he started the book at the age of eighteen, in 1945, approximately two years before arriving in Cartagena: 'and at the time it was called *The house*, because I thought the story would never go outside the Buendía home'.[9] In Cartagena, as he continued writing this book, he regularly read passages from the lengthy and ambitious manuscript to Zabala, Rojas Herazo, and Ibarra Merlano for their reactions and comments.

Rojas Herazo was a particularly knowledgeable and devoted follower of Faulkner, and eventually published a trilogy of novels written in the Faulknerian mode: *Respirando el verano* (1962), *En noviembre llega el arzobispo* (1967), and *Celia se pudre* (1985).[10] Ibarra Merlano was a poet and teacher of classical languages and literatures. García Márquez clearly was reading Faulkner in Cartagena under the tutelage of Rojas Herazo, and classical Greek writers under that of Ibarra Merlano, contrary to the claims of some scholars that García Márquez discovered Faulkner in Barranquilla. Zabala, Rojas Herazo, and Ibarra Merlano have been identified as the 'Group of Cartagena' by one Colombian researcher, and this critic has made a convincing case for the importance of Zabala for the journalistic style of García Márquez, of Rojas Herazo for García Márquez's early readings of Faulkner, and of Ibarra Merlano for the use of Sophocles in *La hojarasca*.[11] The same critic also

---

8  In his *García Márquez en Cartagena*, García Usta provides ample documentation to show that García Márquez had written a very large portion of the manuscript entitled 'La casa' when he was in Cartagena.

9  See González Bermejo, 'And Now, Two Hundred Years', 15.

10  The three novels by Rojas Herazo are well written Faulkner-type novels that are unfortunately relatively unknown outside Colombia. There is a brief analysis of each in Raymond L. Williams, *The Colombian Novel, 1844–1987* (London & Austin TX: University of Texas Press, 1991).

11  In *García Márquez en Cartagena*, García Usta makes direct connections between the presence of Greek writers in García Márquez and his friendship with Ibarra Merlano.

emphasizes the influence of the *greguería* of Ramón Gómez de la Serna on García Márquez's early and later writing.[12]

Immediately after this Cartagena stage, the next period of García Márquez's life was with the Group of Barranquilla. The broad sociocultural backdrop for these two groups' embrace of the aesthetics of cultural modernism, as well as their promotion of it in Colombia, was that nation's deep-seated cultural conservatism. The literary icons in Colombia in the late 1940s were still the nineteenth-century Romantic novelist Jorge Isaacs (author of *María*, the 1867 Romantic classic of Latin America), and the poet and novelist José Eustacio Rivera (author of the 'novel of the land' *La vorágine*, 1924), as well as Colombian poets of the 1940s and 1950s. Many Colombians viewed these poets as the inheritors of the grand tradition of Spanish poetry and, more specifically, as the inheritors of the 'Generation of 1927' in Spain. In Colombia, these poets were known as the 'Piedra y cielo' movement.

For García Márquez, his mentors in Cartagena, and his friends in Barranquilla, these three dominant national icons were exhausted, tired, and basically fraudulent when compared with the cultural modernism that had arisen in Europe and the United States since the 1920s. Colombian culture urgently needed change, renovation, and innovation; these young writers and artists were increasingly excited about being a part of that change, and even promoting it. When García Márquez moved from Barranquilla back to Bogotá in 1954, he soon found a venue to place his modernist agenda into practice on the national front: the cultural magazine *Mito*. In the pages of *Mito*, García Márquez and the poet Alvaro Mutis, as well as other intellectuals and writers of their generation, promoted cultural modernism in general and a radically new writing in Colombia specifically. *Mito* published a broad range of texts by the leading intellectuals and writers in Europe, the United States, and Latin America, becoming the most influential cultural organ in Colombia in the 1950s, in many ways comparable to Fuentes's cultural magazine founded the same year (1955) in Mexico, the *Revista Mexicana de Literatura*.

## Modernism and García Márquez

The aesthetics of modernism that attracted García Márquez were not learned from readings in cultural or aesthetic theory, although he was aware of various cultural manifestos that represented a part of what today is considered 'theory'.

---

[12] García Usta offers a lengthy explanation and analysis of the *greguería* and the work of García Márquez.

Instead, much of his understanding of modernist aesthetics came directly from creative writers. In Faulkner and Kafka, García Márquez perceived and appreciated a fundamental shift in ideas about what was important in a work of fiction. A basic, longstanding assumption of the realist tradition was that the novelist, as a privileged entity more informed and rational than his or her readers, used narrative to communicate the very nature of empirical reality, as well as the details of it, and thus could provide an understanding of this reality. A corollary assumption was that an identifiable 'empirical reality' can, in fact, be described as the totality of what is real. With the rise of the modernist novel and modernist art, these assumptions underwent radical reconsideration. This led the modernist novelist to use techniques such as multiple perspectives, multiple voices, or multiple narrators to question the very idea of one singular understanding of empirical reality, and also to explore other facets of human experience (such as the unconscious and the subconscious) that were not considered a part of 'empirical' reality. This new aesthetic, which García Márquez learned primarily from Faulkner, but also from Borges and Kafka, fascinated the young writer. He has stated on many occasions that it was upon discovery of Faulkner, Borges, and Kafka that he decided to become a writer.[13]

'Modernity is the transient, the fleeting, the contingent; it is one half of art, the other being the eternal and the immutable', Charles Baudelaire had declared in his essay 'The Painter in Modern Life', published in 1863. This contention articulates what García Márquez, his peers in Barranquilla, and an entire generation of Latin American writers desired to find: ways to represent the eternal and the immutable along with the transient, the fleeting, and the contingent.

The commonly accepted tenets of literary modernism that García Márquez discovered primarily by means of reading Faulkner, Borges, and Kafka involve formal innovation (fragmentation, the inclusion of multiple points of view, and the use of neologisms), a breakdown in the nineteenth-century insistence on causality, and an unceasing search for order within a seemingly chaotic world. The British scholar Raymond Williams has questioned European modernism because it gives preference to some writers 'for their denaturalizing of language, their break with the allegedly prior view that language

---

[13] On the surface, García Márquez's declarations about the importance of Kafka, Faulkner, and Borges in his formation as a writer may seem contradictory, for he has claimed, in different contexts, that each was the key to his decision to become a writer. He has been consistent, however, on the importance of all three as writers who freely invented reality rather than merely imitating it.

is either a clear, transparent glass or mirror, and for making abruptly apparent in the very texture of their narratives the problematic status of the author and his authority'.[14] He claims that literary modernism is uncritical of the status quo and has lost the 'anti-bourgeois stance' of some earlier kinds of European literature. This charge, however, certainly is not true for García Márquez and many Latin American fiction writers of his generation. The strong tradition of neo-Marxist thought, as well as the presence of Sartre in the experience of this generation, made this group of writers very different from European modernists, for they have been social critics of consequence.

This European and Anglo-American literary and cultural modernism also became associated with subjective relativism.[15] With this association, literary modernism had increasingly less to do with the world of ideas which may be objectively known, and more to do with what really interested García Márquez: an understanding of the world that can be known and experienced through individual consciousness or other subjective ways.[16] His formative years involved an exploration of many forms of the subjective beyond those found in his key writers. While working at the newspaper *El Universal* in Cartagena, he was fascinated by the news that came from the international press agencies concerning the bizarre or strange. Thus, those surprising and seemingly inexplicable or impossible events or people, such as flying saucers, were often the subject of his commentary in the column he called *La Jirafa* in *El Universal*. Another exploration of a very different type, on the surface, was of the *greguería* (a brief and surprising narrative) of the Spanish writer Ramón Gómez de la Serna (1888–1963). What the surprising bits of news had in common with the *greguería* was the often shocking lack of logic found in this genre. Consequently, García Márquez was also an ardent reader of Ripley's *Believe it or not*. All in all, García Márquez's interests in the unusual or uncanny have many aspects that caution against the reduction of his work to 'magic realism'.

A first generation of modernists in Latin America, consisting of relatively ignored avant-garde novelists of the 1920s and 1930s, such as the Mexican Jaime Torres Bodet, the Chilean Vicente Huidobro, the Peruvian Martín Adán, and others, were as fully committed to this modernist aesthetic agenda as was García Márquez. Torres Bodet's *Primero de enero* (*The First of January*, 1934),

---

[14]  See Raymond Williams, *The Politics of Modernism* (London: Verso, 1989), 33.

[15]  Steven Connor, *Postmodernist Culture: An Introduction to the Theories of the Contemporary* (Oxford: Basil Blackwell, 1989; 2nd edn 1997), 107.

[16]  In chapter 2, I discuss the many ways García Márquez explores beyond the rational without recurring necessarily to the formulas of 'magic realism'.

for example, was just one prominent celebration of subjectivist relativism. In the pioneer fiction of these novelists, empirical or 'objective' reality became a subjectivized part of each individual's psychological experience. The very 'father-figure' of the Group of Barranquilla, a relatively unknown and unrecognized writer interested in modernist aesthetics, José Félix Fuenmayor, published two novels that were noteworthy departures from the conservative, realist mode that dominated the literary scene in Colombia in the 1920s: *Cosme* (1927) and *Una triste aventura de catorce sabios* (1928). The presence of José Félix Fuenmayor and Ramón Vinyes in Barranquilla, as well as the three other mentors of the group of Cartagena during García Márquez's formative years, help explain how a relatively uneducated and provincial adolescent aspiring to be a writer found an way into modernist aesthetics. He did this while living in what was essentially a third-world, conservative and, with respect to avant-garde literature, a backward nation. An amateur poet and essayist, Vinyes had emigrated from Barcelona to Barranquilla, where he had founded the cultural magazine *Voces* (1917–20), which made its readers more attuned to the European avant-garde than intellectuals in the cultural and political epicenter of Bogotá, which had no comparable magazine.

García Márquez has recognized his profound debts to Vinyes as the mentor figure to whom he listened carefully as a reader and emerging writer in the late 1940s in Barranquilla. Along with José Félix Fuenmayor, Vinyes was what García Márquez has described as an 'itinerant' member of the Group of Barranquilla. When the group met together at the Japy Café, Vinyes often presided over the gathering of young intellectuals, offering them his literary insights and the wisdom of his experience. On one occasion, when García Márquez expressed his concern that perhaps Faulkner might be nothing more than an accomplished rhetorician, Vinyes assured the young writer that this was not true by replying: 'No se preocupe Gabito . . . Si Faulkner estuviera en Barranquilla estaría en esta mesa' ('Don't worry. If Faulkner were in Barranquilla, he would be at this table').[17]

García Márquez's most memorable conversation with Vinyes – one that he remembers as a watershed moment of his life – was when he appeared before Vinyes, opened his briefcase, and pulled out the manuscript of a rough draft of a first novel and gave it to Vinyes 'with the audacity I would never be capable of again at any crossroads in life or death'. After reading it with some interest, Vinyes advised García Márquez never again to show his rough drafts to anyone, and then offered some encouraging remarks about the quality of

---

[17] García Márquez, *Vivir para contarla* (Bogotá: Norma, 2002), 140; *Living to Tell the Tale*, tr. Edith Grossman (New York: Knopf, 2003), 125.

this first novelistic effort. Vinyes left Barranquilla for Barcelona permanently in 1950, at the age of sixty-eight.[18]

Besides the Japy Café, a regular meeting place for the Group of Barranquilla was a bookstore called the Librería Mundo. This was the venue for many of the group's readings. On the advice of Vinyes and José Felix Fuenmayor, the group read a wide variety of emerging writers from Latin America and beyond. They ordered shipments of books from Buenos Aires, the publishing capital of Latin America, getting hold of books of writers not easily acquired in Colombia at the time – such as the Argentine Julio Cortázar, the Uruguayan Felisberto Hernández, and the Spaniard Arturo Barea. In addition, they received translations into Spanish of writers such as Graham Greene, Virginia Woolf, and William Irish.

By the time Vinyes left the innocent young García Márquez behind, the Colombian was an informed and committed modernist in the making. At this time, a second generation of Latin American modernist novelists had just emerged quietly but steadily throughout the Americas. Borges had published his literary revolution in the form of the book of short fiction *Ficciones* in 1944, the book which had more impact on the renovation and modernization of Hispanic letters than any other single work written in Spanish in the twentieth century. A number of high modernist novels then appeared in the second half of the 1940s, signalling not merely an important change but a paradigm shift: the Guatemalan Miguel Angel Asturias published his now classic modernist text *El Señor Presidente* (*The President*) in 1946, and this was followed by the Mexican Agustín Yáñez's *Al filo del agua* (*At the Edge of the Storm*, 1947), the Argentine Leopoldo Marechal's *Adán Buenosayres* (1948), and the Cuban Alejo Carpentier's *El reino de este mundo* (*The Kingdom of this World*, 1949). These novels, along with Borges's *Ficciones*, were a reaffirmation of the right of Latin American novelists to use their imagination. For those who, like García Márquez, had felt the heavy burden of the realist tradition and conservative cultural values in their respective nations, this was freedom.[19]

For a young writer aspiring to join in the festivities of modernism that García Márquez had first discovered in the cafes and bars of Cartagena and Barranquilla, the 1950s were an interesting and dynamic time that brought

---

[18] García Márquez provides anecdotes about the importance of Vinyes in various parts of *Vivir para contarla*.

[19] John S. Brushwood discusses the importance of the reaffirmation of the right of invention for Spanish American novelists in the 1940s, 1950s and 1960s in various chapters of *The Spanish American Novel: A Twentieth-century Survey* (London & Austin TX: University of Texas Press, 1975).

the aesthetics of modernism to the forefront of Latin American literature. His early fictions – the short stories of *Los funerales de la mamá grande* (*Big Mama's funeral*) and the short novels *La hojarasca* (*Leafstorm*), *La mala hora* (*In Evil Hour*) and *El coronel no tiene quien le escriba* (*No One Writes to the Colonel*) – were his first works to explore the challenges both of embracing the aesthetics of modernism and of promoting progressive social change.

## Society and *cultura*

Having been born in the Caribbean region of Colombia, which had been dominated by the United Fruit Company during the first quarter of the twentieth century, and having witnessed the civil war of La Violencia, García Márquez was well positioned – seemingly destined – for a career as a writer with a highly developed sense of political awareness. Even when his fictions were not explicitly political in their themes, his commitment to social, economic, and political change was in place: he and his generation of writers, most prominently his friends Belisario Betancur (President of Colombia from 1984 to 1989) and Carlos Fuentes, were firmly committed to the idea that *cultura* (in the broad European sense of *cultura* as culture and education) can change society and that it is, in fact, a key force for social change. García Márquez collaborated with both Betancur and Fuentes on a variety of cultural fronts in which the objectives were political and the assumption was that *cultura* could contribute to progressive change.

In the 1950s, García Márquez and his generation of writers and intellectuals throughout Latin America were also enthusiastic and dedicated readers of Jean-Paul Sartre, and, consequently, committed to the idea of the writer as an *engagé*. Their generation was well aware of the writings of neo-Marxist thinkers, such as the influential Peruvian essayist José Carlos Mariátegui. Since the 1920s, Latin American writers had used literature to portray the social and economic inequities of Latin American society and to reveal its corrupt and undemocratic political systems. They also initiated a search back to the roots of neocolonial society: medieval Spain and the Spanish colonial empire. Thus, writers of the 1930s and 1940s, using the methods of stark realism, had described the injustices suffered by indigenous groups in works now categorized as *literatura indigenista*, including such classics as *Huasipungo* (1934) by the Ecuadorian Jorge Icaza. In Colombia, the prolific José Antonio Osorio Lizarazo – widely read during García Márquez's youth – published a series of novels from the 1930s to the 1950s in defense of the urban proletariate. Given literary precedents such as these, it is logical that

García Márquez and his generation were favorably disposed towards the writings of Sartre on social issues. In García Márquez's journalism and essays, he has been consistently critical of the conservative and elitist political models inherited from Spain. A review of his writing in the late 1940s and 1950s in Cartagena, Barranquilla, and Bogotá reveals an intellectual firmly aligned with the political Left and supportive of progressive social and political thinkers throughout Latin America. Living under the dictatorships of Gustavo Rojas Pinilla in Colombia and Marcos Pérez Jiménez in Venezuela had confirmed this stance. Indeed, after the experience of the 1950s of living under and witnessing these repressive regimes, García Márquez was well prepared later to write his novel portraying and denouncing such dictators, *El otoño del patriarca* (*The Autumn of the Patriarch*).

## The European experience

One dramatic personal experience of the dictatorship in Colombia that affected García Márquez directly took place in December of 1955, soon after he was sent to Paris by the newspaper *El Espectador* as a foreign correspondent. After arriving in Paris, the dictator Rojas Pinilla, in an act of political censorship, closed *El Espectador*. As a direct consequence of this act, García Márquez first worked for a new newspaper, *El Independiente*, but eventually became unemployed in Paris, and experienced extreme poverty. He had been sent a return ticket, but decided to use that money instead as a type of 'grant' to write his novel based on an anecdote he had heard from his girlfriend Mercedes Barcha in the town of Sucre in Colombia. Lampoons had mysteriously appeared on the walls of the town, making various kinds of personal and political accusations. García Márquez wrote the draft for a novel, *La mala hora*, based on this bizarre series of events; this was his first project in Paris, even though the novel did not appear in print in its final form for several years. As he was writing *La mala hora*, another separate story grew from it, and this eventually became the work later published under the title *El coronel no tiene quién le escriba*.

In 1957, the same year he was writing *El coronel no tiene quién le escriba*, García Márquez and his friend Plinio Apuleyo Mendoza took a car trip across the Iron Curtain to East Germany, the first of two such trips into Eastern Europe. They were a revelation about socialism as it was practiced by the Soviets and their satellites, and they were undoubtedly an important factor in García Márquez's later political vision as an open-minded and progressive intellectual. On the first trip, he and Mendoza attempted to be objective and also to enjoy themselves in Berlin, but their visit to a restaurant on the first night was deeply depressing, as was the rest of their brief stay. García Márquez remembered this trip as his introduction to the 'proletariate of Eastern Europe', and he found it inexplicable that, although the workers were in charge of the modes of production, they were still visibly unhappy. On the second occasion, he took a train to Moscow and wrote about his impressions of the people and places he observed. He visited the tomb of Stalin in the Kremlin and was impressed with the very fine hands of the former dictator, a visual image that appeared years later in *El otoño del patriarca*. In his travels through the other Eastern European nations, the city that impressed him the most was Prague, and he was intrigued to discover that the people of Czechoslovakia, as it then was, identified themselves with the nation of Colombia.

After returning to Paris, and making yet another trip, this time to Moscow and to Hungary, García Márquez settled in London and began writing some of the short fiction that eventually appeared as *Los funerales de la mamá grande*.[20]

### Return to the Americas

In 1958 García Márquez went to Caracas to continue his work as a journalist, going briefly to Barranquilla to marry at last the patient Mercedes Barcha, the woman to whom he has been married for his entire life. It was during this period in Caracas that he witnessed the downfall of the dictator Marcos Pérez Jiménez.

The experience of the Cuban Revolution was the next important stage in the formation of García Márquez's political vision. He and Fuentes were among the most outspoken supporters of a revolution that was not only a radical political change for Cuba, but also represented and expressed a vast range of political and nationalistic sentiments that had been growing for over a century from Chile and Argentina to Mexico: the need for political and economic independence from the neocolonial interests of the United States and some European nations; the need to forge an independent national identity; the need for cultural expression valued in itself, without applying foreign criteria; political, economic, and social equality in the face of ruling elites; a rejection of the Spanish medieval and colonial legacy; and a recognition of

---

[20] For an overview and analysis of these stories see Robin Fiddian, *García Márquez, Los funerales de la mamá grande*, Critical Guides to Spanish Texts 70 (London: Grant & Cutler, 2006).

diverse cultural traditions, such as African and indigenous cultures, as essential to national cultural identity. As the Cuban Revolution moved forward in the 1960s, its internal leadership and foreign supporters deftly connected their revolution to these broad Latin American political goals. The writers of the 1960s Boom – particularly García Márquez and Cortázar – visited Cuba frequently, providing political support where possible at the same time as the two were at the forefront of making Havana the *de facto* cultural capital of Latin America. García Márquez also worked as a journalist for the Cuban news agency Prensa Latina, becoming not only an official ally of the Cuban Revolution but also a close personal friend of Castro.

In the period from 1958 to 1961, journalistic assignments took García Márquez from Caracas to Cuba, from Cuba to Bogotá, and from Bogotá to New York. In Cuba, he witnessed the legal proceedings against one of Fulgencio Batista's former generals and closest confidants, Jesús Sosa Blanco. García Márquez and Plinio Apuleyo Mendoza were there in Havana as official observers of the court proceedings, and this experience of seeing from the inside exactly how a dictatorship works was an important experience for the future writing of two fictions about autocrats: the story 'Los funerales de la mamá grande' and the novel *El otoño del patriarca*. In 1960, the year García Márquez returned to Havana to work for Prensa Latina, the first of two children, Rodrigo, was born. Two years later, he and Mercedes had their second child, Gonzalo.

García Márquez's unswerving allegiance to the Cuban Revolution is best understood as part of his background as a person seemingly born to be a leftist, for it relates to his youth in Aracataca: García Márquez grew up in the only region of Colombia ever controlled by foreign neocolonial powers. In 1899 the Colombian Land Company merged with the Boston Fruit Company, and the resulting United Fruit Company operated throughout the first quarter of the twentieth century in the Costa region of Colombia. It had consolidated all banana production in Colombia by the early twentieth century. The United Fruit Company was an economic powerhouse in the region, and was perceived by the populace as a huge, influential, and wealthy presence. Stories circulated about wealthy tycoons lighting cigars with large-denomination bills, and this became the image of the North American in Colombia. In 1928, the year after García Márquez was born, Colombian workers at the United Fruit Company declared a strike, and as a result the Colombian government sent in troops to take over the situation. The troops fired upon the striking workers, and a large number were killed. While exact figures for this massacre have never been available, García Márquez created the number that he needed artistically, as a kind of metaphor: he knew he needed three thousand to fill the boxcar of a train. The real figure was probably in the hundreds. This historical event in the Costa has been profoundly significant in the life, writing, and political vision of García Márquez. The United Fruit Company vacated Colombia soon after the massacre, and for decades no written record of this tragedy existed. The manner in which the personal losses, the regional disaster, and the national tragedy reached the national consciousness in Colombia (and international awareness later) was through fiction: the story of the massacre appeared first in a version novelized by García Márquez's lifelong friend Alvaro Cepeda Samudio in his novel *La casa grande* (1962) and then as a part of a chapter in García Márquez's *Cien años de soledad*. Thus, from an early age, García Márquez learned to be skeptical of the government representation of things, and also to question the work of professional historians. At the same time, he remains willing to trust in the possibility of finding the real truth in the knowlege of the common people and the voices of fiction writers. For him, for Fuentes, and for many writers of his generation, writing fiction was, among other things, a search for an historical truth and a revision of official histories; these writers' fictions can be more truthful than the written record of supposed 'facts'.

### Mexico and the 1960s Boom

The next stage in García Márquez's life was preceded by an important trip that he made on a Greyhound bus with his family from New York City, where he was working as a foreign correspondent for Prensa Latina, to Mexico City, with a stopover in Oxford, Mississippi, to pay homage to Faulkner. García Márquez went to Mexico with a two-fold plan in mind. On the one hand, he had decided that his writing career as a novelist was now over with the publication of a volume of short stories and three short novels. He believed, mistakenly, that he had exhausted the possibilities of stories from the fictional universe he called Macondo. Having published the stories of *Los funerales de la mamá grande* (1962) and the three short novels *La hojarasca* (1955), *El coronel no tiene quien le escriba* (1961), and *La mala hora* (1962), he believed his writing career was now complete and his next direction was not in fiction, but in film. His only success as a writer by 1962 consisted in his having published a second edition of *La hojarasca* and having been awarded a national novel prize, the Esso Prize, worth 3000 US dollars. On the other hand, he wanted to pursue a career in film and hoped his friend Álvaro Mutis would lend him a hand in Mexico to get him into this line of work. He wrote some film scripts on his own and, eventually, some in collaboration with Carlos Fuentes.

However, while living in Mexico City in the early 1960s, partly through his close friendship with Fuentes, García Márquez found himself in the midst of the rise of what soon came to be known as the 'Boom' of the Latin American novel. During this period, Fuentes published *La muerte de Artemio Cruz* (*The Death of Artemio Cruz*, 1962), a novel of political engagement and modernist aesthetics that represented the very best of what a novel could be, as far as García Márquez and many other novelists of his generation were concerned. Soon thereafter, the young Peruvian Mario Vargas Llosa (only thirty years of age at the time) delivered a best-selling bombshell with an equally powerful synthesis of the political with modernist aesthetics, *La ciudad y los perros* (*The Time of the Hero*, 1963). The Argentine master of the short story, Julio Cortázar, published a novel that represented an aesthetic and political revolution, *Rayuela* (*Hopscotch*, 1963). With the appearance of these three novels, three writers who at the time were close friends of García Márquez had launched the internationally recognized 1960s 'Boom' of the 'new' Latin American novel.

Fuentes was the organizer and leader of this Boom, and so García Márquez was an insider at the birth of this cultural phenomenon. The Boom itself was the result of the confluence of several circumstances, institutions, and individuals. Prominent among the institutions and individuals responsible for its success were the Spanish literary agent Carmen Balcells (García Márquez's own literary agent), the publishers Seix Barral in Spain and Harper & Row in the United States (the first English-language publisher of García Márquez), the rise of Latin American studies as an academic discipline in the United States, Europe, and Latin America, and the publication of the literary magazine *Mundo Nuevo* in Paris. Also important was the Cuban Revolution. In his *Historia personal del Boom*, José Donoso pointed out that Carlos Fuentes was the catalyst that brought the group together. Indeed, in the early 1960s Fuentes hosted Sunday afternoon literary soirées at his home, bringing together an often diverse and international crowd of intellectuals. García Márquez was a regular participant in these social, political, and literary gatherings.

A work that predated the Boom and was not associated with it, but which became increasingly recognized in the 1960s, entered García Márquez's life during this period in Mexico. After reading Juan Rulfo's *Pedro Páramo* (1955), García Márquez relates that he could not sleep until he had read it a second time: 'Esa noche no pude dormir hasta que no lo hube leído por segunda vez: no me había sentido tan conmovido nunca, desde aquella noche loca en que leí *La metamorphosis* de Kafka' ('That night I could not sleep until I had read it a second time: I have never been so moved since that crazy night I read Kafka's *Metamorphosis*').[21]

When Castro successfully defeated the dictator Batista, he arrived in Havana in January of 1959 to find that Fuentes, the future leader of the Boom, was already in the Cuban capital, offering his enthusiastic support. As we have seen, García Márquez was also an early ally of the Revolution. However, in the midst of this Boom, García Márquez – unlike Fuentes, Vargas Llosa, and Cortázar – had yet to publish a major novel that might win the sort of international recognition enjoyed by works such as *La muerte de Artemio Cruz*, *Rayuela*, and *La ciudad y los perros*. This situation changed when García Márquez unexpectedly found himself writing the novel that most scholars and critics now consider his masterpiece, *Cien años de soledad*. He had begun a family vacation by taking the highway from Mexico City to Acapulco in 1965. However, before arriving in Acapulco García Márquez had a set of unexpected thoughts, or a type of epiphany: he realized that he had not yet really told the entire story of Macondo in those four volumes of published fiction, and that the way he needed to tell the story was to be in the mode of his grandmother, the master of the oral tale. With this twofold epiphany, García Márquez turned his car around and headed back to Mexico City with his family. The planned vacation to Acapulco never took place. Instead, García Márquez isolated himself in his basement and began writing the 'complete' story of Macondo, which he had begun with the massive manuscript of *La casa* and then rewritten and edited into a first short version of the Macondo story, *La hojarasca*. In 1963, he had attempted once again to narrate that complete Macondo story, but could not find the appropriate voice. This was, then, his third attempt at writing the total story; he worked intensely for a year, often imitating the style of his grandmother, writing what was in essence the final chapter of his Faulknerian cycle on Macondo. He wrote obsessively, while Mercedes took care of all the practical matters of the household, from the care of the two boys to finding ways to obtain loans for the family budget. In their essays, Fuentes and Vargas Llosa had written of their fascination with the idea of writing a 'total' novel, and García Márquez's total Macondo novel had many qualities of that impossible work.[22] During this year of dedication to writing the novel of his life, the young writer in his late thirties also worked through – in one piece of fiction

21  Dagmar Ploetz, *Gabriel García Márquez*, Monografías (Madrid: Edaf, 2004), 86.
22  See the early discussions of the 'total novel' in Carlos Fuentes, *La nueva novela hispanoamericana* (Mexico City: Joaquín Mortiz, 1969), and Mario Vargas Llosa, *Gabriel García Márquez: historia de un deicidio* (Caracas: Monte Ávila, 1971).

– two of his lifelong commitments. The first and most deeply engrained, from his childhood in Aracataca and having heard the stories of the banana workers' strike, was his commitment to progressive social change. Thus, he not only included the massacre of the banana workers in his novel, but also satirized the most venerable political institutions in Colombia, from its two traditional parties to the Roman Catholic church, one of the most powerful political institutions in the nation. The second of his lifelong commitments, one almost as deeply engrained as a result of his many days and often long nights with his mentors in Cartagena, as well as friends from the Group of Barranquilla, was his commitment to modernist literary aesthetics and to 'modernizing' Latin American literature.

After the first chapter of *Cien años* appeared in print in *Mundo Nuevo* in early 1967, there was much anticipation among intellectuals across the Hispanic world about the imminent publication of another major novel of the 'Boom'. When *Cien años* appeared under the label of the prestigious publisher Editorial Sudamericana in Buenos Aires in July of 1967, it was an immediate and overwhelming success. It received swift and enthusiastic critical acclaim from Spain to Mexico and appeared in a record number of new printings for the remainder of 1967, 1968, and in the following years. In Caracas in 1968, at the conference called the 13° Congreso Internacional de Literatura Iberoamericana, García Márquez and Vargas Llosa met for the first time, and soon thereafter gave joint public presentations in Bogotá and Lima. They were treated as celebrities in both countries, as if they were Hollywood actors or soccer players. As *Cien años* was rapidly becoming one of the most widely read pieces of literature in the history of the Spanish language, García Márquez's status changed from marginal participant of the Boom to the star figure among a select group of public intellectuals. In 1970, *Cien años* was named the best foreign book by *Time* magazine. García Márquez was indeed the most widely recognized public intellectual and jetsetting writer of the 1960s Boom. He purchased a home in Barcelona, where he lived frequently in the late 1960s and early 1970s, when relationships among the writers of the Boom were still vital and dynamic.

Unfortunately, however, political and personal differences led to increasing tension. The conflicts often centered on questions about supporting or not supporting Castro's regime. In fact, the last time that García Márquez and the other writers of the Boom were actually together in the same space was in France in 1970. They attended a theater festival in Avignon to enjoy together Fuentes's play *El tuerto es rey* ('The One-eyed Man is King'), which was on the festival program. In the village of Saignon, near Avignon, Julio Cortázar owned a home, and the Spanish writer Juan Goytisolo, José Donoso, Fuentes,

Cortázar, and García Márquez assembled together. Besides the opportunity to see this play, they met in Saignon to make plans for what they intended to be a quarterly magazine, *Libre*, with an emphasis on culture and politics. The six writers believed that creating this magazine would not only help them effect political change, but also bring them together as friends and allies. This was one of the many occasions in which Fuentes and García Márquez collaborated on a political project with the conviction that work in *cultura* could help effect progressive political change. They agreed to name Juan Goytisolo the editor. The effect of the project, however, was the opposite of their original intentions; discussions around issues related to the magazine only accentuated their growing political differences. The arrest of the Cuban poet Heberto Padilla by the Cuban government for writing poetry critical of the regime had created a huge rift among Latin American intellectuals: some, like García Márquez, supported the actions of the Cuban government while others did not. One of the original plans for the magazine *Libre* had been to publish it as an organ to support the Cuban regime from the outside, yet also strengthen the protection for Cuban intellectuals, such as Padilla, who were struggling from the inside for more freedom of expression. It was a narrow and difficult path for the Boom writers to attempt to follow, and the six could not fully agree on just how they might carry out their plan. In the public domain, alliances among these six have often been defined strictly in terms of their respective positions vis-à-vis Cuba, but the reality was that personal frictions among them also contributed to their breakup. García Márquez's distance from Vargas Llosa had partly to do with differences related to Cuba. But there were also personal tensions between them, even though Vargas Llosa had published an informed and exhaustive study on the Colombian writer's work, *García Márquez: historia de un deicidio*.[23]

---

[23] See Vargas Llosa, *Gabriel García Márquez*. In private conversations with Vargas Llosa in the 1990s, it was evident to me that he holds García Márquez in great respect, even though the two do not socialize and in the 1970s and 1980s occasionally made negative public comments about each other. On the surface, it would seem logical that Vargas Llosa's research on the author's entire life and work would contribute to building a solid and lengthy personal relationship between the two. Based on my observation of García Márquez's interaction with literary critics over the years, as well as his public comments about their work, however, I believe that García Márquz misunderstood Vargas Llosa's research, seeing it first as an intrusion into his personal life, and then, once the book appeared, as an imposition of concepts related to literary theory and literary criticism that were foreign to the Colombian writer. Thus, as political differences accentuated the tensions between the two in the later 1960s and early 1970s, the publication of *Gabriel García Márquez: historia de un deicidio* probably made the situation worse.

In the 1970s, basking in the glory of the phenomenal success of *Cien años*, García Márquez enjoyed the respect of many intellectuals on the political left in Colombia; however, at the time he was generally criticized and rejected by many middle-class Colombians and by some intellectuals. In addition to his leftist politics, he did not fit the Bogotá model of the elite intellectual, who generally had more class credentials and more formal education. Colombian citizens supporting the two traditional parties (Liberal and Conservative) tended to consider him too mucn of a revolutionary – and even labeled him as 'unpatriotic' – because of his ties with Castro, and also because he had founded and directed the political magazine *Alternativa* that supported armed revolution.

In 1972, García Márquez felt once again, as he had done in the early 1960s, that he had completed all of the fiction writing that he needed to do. He often told journalists and others that he was essentially a journalist and not really a novelist at all. These statements were one of his ways, as a young writer with humble roots, to deal with his extraordinary success and his new celebrity status. Such statements were a form of denial; he had indeed completed the narration of the entire Macondo story, so it is understandable that he claimed that his career as a fiction writer was completed. He did, however, have two lingering projects from the 1960s that he had yet to complete. The first was a set of short stories of the fantastic or supposed 'magic realist' ilk that, in reality, had been written in the 1960s as rough drafts for children's stories. He eventually rewrote, edited, and polished these, publishing them in 1972 under the title *La increíble y triste historia de la cándida Eréndira y su abuela desalmada* (*The Incredible and Sad Tale of Candid Erendira and her Heartless Grandmother*). This was the first work he had published since *Cien años*. It consisted of seven stories set vaguely on the Caribbean coast, but it is important to note that these are not Macondo stories and that García Márquez himself has described them as 'piano exercises'.[24] They are set in the coastal area of García Márquez's Caribbean Colombia, not in the fictional setting of Macondo. The space is vaguely Riohacha, in the Caribbean region along the coast stretching from Santa Marta to the Venezuelan border. The stories reveal García Márquez's growing awareness of the African roots of Caribbean culture. Vera Kutzinski has made subtle connections between one of the stories of this volume, 'Un señor muy viejo con unas alas enormes' ('A very old man with enormous wings') and Afro-American folklore.[25] She

[24] See González Bermejo, 'And Now, Two Hundred Years', 16.
[25] See Vera Kutzinksi, 'The Logic of Wings: Gabriel García Márquez and Afro-American Literature', in *García Márquez*, ed. Robin Fiddian, Modern Literatures in

points out that there are many tales about flight in African oral tradition, and that these stories are deeply indebted to the oral tradition of this tri-ethnic region, and are clearly more than mere 'exercises'.

García Márquez's more important unfinished project from the 1960s was a novel about a fictional dictator. The idea had arisen during conversations with the other writers of the Boom about collaborating on a novel that would focus on a protodictator figure from Latin America. As we have seen, García Márquez had first-hand experience of the dictatorships of Rojas Pinilla in Colombia and of Pérez Jiménez in Venezuela, and many other writers of his generation had witnessed the iron rule of dictators directly. Augusto Roa Bastos in Paraguay, Alejo Carpentier in Cuba, Demetrio Aguilera Malta in Ecuador, as well as Vargas Llosa, were just a few of the Latin American writers interested in writing about dictators. García Márquez began this project of writing about a dictator figure in the 1960s, and talked about it with other writers as dictators began taking power throughout the Americas in the early 1970s. The proceedings in Cuba against the former general of Batista, Jesús Sosa Blanco, had given García Márquez specific and detailed insights into the actual workings of such dictatorships. In 1973 and 1974, he dedicated long hours to the completion of the work that represented a fictional composite of several historical figures, and which appeared in print in 1975 under the title of *El otoño del patriarca* (*The Autumn of the Patriarch*). With this novel, the writer's break with his Macondo fiction was definitive; none of the characters are from the Macondo stories and the setting is vaguely Caribbean, with allusions to an island setting. The style of the novel has less affinity with oral culture than it does with other, more complex kinds of writing, such as the poetry of Rubén Darío and the fiction of Valle-Inclán. In the powerful opening scene of *El otoño*, a cow's corpse is being devoured by vultures at the entrance to a dilapidated palace, a recurrent image in the novel; here, García Márquez is using a visual image from a drawing rather than an actual setting from the Aracataca area. With the change of setting and the predominance of the literary over the oral, García Márquez broke with the fiction of the Macondo cycle (see Chapter 3, below).

After having completed all his fictional projects from the 1960s – both the Macondo story and the two unfinished projects (the stories of *La cándida Eréndira* and the novel *El otoño*) – García Márquez once again adopted the stance that he was not really a novelist but a journalist, and that his career

Perspective (London: Longman, 1995), 214–28, an essay reprinted from *Latin American Literary Review*, 13 (1985), 133–46.

as a fiction writer was, once again, basically over.[26] He declared in 1975, in one of his most cited public statements of the 1970s, made soon after the publication of *El otoño*, that he would not write another novel until after the fall of General Pinochet in Chile. This declaration circulated widely in media circles throughout the Hispanic world. García Márquez and the writers of the Boom had witnessed the democratic election of Salvador Allende's Unidad Popular in 1970. Subsequently, after General Pinochet led a military coup against Allende's government, they had all aligned themselves in solidarity with the populace that had elected Allende in September 1973. The massacre of Allende and his supporters, which began on 11 September 1973 and continued throughout the mid-1970s, was as dramatic for García Márquez as had been the massacre of the striking workers on the Costa in 1928. When he made his statement in 1975 about not writing again, he was taking a symbolic political stance against all such genocides, rather than making a literal statement about his writing plans.

This declaration was politically consistent and coherent, and it reflected García Márquez's own sense of himself as a person and as a writer. But it also stated the truth. He had completed all his fictional projects: both his Macondo story and his other previously unfinished work had been written and published. He had begun his writing career as a journalist and had every reason to believe that he was at heart more of a journalist than he was a novelist. In any case, both kinds of writing, journalism and fiction, involved taking everyday events and making out of them an engaging story.

Though he was, from an early age, a writer with political concerns and a political agenda, García Márquez has never allowed that agenda to distract him from his fascination with the basic act of telling a story. Despite his political commitments and despite his claim about not writing another novel until the fall of Pinochet, García Márquez did in fact write fiction after 1975, primarily out of that desire or need to tell a good story. When criticized by Latin American intellectuals for this contradiction, he pointed out that his six-year ban on publishing fiction had had no effect on the longevity of the Pinochet regime, and he had become, in effect, a prisoner of that regime. On one occasion, when questioned by a journalist about the 'commitment' of the writer, García Márquez responded that the writer's commitment is to tell a good story. Consistent with his view of himself as a political journalist, in 1976 and 1977, he traveled to Angola and published a series of articles,

---

[26] In an interview with García Márquez in October of 1975 in Bogotá, he explained to me also that he considered himself primarily a journalist and had no imminent plans to write any more novels. (For more information about this interview, see Chapter 6, below.)

which appeared throughout the Hispanic world and in the *Washington Post* on the situation there. This trip was a revelation and it renewed his lifelong interest in the African presence in the Caribbean. He has described it as one of the most 'fascinating' experiences of his life, saying 'I believe that it divided my life into two halves'.[27] He also affirmed that on this trip he discovered that he was not only a Spaniard (as he had always been told) but also an African. It was at this point in his life that he came to realize that the oral storytelling tradition that had been so important for the Macondo fiction was also a part of the African tradition. In this sense, he was 'also an African'. After this new awareness of the African presence in his Caribbean society and culture, his writing underwent a subtle change: African culture and Afro-American characters were more explicitly present.

### New novels and the Nobel Prize

His next two books, *Crónica de una muerte anunciada* (*Chronicle of a Death Foretold*, 1981) and *El amor en los tiempos del cólera* (*Love in the Time of Cholera*, 1985), were two of García Márquez's most basic and impressive acts of telling a story. They both contain elements of the accomplished professional writer making a tour de force out of storytelling itself. In *Crónica de una muerte anunciada*, he announces that tour de force in the very first line of the novel, with a sentence that makes the reader aware of exactly what the outcome of the plot will be: the protagonist will be assassinated at the end, an act that takes place on the last page of the novel. The tour de force consists of revealing the entire plot in the first line (the opposite of detective fiction or the 'pot boiler') and then having the pure storytelling *savoir faire* and technical mastery to keep the reader not only interested until the end, but fully engaged. Additionally, this novel also contains pointers to the Spanish medieval and neocolonial mentality that has pervaded Colombian society well into the twenty-first century. Finally, it was also a statement, just one year before he was awarded the Nobel Prize for Literature, that García Márquez was as accomplished as the very best professional storytellers.

Given the author's ongoing contention that he was really just a journalist at heart, *Crónica* is also a masterpiece of journalism, a direct inheritance of the early journalist-cum-storyteller who engaged thousands of Colombian readers and kept them intrigued for weeks with the tale of a shipwrecked sailor (see Chapter 5, below). The background to *Crónica* was García

---

[27] Kutzinski, 'The Logic of Wings', 216.

Márquez's recalling having read a newspaper account of a story of love and revenge involving some individuals whom he had known personally in his youth. Narrated as a day-by-day and even hour-by-hour 'chronicle', it is not really either a 'chronicle' or just a newspaper account, but, in it, he makes gestures toward both genres by imitating much of their respective styles. Shortly before the publication of *Crónica*, and under threat of physical danger for political reasons, García Márquez went into political exile in Mexico, for it was rumored that the government was going to make a case that he was connected with certain members of the armed revolutionary group M–19 who had been arrested.

Since 1967 and the publication of *Cien años*, García Márquez had received worldwide recognition and critical acclaim, and he was awarded many literary prizes and had become the focus of more scholarly studies than any other living writer of the Spanish language. His most significant recognition by far, however, came in 1982, with the award of the Nobel Prize for Literature. At the time, he was the author of six novels and two volumes of short fiction, but there was a consensus among scholars that the award was given primarily in recognition of his final Macondo novel, *Cien años de soledad*. In his acceptance speech in Stockholm, García Márquez clearly delineated the devastating social, economic, and political implications of the Spanish colonial legacy and the neocolonial legacy that followed. He spoke on behalf of the impoverished masses in Colombia and other regions of Latin America and questioned why European systems of social justice have been imposed on the region. Despite this circumstance and in the face of 'oppression, pillage, and abandonment', García Márquez, like his valiant Balthazar and his Colonel Aureliano Buendía, seems to be suggesting that the appropriate response is to carry on living one's life.

García Márquez's life changed once again after he received the Nobel Prize, almost as much as it did when he went to Mexico in 1962 or in the period following 1967 with the overwhelming success of *Cien años*. Before the prize, he had lived intermittently in Colombia, originally to create the psychological distance necessary for his writing, and later for security reasons. Nevertheless, with the award of the Nobel Prize during the early stages of the presidency of his long-time friend Belisario Betancur, a formidable intellectual in his own right, he was now comfortable for the first time in many years with the idea of actually living in his homeland. He accepted Betancur's invitation to end his political and psychological exile, soon after the ceremony in Stockholm, as the honored guest of Colombia's national celebration of the Nobel Prize. In the early 1980s, García Márquez and his wife Mercedes began residing more often in Colombia than they ever had in their adult lives. During this period, he often took up residence in Cartagena in the condominium of his old friend Alejandro Obregón (an occasional participant in the activities of the Group of Barranquilla), and he made brief visits to nearby Barranquilla, as well as to highland Bogotá.[28] Of his mentors of the original group of Cartagena, Zabala had died in 1963, Rojas Herazo was living in Cartagena and Bogotá, and Gustavo Ibarra was still in Cartagena. In Cartagena, García Márquez assumed a challenge almost as daunting as the writing of *Crónica*: to tell an unlikely and romantic love story in a novel by a world-class writer of modernist and postmodern-type fiction, and to direct it to the broad, worldwide readership he had developed over the years. The real challenge was to do so without giving the appearance of merely having produced nothing more than a soap opera or a popular romance novel.[29]

In the early 1980s, García Márquez wrote the manuscript of *El amor en los tiempos del cólera* (*Love in the Time of Cholera*, 1985) in Cartagena, the setting for most of the novel, and at the same time carried out historical research on nineteenth-century Colombia. In this novel, as in *El otoño*, he used nineteenth-century drawings as key images for some of the settings. His elderly protagonist, Florentino Ariza, writes love letters to Fermina Daza for years after she rejects him and marries a wealthy doctor, thus creating a strictly epistolary love affair that lasts for decades. With occasional self-parody of his own Macondo cycle, *El amor* refers back to several of the characters of *Cien años* and contains several of the stylistic traits that, by the mid-1980s, had become trademarks of the García Márquez fictional repertoire. He even refers to an exotic parrot as an 'estorbo ornamental' ('decorative annoyance'), thus warning readers of the exotic fictions of Macondo to be cautious about overinterpreting the exotic flora and fauna to be found in

[28] I met with García Márquez in May of 1984 in the condominium of Alejandro Obregón in Cartagena. He was living there at the time, apparently finishing the writing of *El amor*. He indicated that he had frequently stayed there in the 1980s when he was in Cartagena.

[29] Several world-class writers from Latin America had already published parodies of popular romance novels. Among the most widely read were Manuel Puig's *La traición de Rita Hayworth* (*Betrayed by Rita Hayworth*, 1968) and Mario Vargas Llosa's *La tía Julia y el escribidor* (*Aunt Julia and the Scriptwriter*, 1977). For an introduction to these and similar novels, see Raymond L. Williams, *The Twentieth-century Spanish American Novel*. For the writers of the 1960s Boom, and others writing in the 1970s and 1980s, the publication of these popular fictions was a reaction against the experimental and ambitious 'total' novel projects of the 1960s, including some of their own. García Márquez and each of the writers of the Boom published at least one novel that was a dialogue with popular forms. Both *Crónica* and *El amor* fit this pattern.

his fiction. Written in the years following his trip to Angola and his redis-
covery of African culture, *El amor* has a subtle African presence that functions as an integral yet almost invisible element in the novel, as were the
Africans in the white, upper-class society of nineteenth-century Cartagena.

*El amor* is an improbable love story constructed by an accomplished
writer in the glory of his artistic maturity; it is part of García Márquez's
lifelong reflection on the role of the Spanish colonial legacy, as well as the
contributions of African tradition to Latin American society. Of the author's
works, this is the one that is located most closely to the colonial setting; it
takes place in the city of Cartagena, a small city of former colonial splendor.
Much of the plot deals with a nineteenth-century society still living, to a large
degree, the Spanish colonial legacy that was strongly present in nineteenth-
century Colombia, and particularly in Cartagena. García Márquez published
this novel at the age of fifty-eight, and it was also the first of several writings to deal with ageing; in this sense, it is a forerunner of *Del amor y otros
demonios* (*Of Love and Other Demons*, 1994) and *Memoria de mis putas
tristes* (*Memories of my Melancholy Whores*, 2004).

The author's ongoing commitment to political and social change took a
different twist after the Nobel Prize; this active public intellectual began
to assume the role of elder statesman and mediator in the political process
in Colombia and Latin America. With his strong personal associations with
Fidel Castro and Carlos Fuentes, as well as his ample connections with the
political Left in Colombia, Latin America, and Europe, he was well positioned to serve as intermediary or mediator in those political processes in
which a lack of trust between political foes made direct dialogue, or any other
form of communication, difficult at best. The fact that President Belisario
Betancur was also García Márquez's trusted friend made the writer an effective and useful player in many different kinds of political dialogue. More
specifically, armed guerrillas such as the FARC (Fuerzas Armadas Revolu-
cionarias de Colombia) in Colombia, who had strong ties to Cuba and a
deep mistrust of the traditional political parties and institutions in Colombia,
were difficult for the government to approach for the construction of a peace
agreement. Betancur was fully committed to such a peace process and some
of the armed revolutionary groups were more willing to speak or meet with
García Márquez than they were to communicate with anyone in an official
institutional capacity.

García Márquez and his generation had been marked by the intense political experience of the 1950s when the nation was living a violent civil war
that resulted in over 300,000 deaths, as well as by the military dictatorship
of Gustavo Rojas Pinilla. With the peace agreements of 1958, this civil war

between the traditional forces of the Liberal Party and the Conservative Party ended and the nature of political conflict in Colombia changed. With this peace, most members of the traditional parties ended their participation in armed conflict and assumed their roles as voting members of the two parties that, in turn, agreed to a form of shared governance in which they alternated in holding the presidency. Some groups, however, found the institutional political process incapable of providing social and economic justice. In his Nobel Prize acceptance speech, García Márquez questions the ability of traditional European models to respond to the enormous social and political needs of Latin America. Colombians adhering to this line of thought in the 1950s and 1960s, and who did not believe in the ability of the traditional parties to find social and economic justice, chose to join forces with a variety of rural guerrilla movements, the largest of which was the FARC. By the 1980s, these same guerrilla groups had grown into a serious threat to Colombia's major institutions, including its political parties. The armed guerrillas had connections with entities as disparate as the Cuban government and the drug cartels, and so were capable of operating in some regions of Colombia with arms and personnel superior to those of the government.

Betancur's strategy in the early 1980s was not only to find a way to reach peace agreements with these armed groups, but to do so by reintegrating marginalized groups into Colombian society – integrating guerrillas, for example, into the economic system and the institutional political process. Betancur did enjoy some success in the early stages of this process, and García Márquez functioned as an intermediary. In this process and others, Colombia's most prominent public intellectual became an informal and unofficial member of Betancur's cabinet, providing informed advice and key contacts for this national and international dialogue.

In recent years, García Márquez has suffered from ill health, and in 1999 he underwent successful surgery in Los Angeles for lymphatic cancer. In the early 1990s, he planned to live in Cartagena and built a house there as a retirement home. Nevertheless, in 1997, during the presidency of Ernesto Samper, García Márquez found the security situation in Colombia so fragile that he moved back to Mexico City. On several occasions during this period, his ability to live in Colombia was determined by whether or not the nation's president could assure his safety, despite the daily kidnappings and political assassinations. In 2000 he published a journalistic report on the case of the Cuban boy Elián González, who was temporarily in Florida and then was taken by U.S. officials back to his father in Cuba. That account of the adventures of the young boy and the bungling of this case by the two governments is reminiscent of García Márquez's early success in journalistic writing about such adventures in his *Relato de un náufrago* (*Story of a ship-wrecked sailor*).

In 2002, García Márquez published the first part of his autobiography, *Vivir para contarla* (*Living to Tell the Tale*). In it, he writes of his childhood in Aracataca, his experience in the boarding school in Zipaquirá on the outskirts of Bogotá, the conservative, stifling cultural scenario in Colombia in the late 1940s, and his early readings and writings in Cartagena and Barranquilla. In the latter part of the book he relates anecdotes involving his friends German Vargas, Alfonso Fuenmayor, Alvaro Cepeda Samudio, the elder Fuenmayor (José Félix), and Ramón Vinyes, and his becoming acquainted with his future wife Mercedes Barcha. This book also relates the rejection of the manuscript of his novel, which came in a letter signed by Guillermo de la Torre on the headed notepaper of the Losada publishing house, his move to Bogotá to work at *El Espectador*, the scandal created by the publication of his story of a shipwrecked sailor, and his departure to Europe.

## Conclusion

García Márquez has cited the discovery of Kafka and Faulkner as the keys to his becoming a writer. When he read the first page of *Metamorphosis*, he decided that if this was what novelists could do – radically transform reality – then he wanted to become a writer. Since then, he has written about the realities he knows, using a free hand for whatever his imagination might bring with respect to invention, transformation of that reality, or what some readers consider the fantastic, or 'magic realism'. All along, he has tended to insist upon the 'real' base for his stories. His literary formation was deeply affected by the oral tales of his grandmother and aunts, by his grandfather's stories of the nineteenth-century civil wars, by his mentor figures in Cartagena, and by his mentors and peers in Barranquilla. The writers that were embedded into his very being from the experience in Cartagena and Barranquilla from 1948 to 1952 were Faulkner, Borges, Kafka, and Ramón Gómez de la Serna. The most important literary revelation later in his life (but before writing *Cien años*) was Juan Rulfo's *Pedro Páramo*. While García Márquez's political experience has been vast and rich, the key points of his development were the 1928 banana workers' strike, the uprising or 'bogotazo' that followed the assassination of Gaitán in 1948, the dictatorship of Rojas Pinilla, the Cuban Revolution, the related legal process against General Jesús Sosa Blanco, and the Padilla case later in Cuba.

García Márquez began writing his first, amateurish stories in the 1940s.

However, the foundation of his career as a fiction writer was his Macondo cycle, a set of four novels and one book of short stories that eventually culminated in his masterpiece *Cien años*. His other major novels are a book about power, *El otoño*, and one about ageing, love, and writing, *El amor*. In the second half of his writing career, after the Macondo cycle, there is a subtle yet consistent presence of African culture. The chapters that follow will offer some general directions for reading his complete fiction, as well as suggestions about how to proceed with caution in this reading.

2

# Cien años de soledad
# and the Macondo Cycle

García Márquez is best known for his novel *Cien años de soledad (One Hundred Years of Solitude)*. This was the centerpiece of his writing career when he was awarded the Nobel Prize for Literature in 1982. This novel was the culmination of the 'cycle of Macondo' fictions that García Márquez began constructing in the early 1950s and continued to elaborate, in short fictions and novels, until 1967. What is exceptional in this novel is its unique combination of seemingly incongruous elements, for it is both traditional and modern, at the same time modern and postmodern, and also heavily indebted to the traditions of both oral and written cultures. The synthesis of these seemingly opposite elements invites the reader to question the binary thinking typically used to discuss literature. The Macondo fictions that preceded this novel – *La hojarasca* (*Leafstorm*, 1955), *El coronel no tiene quien le escriba* (*No One Writes to the Colonel*, 1961), *La mala hora* (*In Evil Hour*, 1962), *Los funerales de la mamá grande* (1962, with its cover story translated in *No One Writes to the Colonel and Other Stories* under the title *Big Mama's funeral*) – are also the subject of this chapter.

García Márquez has become widely celebrated for his creative imagination, for his commitment to progressive social change in Latin America, and, for better or for worse, as the paradigmatic 'magic realist' author.[1] Writing under the tutelage of a group of intellectuals recently identified as the Group of Cartagena, he began the creation of Macondo in Cartagena during the years 1948 and 1949. He completed the first Macondo novel, *La hojarasca*, in Barranquilla while in dialogue with his friends of the Group of Barranquilla; it appeared in print in 1955. According to Oscar de la Espriella, one of his friends from Cartagena, the young García Márquez did not seem to fit among

---

[1]   Magic realism can be defined, in the simplest of terms, as a writing style in which the author blends elements of the rational world of empirical reality with elements of the irrational world of fantasy. When Latin American writers use this style and the irrational elements tend toward the exotic, the writing is often described as 'magic realism'.

intellectuals in Bogotá: he was always dressed informally, in bright-colored Caribbean clothes, in contrast to the formal and dark clothes of the residents of Bogotá. More importantly, according to De la Espriella, he showed signs of intellectual brilliance and literary talent.[2] The five books of the cycle of Macondo made that observation prophetic.

'La prodigiosa tarde de Baltazar' ('Balthazar's Prodigious Afternoon') and 'La siesta del martes' ('Tuesday Siesta'), two short stories from the volume *Los funerales*, serve as an ideal introduction to *Cien años*. In addition to being important groundwork for the novel, they are also well-wrought short fictions in their own right. Baltazar's epic experience in 'La prodigiosa tarde' is a forerunner to a wide range of epic events in *Cien años*, from military battles to experiments in the 'scientific' laboratory of José Arcadio Buendía. In the story, the construction of a birdcage – seemingly an ordinary event – assumes epic proportions when its creator, Baltazar, attempts to make it a fine piece of art and some of his friends agree that he has indeed accomplished his lofty aesthetic goal. His wife Úrsula – the prototype for the Úrsula in *Cien años* – is less interested in the cage's artistic qualities than she is in a strictly practical matter: its monetary value. The Úrsula figure is the practical-minded pragmatist in all situations. Thus, the prototype Úrsula in 'La prodigiosa tarde' is pushed beyond her limits to avoid losing her patience with Balthazar when he seems disposed to sell his cage at a quite moderate price; this is the same Úrsula who in *Cien años* loses patience with José Arcadio early in the novel when he declares, after lengthy scientific deliberations, that the world is round like an orange.

The story begins with a description of what is, according to locals, the most beautiful birdcage in the world ('la jaula más bella del mundo'); masses of people congregate in front of the house just to see Balthazar's masterpiece. This description is one of García Márquez's early uses of hyperbole to underline the basic simplicity and innocence of the people of Macondo. The first page is also an early example of the narrator juxtaposing the exaggerated adventures of the Baltazar/José Arcadio figure and the reactions of the down-to-earth Úrsula. After the hyperbolic description of Balthazar's cage in the first paragraph, Úrsula brings matters back down to earth with her first comment; ignoring the cage, she informs Baltazar that he needs to shave ('Tienes que afeitarte').[3]

[2]   See Jorge García Usta, *García Márquez en Cartagena: sus inicios literarios*, Los Tres Mundos (Bogotá: Planeta Colombiana, 2007), 35–36.
[3]   García Márquez, *Los funerales de la mamá grande* (Bogotá: La Oveja Negra, 1982), 65. All quotations from stories in this volume are from this edition.

The characterization of Baltazar in the story's opening pages contains examples of García Márquez's ability to reveal the essence of a character with a succinct phrase or anecdote. In this case, the brief phrase describes a protagonist who has the expression of a scared child ('una expresión general de muchacho asustado', *Los funerales*, 65). The narrator then explains that this initial expression is false, for life had given Baltazar reasons to be alert, but none to be scared ('muchos motivos para estar alerto, pero ninguno para estar asustado', *Los funerales*, 65).

As the story develops, Úrsula is displeased, for Baltazar has spent too much time working on the birdcage and not enough time on his carpentry. Thus, once again, the practical-minded Úrsula rejects the importance of Baltazar's 'art' in favor of the more utilitarian. She does regain some interest in the birdcage when she realizes its potential monetary value and begins discussing possible prices that Baltazar might demand. He considers the possibility of charging the wealthy José ('Chepe') Montiel thirty pesos, but Úrsula insists that he should demand at least fifty or sixty.

When the local doctor visits the home to inspect the cage, he confirms its status as art, calling it an 'adventure of the imagination' ('una aventura de la imaginación', *Los funerales*, 67). The doctor attempts to convince Baltazar to sell him the cage, but both Baltazar and Úrsula insist that it has already been sold to the wealthy José Montiel, who they claim has paid sixty pesos for the cage he had ordered built. This lie is the first of Baltazar's several innocent self-deceptions.

The doctor's response to the situation is noteworthy. Moving toward the door, the doctor hides his real reaction, beginning to fan himself energetically, smiling, and forgetting the episode forever ('empezó a abanicarse con energía, sonriente, y el recuerdo de aquel episodio desapareció para siempre de su memoria', *Los funerales*, 70). Just as Baltazar is false in his deception, the doctor, defeated by the upper-class José Montiel, is also disingenuous, hiding his sense of loss with a smile. Instead of simply 'forgetting' this episode, García Márquez captures another essence of the human moment by asserting that the event disappears forever from the doctor's memory, a phrase that suggests something more powerful than simply forgetting. This is an early use of a phrase that García Márquez often employs in his Macondo fiction – today a signature phrase for this author – to create this powerful effect: 'para siempre' ('forever'). The doctor's departing words are 'Montiel es muy rico' ('Montiel is very rich'), affirming an apparent difference between the economically solid (upper-middle-class) doctor and the more historically wealthy (rural-elite) Montiel.

Nevertheless, Montiel's class credentials turn out to be as dubious as

Baltazar's sale, for the narrator describes him as someone who is not as rich as he seems, and with a questionable background ('En verdad, José Montiel no era tan rico como parecía, pero había sido capaz de todo por llegar a serlo', *Los funerales*, 70). Montiel is not as wealthy as he appears, yet he seems to exercise power on the basis of the financial resources that he does possess. Thus, Montiel clearly is a member of an upper class that a doctor and a carpenter recognize has the means to exploit others, a model that appears in *Cien años* and much of the Macondo fiction.

This class difference is described with Baltazar's arrival at Montiel's home as the innocent face of the poor that arrive at the home of the rich. One phrase, 'En verdad, José Montiel no era tan rico como parecía, pero había sido capaz de todo por llegar a serlo' (*Los funerales*, 69), captures the basic class difference between Baltazar and Montiel, emphasizing how Baltazar's facial expression reveals the humility he silently feels upon arriving at the home of someone belonging to the local elite.

Inside Montiel's home, more subtle class differences emerge. Montiel's wife claims that the cage is 'marvelous' ('maravillosa'), but is indignant about the masses of people at the door. She proceeds to order Baltazar to take the cage further inside, lest the living room become a chicken coop ('gallera'), thus maintaining the refinement of her elite household. Baltazar's class-consciousness surfaces immediately when he states that he never felt well among the rich ('Nunca se sintió bien entre los ricos', *Los funerales*, 71). Then Montiel's wife lies to Baltazar, claiming that her son Pepe is in school and José Montiel is bathing. All in all, García Márquez portrays the upper class as false and conniving. In contrast, Baltazar, although simple and innocent, appears honest and forthright in his dealings with those wealthier than he and in the sale of this piece of art.

In this introductory section of the story, class distinctions and the delineation of the characters are clear and unequivocal. In the next scene, however, Baltazar gives the birdcage to Montiel's son as a gift, creating an ambiguity of the sort that will become a cornerstone of García Márquez's novelistic repertoire. When Montiel discovers that his twelve-year-old son had, in fact, ordered the birdcage to be built, Montiel unequivocally rejects any possibility of purchasing the cage. Montiel's son throws a fit, falling to the floor and crying, whereupon Baltazar gives the cage to the son at no charge, ignoring Montiel's insistence that he take it, and leaves the home without the cage. The narrator provides no indication of what Baltazar is thinking as he stands before Montiel and his son, what Baltazar's understanding of the situation may be, or what his motive is when he gives the cage away.

At least two interpretations are possible at this point in the story. Using

Baltazar's innocence and kindness as textual evidence, it is possible to argue that Baltazar is more sympathetic toward the child than is the boy's own father and that, by giving away the cage, he gains moral superiority over Montiel: that Baltazar 'wins' even though he does not profit. On the other hand, it is also possible to use textual evidence to support an interpretation based on social class: despite feeling his class inferiority, Baltazar transcends the material by ignoring payment, thus 'winning' a class conflict. In the first reading (of Baltazar as the morally superior human being), the subsequent unfolding of the story underscores the potential fragility of moral positions. After establishing his moral superiority over Montiel in the late afternoon, Baltazar goes to a local bar, where he loses the moral terrain he had gained. He begins drinking and celebrating his lie: he claims in the bar to have sold the cage for the optimum possible price of sixty pesos. Initially, acquaintances at the bar buy him a beer to celebrate his defeat of Montiel (his class victory), but once Balthazar becomes drunk, he himself pays for all the drinks, as well as paying to keep the jukebox playing all night. By the end of the evening's celebration, he is required to leave his watch at the bar as collateral. The act of leaving his watch is a sign of his degradation, a visible indicator that a verbal commitment to pay off his debt is not sufficient. This reading of the story as a moral tale ends not only in a moral loss but degradation, for Baltazar not only has to leave his watch at the bar like a common drunk, but is later seen sleeping in the street by women walking to early morning mass. In the end, as in *Cien años*, this is a story of loss, degradation, and trauma.

In a more political reading of this story, Baltazar makes comments about Montiel that indicate a class-consciousness and desire for revenge. In the glory of his inebriation, Baltazar articulates his fantasy to build thousands of cages to sell at sixty pesos each and states that all the wealthy are sick ('enfermos') and are going to die. Then, after listening to the jukebox play for two hours on Baltazar's account, the bar's patrons have one more drink in Baltazar's honor, and then another for the death of the rich, thus reaffirming a kind of class solidarity. This passage also evokes the colonial legacy that these characters have inherited. Baltazar's degradation at the end exhibits the neocolonial mentality from which the characters all suffer as they abandon Baltazar in the bar. He is left alone with nothing but a drunken sexual fantasy – going to bed with two women. The nature of this fantasy operates in ways parallel to the power game in which he was involved with Montiel and the fantasy of power and control that he promulgated in the bar.

These two readings of 'La prodigiosa tarde' are not mutually exclusive, and both lend themselves to further analysis of Baltazar as a human being on what is sometimes called the 'human' level of understanding this fiction.

Such an analysis evokes the unresolved ambiguity concerning Baltazar's act of supreme generosity in gifting his artistic masterpiece to Montiel's son. In the first reading, we assume that Baltazar turns over the cage to gain moral superiority over Montiel. In the second reading, he acts out a class conflict, the victory of which he celebrates at the bar with his working-class friends. It is also possible, however, that this act of either generosity or class tension was actually just an act of ego; Baltazar preferred to give away the cage rather than walk out of Montiel's house carrying his rejected masterpiece. In this view, the celebration at the bar was simply a classic story of excessive ego and pride. His sexual fantasy of being in bed with two women does not fit into the moral tale, but it does fit into a reading of this story as a tale about excessive ego (and into the reading of it as a power game between social classes). This third variant on the first two readings, recognizing Baltazar's defect as excessive pride, is reminiscent of Greek myth. As in an allusion to Sophocles in *La hojarasca*, Greek mythology is present in this tale as an outgrowth of García Márquez's days with his mentors of the Group of Cartagena, and the classicist Gustavo Ibarra Merlano, in particular.

Several critics have pointed out that some of García Márquez's most accomplished stories are contained in this volume; for the writer himself, 'La siesta del martes' ('Tuesday Siesta') is the best piece in the volume. He had learned the technical tricks for this fiction from Hemingway, this being the story with the most sparse and minimal language of the book. The choice of Tuesday could well have its origin in the Spanish proverb 'martes, ni te cases ni te embarques, ni de tu familia te apartes' ('Tuesdays, don't get married or take a trip, or leave your family').

'La prodigiosa tarde' was an early step in the construction of the world of Macondo. The pragmatic Úrsula figure and the figure of the innocent genius – an *idiot-savant* in the character Baltazar/José Arcadio – begin assuming their respective characteristics in this early fiction. In this story, García Márquez constructs a tale with unresolved ambiguities that allow multiple levels of interpretation that are not mutually exclusive. The ability to create the multiple levels of meaning that cohabit the text is part of the special and universal quality of the Macondo fiction, from the beginning in *La hojarasca* to the culmination in *Cien años*.

'La siesta del martes' offers another window into the world of Macondo, even though, on the surface, there is little direct connection between this story and *Cien años de soledad*. The only obvious link is a minor element of the story: the protagonist remembers the days of Colonel Aureliano Buendía and the civil wars that are a part of Macondo's history in both *Cien años* and *El coronel*. No other character from 'La siesta del martes' appears in *Cien años* and the anecdote on which this short story is based does not appear in the novel either. Nevertheless, in this story García Márquez develops some of his most basic practices for his Macondo novel masterpiece.

'La siesta del martes' begins with a neutral description of the region of Macondo as seen through the window of a train rolling slowly past banana plantations and buildings, ranging from modest to impoverished. This neutral description limited strictly to what is seen – with no human characters identified yet as the subjects seeing – is part of García Márquez's early exploration of the technical devices of micromanaging the act of seeing (as opposed to speaking, narrating, or writing). This is a modernist strategy that García Márquez exploits deftly in the remainder of his Macondo fiction and later in *El otoño* and *El amor*.

The story goes on to portray the two main characters – a mother and her twelve-year-old daughter – who are traveling by train to visit the cemetery where the mother's son has recently been buried. He had been shot and killed when caught in the act of petty theft in a private home. The mother and daughter visit the town's priest in order to be directed to the exact place where the son was interred, and where they can pay their last respects.

The initial description of the mother and the daughter on the train reveals two passengers in a bare, third-class wagon ('Eran los únicos pasajeros en el escueto vagón de tercera clase', *Los funerales*, 7). This sentence underlines not only their isolation on the train, but also their modesty and impoverishment. Their isolation and their humility are among the most noteworthy character traits in the unfolding of the story and are key to the denouement. The paragraph ends with a sentence that captures the essence of their being and their circumstance, as two characters involved in a serious and rigorous, yet impoverished mourning process ('Ambas guardaban un luto rigoroso y pobre', 8). Their rigor and their poverty increase in significance as the story progresses. The narrator then offers a succinct observation about the mother as someone who has the kind of serenity of people accustomed to poverty ('Tenía la serenidad escrupulosa de la gente acostumbrada a la pobreza', 8). This observation not only portrays the mother effectively with a minimum of words, but also shows an attitude that is constant throughout the Macondo cycle of fiction: the impoverished and the common folk have the most admirable basic human qualities, such as serenity. The portrayal of the mother here demonstrates how intimately familiar the implied author is with the impoverished and the working poor. The interaction early in the story between the mother and the daughter prefigures what proves to be an important virtue for the mother: dignity. Thus, early in the story, she instructs the young girl to take care of all of her basic needs (such as relieving herself or drinking water) immediately, for she is not to request anything at all once they reach their destination. From the mother's perspective, asking for anything at all could potentially be a humiliation that her acute sense of dignity could not tolerate.

As the train halts in the small town, and the mother and the child descend, the story assumes a mythical, almost epic quality that is also an element that García Márquez began developing in this early Macondo fiction. In this story, the image of the nameless mother and the nameless child descending from the train lends a mythic quality to the scene, for there is a sense that this could be any mother with her child; their simple personas, with their aura of honesty and dignity, lend more power to their mythic representation.

In this story, as in the Macondo fiction and *Cien años*, this mythic content is not fully developed. Rather, 'La prodigiosa tarde de Baltazar', 'La siesta del martes', and much of the other Macondo fiction only allude to things with mythic and epic qualities. But by making these allusions, these fictions are about myth.[4]

As the mother looks at the town before her, she sees a poor village that is typical of the Caribbean coast in mid-afternoon; the severe summer heat quietly penetrates human bodies during the afternoon *siesta*. The only historical referent in the story is the description of townhouses, obviously alluding to the type of homes built by the foreign United Fruit Company in the first quarter of the century.[5] By not naming the fruit company, however, García Márquez maintains the mythic and universal quality of the story as the mother and her daughter walk humbly through the town in search of the grave of the lost son. Their first act is to look for the town priest.

The last part of 'La siesta del martes' deals with the subtle interaction between the mother and the priest. When the mother locates the priest, she establishes her moral superiority with the calmness of her voice and the neutral tone that she uses to provide the information he needs to identify her as the mother of the young man. A week earlier, an elderly widow had heard the noise of someone forcing himself into her home and she used a revolver

---

[4]  In his discussion of *Cien años*, Roberto González Echevarría has suggested that this novel is really about myth rather than being myth. I agree with this observation, and propose that it also applies to these stories. See González Echevarría, '*One Hundred Years of Solitude*: The Novel as Myth and Archive', in *García Márquez*, ed. Robin Fiddian, Modern Literatures in Perspective (London: Longman, 1995), 79–99.

[5]  When García Márquez traveled through the southern region of the United States in order to visit Oxford, Mississippi, he saw homes built on the same model as those he had seen constructed by the United Fruit Company in Colombia in the first quarter of the century.

to kill him instantaneously. The mother hears the story from the priest and provides the full name of her son, Carlos Centeno Ayala. The priest, in turn, asks the mother if she had ever tried to put him on the right path, to which she responds that she had told him never to steal anything that someone might need to eat. The son, who had suffered attempting to survive as a boxer, had always followed her guidance.

At the end of the story, the townsfolk have realized that the criminal's mother is present in the town; they stare through windows and their children are on the streets to observe the mother and the child. The priest offers a parasol to the mother so that she can hide from them. However, the mother, in her final act of affirming her sense of self-dignity, rejects the parasol, takes her daughter in hand, and strides into the street.

Once again, García Márquez has created a patently ambiguous story by leaving unresolved the moral question of the son's guilt vis-à-vis that of the widow. Is it a serious crime to steal for survival if the person committing the crime respects the needs of others to survive also? Should the widow be prosecuted for the use of excessive force? Should the priest support the widow? These are all questions that the story leaves open enough to lend themselves to considerable discussion, thus making this story another of García Márquez's early masterpieces in creating unresolved ambiguities.

Despite the ambiguities and potential moral questions concerning the relative justifiability of stealing and of murder, García Márquez does lead the reader to sympathize with the family of the deceased and with Carlos Centeno himself. On the one hand, the mother is the most admirable figure of the story, with her humility combined with her refined sense of dignity (she prefigures other characters of great dignity in the Macondo cycle, such as the Colonel in *El coronel*). On the other hand, the priest is not an admirable character. He seems embarrassed to speak with the mother, and he is unsure and skeptical about his own statements about the will of God. Thus, the priest is an early instance of a number of representatives of the Catholic church that García Márquez places under scrutiny in his fiction. In the end, the author consistently portrays the human spirit of the common people as superior to institutional doctrines brought by the elite from Spain to the Americas.

These two stories, 'La prodigiosa tarde' and 'La siesta del martes', are important texts (of the kind sometimes termed foundational fictions) not only for *Cien años* but also for the entire cycle of Macondo. They introduce characters and situations that are more fully developed in *Cien años*. More importantly, the author found his first early success in exploiting narrative strategies that have become 'trademark' García Márquez (and have been often associated with his supposed 'magic realism'), such as the use of attractive and enigmatic beginnings and a narrative point of view similar to that of the common folk or the average person on the street.

### Synthesis: *Cien años de soledad*

The first chapter of *Cien años* introduces the two characters modeled after Baltazar and Úrsula, José Arcadio Buendía and Úrsula. José Arcadio is the scientist and inventor whose wild imagination makes him a figure very comparable to Baltazar, whose fantasy creates an incredible birdcage, and whose wild imagination leads him into his night of fame that eventually turns into ignominy. José Arcadio's imaginative way of thinking clashes with the pragmatic thinking of Úrsula in the first chapter, when he declares, after intense study and thought, that the world is round 'like an orange'. His declaration is followed immediately by Úrsula's pragmatic reaction, losing her patience ('Úrsula perdió la paciencia').[6] This contrast of characters, similar to that in 'La prodigiosa tarde', is developed throughout *Cien años*, not only in the contrast between these two characters in particular but in other sets of dual and contrasting characters as well.

The affirmation of the spirit of the common people shown in the story 'La siesta del martes' is the constant world view developed more fully in *Cien años de soledad*. In 'La siesta del martes', the solitary and humble woman faces the rebuff of the local priest, as well as the scorn of the town's citizens. Similarly, in *Cien años*, the people of Macondo are the common folk who endure as best they can in order to survive the traditions of the Catholic church that impose the values of medieval Spain. They also survive the vicissitudes of institutional politics, as well as the numerous individual failures and collective tragedies of the underclass. The people of Macondo suffer the isolation and solitude of the mother in 'La siesta del martes', and many of them not only endure, but the most admirable of them do so with her sense of dignity.

The basic plot of *Cien años* tells the story of the Buendía family and the history of the town of Macondo. José Arcadio Buendía marries Úrsula, his cousin, and they are the first of seven generations covered in the novel. Macondo progresses from a simple village to a modern town. The town suffers from a succession of civil wars that replicate the real history of

---

6  The English version reads, 'Úrsula lost her patience': García Márquez, *One Hundred Years of Solitude*. tr. Gregory Rabassa (New York: Avon, 1971), 11. All quotations in English are from this edition.

nineteenth-century Colombia. At the end of the novel, a member of the family succeeds in translating some mysterious parchments that, as it turns out, tell the story of the family exactly as its members have experienced it in real life.

Few Latin American novels have been the subject of as much scholarly attention as *Cien años*. Critical readings of the novel have been exhaustive; explorations range from minute, close readings of the novel's first sentence to broad approaches to its mythic and historical qualities. From his days as a journalist in the 1950s, García Márquez has been a master of the arresting opening sentence. *Cien años* begins as follows: 'Muchos años después, frente al pelotón de fusilamiento, el coronel Aurelano Buendía había de recordar aquella tarde remota en que su padre lo llevó a conocer el hielo' ('Many years later, as he faced the firing squad, Colonel Aureliano Buendía was to remember that distant afternoon when his father took him to discover ice'). Not only is this one of García Márquez's most engaging opening lines, it is also one of the most memorable opening lines to be found in modern Latin American fiction. In his reflections on the opening, on time, and on memory in the novel's multifaceted textual representations, Julio Ortega has suggested that García Márquez's loosening of the limits of traditional literary language subverts the memory of Latin American history as it has been written in official histories of the nations in the region. Another critic has pointed out that, in the first sentence, García Márquez involves the reader in three aspects of time: the future of 'many years later', an assumed present, and the past of 'that distant afternoon', Consequently, from the outset, time itself is a problematic issue. The reader is left to speculate in which of these three times the story begins. From this sentence, it appears that time has a special quality and its exact nature is elusive. This opening line will be evoked throughout the novel, as García Márquez continues his play with time, and time will escape clear description or definition. With respect to elements of the plot foreshadowed in this opening line, the reader is left wondering what the role of the firing squad may be. The ambiguous use of time may lead the reader to question whether this firing squad will be something significant in the novel or a ruse used as a dramatic device just to create suspense. As the reader discovers, there are seven references to this event in the first four chapters, confirming as legitimate the level of interest created in the first line. Those references build the suspense throughout these four chapters. Finally, in the seventh chapter, when the colonel does face the firing squad, he does not actually die, for his brother rescues him at the last moment. In another surprising twist of the plot, the soldiers at the firing squad are so intimidated that they join the two Buendías in their crusade against the conservatives.

The manner in which the author handles this firing squad episode indicates from the first sentence that minute details are worthy of careful note and are not gratuitous, as they might be in some realist fiction that often uses details for nothing more than creating realist effects. Early on, García Márquez establishes that this novel has one of those trademark qualities of modernist fiction: some initially incoherent details appear and reappear, eventually fitting into some kind of pattern. On the other hand, the reader learns to proceed with caution and doubt, for the seven references to a death scene lead not to the anticipated execution, but to more repetitive action of the sort the reader has already experienced.

The first sentence also introduces the matter of 'discovering ice'. With these words, the author begins a portrayal of Macondo as a primitive, innocent place that is a type of biblical paradise. Further construction of this biblical paradise continues in the first paragraph when the narrator states that 'el mundo era tan reciente, que muchas cosas carecían de nombre, y para mencionarlas había que señalarlas con el dedo' ('the world was so recent that many things lacked names, and in order to indicate them it was necessary to point'). As it turns out, the Buendía family is still in the process of learning the names of even the most basic things, including ice. The novel becomes, eventually, a celebration of the act of creation, and this will prove to be one of its universal themes. This mention of ice will become another of the novel's most memorable passages, whose significance is both thematic and structural. With respect to structure, the ice becomes the main element in the chapter's organization: from the mention of it the narrator turns quickly to Melquíades's other inventions, and the chapter closes with the anecdote of the introduction to ice. The ending of that first sentence is developed later, affirming for the reader the pattern suggested by the anecdote of the firing squad. The presence of ice, then, creates a circular structure in the first chapter, and that circular structure is repeated throughout the novel.[7]

Scholars and critics have also given a considerable amount of attention to the last three pages of *Cien años*, which offer several surprises and twists. Near the end of the novel references begin to appear that clearly emphasize the book's status as fiction. Parallel to these references in the last three pages, there remains, above all, a story of a family and a town, as opposed to a fully developed metafiction. In the fifteenth chapter, García Márquez inserts a character from Fuentes's *La muerte de Artemio Cruz*, Lorenzo Gavilán.

[7]   See John S. Brushwood, *The Spanish American Novel: A Twentieth-century Survey* (London & Austin TX: University of Texas Press, 1975), 287–88; also Seymour Menton, 'One Hundred Years of Solitude', an unpublished lecture presented in the Distinguished Faculty Lecture Series, University of California, Irvine, 24 January 1980.

García Márquez's cohorts from his youth in Barranquilla, Álvaro Cepeda Samudio, Alfonso Fuenmayor, and Germán Vargas, actually appear in the novel as Álvaro, Alfonso, and Germán. Aureliano Buendía finds the key to deciphering some mysterious parchments that Melquíades has left. The entire family history has been written: every action from one generation after another was predetermined. Consequently, the fact that the family story is discovered to be a fiction adds a new level of fictionality. Aureliano Buendía's discovery concerning the fictionality of the Buendía family runs parallel to the reader's discovery and experience at the end of the novel. As an ideal reader-figure, Aureliano isolates himself in order to concentrate on his parchments. As reader, he is able to see the family destiny from the beginning of its story to the immediate present of himself reading and living the moment:

> Sólo entonces descubrió que Amaranta Úrsula no era su hermana, sino su tía, y que Francis Drake había asaltado a Riohacha solamente para que ellos pudieran buscarse por los laberintos más intricados de la sangre, hasta engendrar el animal mitológico que había de poner término a la estirpe.
> (*Cien años*, 350)

> Only then did he discover that Amaranta Úrsula was not his sister but his aunt, and that Sir Francis Drake had attacked Riohacha only so that they could seek each other through the most intricate labyrinths of blood until they would engender the mythological animal that was to bring the line to an end.   (*One Hundred Years*, 416)

The reference to the mythological animal is to the Buendía with the pig's tail that Aureliano had engendered. Reading himself in the text, realizing that he himself is a fiction, he leaps forward in the final paragraph of the novel in order to read about the very moment he is living, as a reader 'descifrándolo a medida que lo vivía, profetizándose a sí mismo en el acto de descifrar la última página de los pergaminos, como si se estuviera viendo en un espejo hablado' ('prophesying himself in the act of deciphering the last page of parchments, as if he were looking into a speaking mirror'). Here, the reader and Aureliano are reminded of the fictionality of the Macondo story, at the same time that it becomes evident that the reader and Aureliano play identical roles as readers of fiction.

In addition to the beginning and the end of *Cien años*, the issue of 'magic realism' in the work has also been a matter of critical attention. Over the years, this novel has become known as the paradigm of magic realist fiction. Nevertheless, the term 'magic realist' originates not with García Márquez but with the Swiss art critic Franz Roh who, in 1925, coined the term to refer to a magic insight into reality. Magic realism expressed human astonishment before the wonders of the real world. Thus, José Arcadio Buendía's reaction to Melquíades's ice seems appropriately related to the term 'magic realism'.[8]

In Latin America, intellectuals have been engaged in attempts to define the reality of this region as something special, uniquely different from Europe, and 'magic' in a variety of ways, since the 1940s. The Cuban writer Alejo Carpentier was a leading voice in these early discussions, and he used the phrase 'lo real maravilloso' ('marvelous American reality') in the prologue to his novel *El reino de este mundo* (*The Kingdom of this World*, 1949).[9] This special reality, for Carpentier, has its roots in the 'marvelous' nature of the cultural experience and history of the Americas. He suggests that his self-defined 'marvelous American reality' has much in common with poetic epiphany. In the 1950s and 1960s, several critics of Spanish American litera-ture adopted and popularized the term 'magic realism', and the critic Ángel Flores published an oft-cited article on the subject in 1955. Since the 1960s, magic realism has been used as a point of reference, for better or for worse, in discussions of a wide and diverse set of writers. Often, the appearance of even the slightest element of the fantastic or irrational in a Latin American fiction has led some critics – often book reviewers – to the conclusion that the book is yet another example of the now overused term 'magic realism'. Some scholars of Latin American literature have simply defined magic realism as a blend of reality and fantasy, and *Cien años*, by this definition, can be consid-ered a prime example: the broad appeal and aesthetic value of this blending of reality and fantasy justify this description of the novel. In recent years, scholarly discussions of magic realism have waned.

Aspects of the empirical reality (or 'the real') in Colombia and Latin America, as well as other elements often considered 'fantastic' according to Western European definitions, do indeed appear in *Cien años*. Remedios la bella (Remedios the Beauty), who is portayed as a 'real' person in the world of Macondo, inexplicably appears to fly off into the sky. By the time this event occurs in the novel, the reader has been given descriptions of her exceptional beauty, which seems to make her something other than human. There are other incredible anecdotes which are never explained as well, such as Melquíades's return from the dead. Equally inexplicably, Melquíades is

---

[8]   For a set of well informed readings on magic realism, see *Magic Realism: Theory, History*, ed. Lois Parkinson Zamora and Wendy B. Faris (Durham NC: Duke University Press, 1995).

[9]   For an analysis of the broad importance of the writings of Alejo Carpentier in Latin American literature, see Roberto González Echevarría, *Alejo Carpentier: The Pilgrim at Home* (Ithaca NY: Cornell University Press, 1977; reissued, with updated introduction and bibliography, Austin TX: Texas University Press, 1990).

somehow present even when he is absent, and his room remains well kept even though no one physically takes care of it. An incredible anecdote of a different nature is Colonel Aureliano Buendía's engendering of seventeen illegitimate sons by seventeen different women. This is an example of an only slightly hyperbolic representation of something that does happen in Latin America, and has cultural origins in the strongly patriarchal and male-oriented roots of the medieval and Hispano-Arabic past of the region. In the social and political realm, thousands of striking workers die in a massacre, yet seemingly no one sees or hears anything and the workers seemingly never existed.

The use of terms such as 'magic realism' represents an attempt to concep-tualize a narrative process in which even the most unlikely and seemingly incredible people, events, and things are not presented as 'fantastic' by the narrator or the characters. Akin to Roh's original concept of magic realism, these people, events, and things are often commonplace. This ongoing narra-tive strategy can be understood by recalling García Márquez's insight into the importance of the stories his grandmother and aunts told him to explain things when he was a child. In his book, *El olor de la guayaba: Conversaciones con Plinio Apuleyo Mendoza* (1982, translated as *The Fragrance of the Guava*), he frequently mentions the importance of his grandmother and aunts, and he has mentioned them in interview after interview ever since the 1970s.

What García Márquez has explained, in effect, in his numerous recogni-tions of the storytelling prowess of his aunts and his grandmother, is the central importance in his writing of the oral tradition in which he was steeped in his childhood. The orality of *Cien años* can be placed into two general categories: the orality of the folk tale, comparable to the 'tall tale' in the United States, and 'primary orality'. The stories that García Márquez heard from his aunts and his grandmother are related to the tradition of the tall tale. One technique that the narrator of *Cien años* shares with the teller of the oral tall tale is an absolute coolness or understatement when describing incredible situations and, on the other hand, a penchant for exaggeration when dealing with the commonplace. In the ice episode of the first chapter, for example, the narrator's language shares the character's exaggerated reac-tion to Melquíades's new discovery.

When the narrator reacts to the most marvelous and fantastic people, events, and things with exceptional passivity, he is also imitating the manner of the tall tale. In the first chapter, José Arcadio and his children experience the disappearance of a man who becomes invisible after drinking a special potion. As incredible as this event is, neither the narrator nor the characters find it in any way extraordinary, and they do not pay particular attention to it.

What has often been identified as magic realism is best understood, in many instances, as a manifestation of the mindset of primary orality. Walter Ong has observed that many cultures and subcultures, even in a high-technology ambience, preserve much of the mindset of what he calls 'primary orality', and this was the case of the Caribbean region of Colombia in the early twentieth century.[10] García Márquez juxtaposes the mindset of a writing culture with the mindset of the residually oral milieu of his youth in Aracataca. The elaborate culture of numerous literary traditions and of primary oral culture permeate *Cien años*, sometimes creating humorous juxtapositions. Much of what happens in this novel, in features frequently described as instances of magic realism, is actually a recreation, in one way or another, of precisely that shift from orality to writing: the shift from orality to various stages of literacy and, in turn, to various stages of literary culture.[11]

The shift from orality to literary culture is an important element in *Cien años* and is most evident in the early chapters of the novel. In those early chapters, a mindset of primary orality predominates; in the last chapter, the complex maneuvers of writing culture are fully in evidence. In the first chapter, the two cultural extremes are represented by Melquíades, with a writing culture originating from the outside, and by Úrsula, whose mindset is oral. As Macondo is portrayed in the first paragraph, it is a town of paradisiacal primary orality in which stones are 'white and enormous, like prehistoric eggs'. The word 'prehistoric' associates the milieu with a prewriting stage of prehistory, even bordering on pre-speaking: 'The world was so recent that many things lacked names, and in order to indicate them it was necessary to point'. Located in a space between the two extremes of Melquíades and Úrsula, José Arcadio Buendía provides a special link between them, because, paradoxically, he belongs to both: he reacts in some situations as an oral-culture person and in others as the only lettered person in a predominantly oral milieu. José Arcadio Buendía is literate, but he deals with science with

---

[10] Ong introduces the concept of primary orality in *Orality and Literacy: The Technologizing of the Word*, New Accents (London: Methuen, 1982); see especially Chapter 2.

[11] I have explored this shift from orality to literacy in more depth in the Costa region and in the work of García Márquez in *The Colombian Novel, 1844–1987* (London & Austin TX: University of Texas Press, 1981). One of the most revealing studies about the presence of oral culture in the Costa region of Colombia is Orlando Fals Borda's *Historia doble de la costa*, 4 vols (Bogotá: Carlos Valencia, 1979–86). In that book, Fals Borda, a sociologist by training, transcribes two basic versions of the history of this region. One is based on research into the history of the region using the written documentation of writing culture. The other is based on interviews with mostly illiterate people who relate to him the stories that have been transmitted through what remains of the region's oral tradition. Fals Borda provides these two versions in alternate chapters (see especially Chapter 4).

some ingenuousness as an oral-culture person, conceiving Melquíades's magnets, for example, as a 'weapon of war'. Equally typical of an oral-culture person's reaction to a writing mindset is his reaction to Melquíades: 'Hasta el proprio José Arcadio Buendía consideró que los conocimientos de Melquíades habían llegado a extremos intolerables' ('Even José Arcadio Buendía himself considered that Melquíades's knowledge had reached unbearable extremes', *One Hundred Years*, 12). Oral-culture persons tend to view many facets of writing culture as irrelevant or even ridiculous.[12] In the first chapter, for example, Úrsula is uninterested in abstract conceptualization; thus, as mentioned earlier, she loses her patience with José Arcadio Buendía when he defines the world as round like an orange.[13] As Ong has pointed out, the oral mind is not abstract but situational, the latter being Úrsula's mode of thinking throughout the novel. José Arcadio Buendía attempts to convince her to move from Macondo, using several arguments in the abstract mode, and her reaction is to bring him down from his high level of abstraction to the reality of the immediate situation: 'En vez de andar pensando en tus alocadas novelerías, debes ocuparte de tus hijos' (*Cien años*, 20) ('Instead of going around thinking about your crazy inventions, you should be worrying about your sons', *One Hundred Years*, 22). The world of this first chapter, then, emerges as the oral culture of Úrsula, the writing culture of Melquíades, and the humorous semi-orality of José Arcadio Buendía that bridges the gap between the two.

Macondo moves from preliteracy to literacy after the initial chapter; and the narrator's mindset shifts from the feigned pre-orality of the first chapter to the historicity of the second. The pre-literacy image of 'prehistoric eggs' used in Chapter I can be compared to the second chapter's historical discourse of writing culture: 'Cuando el pirata Francis Drake asaltó a Riohacha, en el siglo XVI, la bisabuela de Úrsula Iguarán se asustó tanto con el toque de rebato y el estampido de los cañones, que perdió el control de los nervios y se sentó en un fogón encendido' (*Cien años*, 24) ('When the pirate Sir Francis Drake attacked Riohacha in the sixteenth century, Úrsula Iguarán's great-grandmother became so frightened with the ringing of alarm bells and the firing of cannons that she lost control of her nerves and sat down on a lighted stove', *One Hundred Years*, 27). In the last chapter, the novel announces itself

---

[12] See Ong, *Orality and Literacy*, Chapter 2.

[13] Ong has explained how individuals in oral cultures, like Úrsula, are not interested in definitions: 'Oral cultures of course have no dictionaries and few semantic discrepancies. The meaning of each word is controlled by what Goody and Watt call 'direct semantic ratification', that is, by real-life situations in which the word is used here and now. The oral mind is uninterested in definitions' (*Orality and Literacy*, 47).

as not only focused on writing culture, but also as an example of complex forms of self-conscious fiction: it incorporates characters from modern Latin American literature, and Aureliano's role as reader of the parchments also focuses, obviously, on writing culture.

*Cien años* offers numerous examples of oral processes that are noetic (that require, that is, abstract intellection if they are to be understood). Typical of the tall tale of the United States is the use of 'heavy characters': people whose deeds are monumental, memorable, and commonly public.[14] The lengthy account of José Arcadio Buendía's exploits after his return from sixty-five trips around the world (see Chapter 5) and Colonel Aureliano Buendía's military exploits, including his losing all thirty-two of his battles, are perhaps the best example of this oral noetic process.

The oral process already mentioned as it pertains to Úrsula makes use of concepts in situational frames of reference that are minimally abstract in the sense that they remain close to life as humans beings live it.[15] The narrator takes on his role as an oral-culture person throughout much of the novel, often using animal imagery that keeps the anecdotes close to the life of humans. When the narrator assumes such positions, he is often taking on a role that is also similar to the ones played by his characters. He employs animal imagery in his early description of Amaranta: 'Era liviana y acuosa como una lagartija, pero todas sus partes eran humanas' (*Cien años*, 33) ('She was light and watery, like a newt, but all her parts were human', *One Hundred Years*, 37).

The narrator's treatment of Remedios la bella, both in form and content, is that of an oral person, and is but one example of his many other strategies that are typical of an oral mindset. The narrator uses the epithet *la bella* for her in Spanish, a common usage in oral storytelling. The anecdote in which Remedios la bella rises into the sky is a typical description of how a person in an oral culture would view such an event. The narrator's copiousness is another noteworthy oral element of his storytelling. Ong points out that oral performance demands flow: repetition and redundancy create oral flow and hesitancy is a negative element. One of the best examples of this copious-

---

[14] Ong explains the function of 'heavy' characters as follows: 'The heroic tradition of primary oral culture and of early literate culture, with its massive oral residue, relates to the agonistic lifestyle, but it is best and most radically explained in terms of the needs of oral noetic processes. Oral memory works effectively with 'heavy' characters, persons whose deeds are monumental, memorable and commonly public' (*Orality and Literacy*, 70).

[15] Ong describes the relationship between oral cultures and closeness to the human lifeworld (*Orality and Literacy*, 42–43).

ness or flow is Fernanda's two-page, single-sentence diatribe (*One Hundred Years*, 298–300).

Clearly, the narrator and Úrsula are the most prominent examples of oral-culture entities, but there are other characters who react as participants in oral environments. For example, by the twelfth chapter, Macondo's inhabitants seem to be modern in some of their attitudes and some of them are lettered as well. This chapter begins, however, with a humorous anecdote describing an oral-culture person's reaction to modern technology: the inhabitants of Macondo become outraged and destroy the seats in the movie house because an actor who died and was buried in one film reappeared later in another – alive, and as an Arab.[16]

Oral cultures also tend to be verbally 'agonistic': that is, they contain verbally combative exchanges. It is as a result of Prudencio Aguilar's verbal challenge to José Arcadio Buendía – questioning his masculinity – that the Buendía family history begins. The males of Macondo tend to be lettered and the females usually belong to oral culture. In the last chapter, the women begin to read, often finding themselves unprepared for masculine writing culture. The loss of feminine oral culture brings about the novel's denouement: the lettered Amaranta Úrsula and Aureliano conceive a baby after their final defeat within a lost oral culture; he had abandoned his analyses of the parchments at the point where he would have discovered their blood relationship.

The special blend of traditionalism and modernity in *Cien años* needs to be associated with the various roles the narrator assumes as oral story-

---

[16] I consider it significant that the character against whom Macondo's inhabitants react is an Arab, even apart from the oral culture under consideration. I would propose (as a matter for future study) that there is a strong and consistent undercurrent of Arab culture in *Cien años* in particular and in García Márquez's work in general. The presence of the Arabic tale *A Thousand and One Nights* in *Cien años* has been amply documented. In addition, linguists have proposed that the word *gitano* has etymological roots with an antiquated Arabic word for 'Egyptian'. Thus, Melquíades might be seen as an Arab. More importantly, however, are the profoundly Arabic elements in the 'Spanish medieval' culture transplanted into the colonial society in the Americas. Contrary to the dominant ideology of a 'pure' Spanish culture imposed on the indigenous cultures of the Americas, the line of thought developed from the writings of Américo Castro to books such as *Terra nostra* and *Valiente Mundo Nuevo* of Carlos Fuentes emphasize the strong and diverse semitic presence on the Iberian Peninsula in the Middle Ages. The codes and actions of characters of Macondo that seem so anachronistically 'medieval' are best understood as 'Hispano-Arabic', from the first chapter in which José Arcadio feels compelled to engender a child to prove his virility and protect his Arabic sense of honor. The undercurrent of the novel is the constant fear of the residents of Macondo that they will discover, as they did in the movie theater, that their dead past will somehow be resuscitated and be revealed, to their horror, as Arabic.

teller in the manner of the tall tale, as narrator with a primary oral-culture mindset, and as the modern narrator of a self-conscious (written) fiction.[17] Among the factors that contribute to the special qualities of *Cien años* (and its supposed magic realism) is the *greguería* of Ramón Gómez de la Serna; there are connections between oral noetic processes and the logic (or lack of logic) of the *greguería*. When José Arcadio Buendía proclaims that 'La tierra es redonda, como una naranja' ('The world is round, like an orange'), he is making a statement that is as illogical to the illiterate Úrsula as is a *greguería* to a lettered person.

## Colonial legacy and the plot

*Cien años* is García Márquez's most comprehensive novel dealing with the Spanish medieval and colonial legacy in Latin America. The family story, the town's story, the story of Colombia, and the story of Latin America are all implied in the novel's plot. It has often been called a history of Latin America, but García Márquez has pointed out correctly that, rather than being a history of Latin America, it is a metaphor for Latin America. Medieval honor systems appear directly in *Cien años*, *Crónica*, and others of García Márquez's fictions. The family story begins in a Spanish medieval duel of honor: José Arcadio Buendía engenders his first child as a response to a challenge to his masculinity, even though there were serious questions about the possible incest involved in the sexual union. This act also establishes a local version of the Spanish patriarchal order from the beginnings of the Buendía family, from the foundation of Macondo, from the colonial period in Colombia, and from the conquest of the indigenous peoples in Latin America. The medieval duel of honor (actually an Hispano-Arabic tradition) is replayed later as the central event of *Crónica*.

The twenty-one unnumbered and untitled chapters of *Cien años* narrate the story of the Buendía family and the story of Macondo in a basically linear fashion, with the occasional diversions into the past and future suggested in the opening sentence. The first two chapters provide the family's background. The first focuses on José Arcadio Buendía's methods for understanding the world, presented as a parody of Western science. At the same time, this parody communicates an underlying fear of recognizing Arabic culture, for the roots of Western science are also Arabic. After studying the magnet that

---

[17] I have discussed the relationship of writing and orality in the context of the modern in *The Colombian Novel*, Chapter 4.

Melquíades brought to Macondo, José Arcadio declares it useless except to extract gold from the earth. The gypsies from outside Macondo then bring a telescope and a magnifying glass, and he attempts to make use of these new objects, which are as novel to Macondo as was the magnet. If Melquíades is understood as an Arabic character, all of his 'inventions' of science brought to Macondo have an Arabic source. José Arcadio then goes into his private readings and research, leading him to declare, as noted earlier, that 'the earth is round, like an orange'. The gypsies eventually return to Macondo and bring their inventions, but relatively little changes at the outset in this idyllic town, living a prehistorical utopia in which no one is over thirty years old and no one has yet died. Each of the family members is described as a 'heavy' character (in Ong's terms), with just a few characteristics, but very outstanding ones. Of the children, the older son, also named José Arcadio, is exceptionally well endowed, and the youngest son, Aureliano, has supernatural powers, predicting, for example, that a pot will fall from a table seconds before it actually does so.

In the second chapter, the narrator moves back in time and in the family history, describing the foundation of Macondo. This chapter takes the history of the family back to the sixteenth century and the Spanish colonial empire, when Sir Francis Drake attacked the Colombian coastal region of Riohacha. In this novel the author does not name the 'Spanish colonial' legacy *per se*, but he does refer to it directly in essays and interviews, and he actually names Sir Francis Drake, thus changing the nature of the text in the second chapter: it is now 'historical' in a way that it was not in the first. This narrative now becomes the historical account of colonial powers in competition and conflict in the Caribbean region. This setting was also the major Caribbean venue for the African slave trade, for Cartagena was a busy distribution point for the slaves brought from Africa. (The historical details of the slave trade are elaborated in a later novel set in Cartagena, *El amor en los tiempos del cólera*; see Chapter 4, below.) García Márquez connects the empirical history of Latin America with the Buendía fictional story by having Úrsula's great-great grandfather wounded in the battle against the invading forces of the historical figure Sir Francis Drake. Soon after this battle with the British Colonial forces, she and her husband move inland from the Caribbean coast, where her spouse becomes engaged in business relations with Don José Arcadio Buendía, a tobacco farmer. Several centuries later, Úrsula's great-grand daughter, also named Úrsula, marries the great-grandson of Don José Arcadio Buendía, also named Don José Arcadio Buendía. Given the incestuous relations already in place, and in parody of the incestuous family relations of the founding Spanish aristocracy, it is not surprising that an uncle of José Arcadio Buendía had married an aunt of Úrsula, and this eventually results in the birth of a child with a pig's tail. Because of this family history, José Arcadio Buendía has at the beginning of the novel been married to Úrsula for months before they consumate their marriage. As we have seen, once José Arcadio Buendía's masculinity is ridiculed in public by his friend Prudencio Aguilar, José Arcadio exhibits his sexual prowess and his first son is born without the predicted pig's tail. With his Spanish medieval and Arabic sense of honor, José Arcadio also feels the need to kill Prudencio Aguilar, which he does. This act haunts José Arcadio and Úrsula so intensely, however, that they decide they must leave town, and they name the place where they arrive 'Macondo'. (The name in itself is not significant; García Márquez once saw a ranch in Colombia with that name, which might or might not have been a name adopted from an indigenous language.) Among the more mundane (and less fantastic) events is the birth of their daughter Amaranta, followed by the birth of their son José Arcadio, who falls in love with Pilar Ternera. As the family grows, José Arcadio Buendía remains dedicated to his scientific research. Úrsula then disappears unexpectedly, returns unannounced five months later, and discovers a route to a nearby town which can offer some of the amenities of modern life, such as access to a mail system.

In the third chapter, outsiders continue to arrive in Macondo and the town begins to modernize, setting up ongoing contrasts between colonial ways and signs of nascent modernity. From Chapter three onwards, part of the novel's tension is based not only on conflict of action, but on the conflict between a pervasively colonial mentality and an emergent modern one. Rebecca is the first of the outsiders, arriving at the Buendía home with a note from a distant relative of the family. She likes to eat dirt, which is a trait characteristic of the people of Macondo: they inexplicably do seemingly irrational things and the text seemingly has no need to explain them. In effect, they act out the verbal constructs that are the surprising *greguerías* of Gómez de la Serna. In *La hojarasca*, for example, the doctor requests grass to eat, and the other characters do not react in any way to this bizarre need any more than they do to Rebecca's eating dirt in *Cien años*. In both cases, the narrator also remains aloof from activities that would in conventional fiction require explanation by either the narrator or the characters. Even fragmented and innovative modernist texts not constructed on the basis of immediate causality eventually provide the reader with some means for more understanding or interpretation. Herein lies a special quality of García Márquez's brand of modernism (and what some have called magic realism): rather than just inverting causes and effects (a common strategy of many modernist narratives and one which García Márquez himself employs often), he often never offers any causal explanation at all. Instead, he uses an oral-culture approach that imitates the strong primary oral culture that had developed over the centuries in this region of Colombia. Oral storytelling is replete with stories such as characters eating dirt and grass for no apparent reason; they are simply acts that occur in the most immediate human lifeworld that no one questions. The early Macondo of the initial chapters is populated by a tri-ethnic people of an oral culture blended from an illiterate medieval Spanish culture, illiterate indigenous cultures, and illiterate African cultures. Rebecca's eating dirt in Chapter 3, then, is a manifestation of an oral-culture treatment of an event seemingly within a modernist text and containing the surprise of the *greguería*. It is a unique case of a modernist writer who found ways to narrate traces of disparate cultures such as those of medieval Spain and Africa.[18]

In the third chapter, a character from the first, Melquíades, returns to Macondo, even though is already dead. This event is not totally unexplained, for the narrator and the characters understand this return to Macondo as a result of his having been bored to death. All of this is typical of the humor employed in the journalism of García Márquez's mentor in Cartagena, Clemente Manuel Zabala. Since such an explanation is not fully rational, the anecdote also involves an oral-storytelling approach. The nature of the explanation is interesting in an oral-culture world: death, the ultimate human fear, is trivialized and discarded as oral cultures often do with the most challenging paradoxes of writing culture. The figure of Melquíades in itself is also paradoxical, for the roots of the word *gitano* have been associated with a word for 'Egyptian', and there is a vaguely Arab quality to Melquíades.

The political implications of the colonial legacy surface directly in Chapter 3. When the distant 'government' sends a representative to Macondo, it is in the form of a 'magistrate', Don Apolinar Moscote. This new presence functions as a fundamentally irrelevant political element in Macondo, for Moscote's role in the real life of the town is of little substance. Moscote is a representative of the colonial bureaucracy and is appointed from above; as an outsider, he has little or no connection with the local people. (The colonial model of centrally controlled government is still in place in the 1950s Colombia of the story 'Un día de éstos'.) García Márquez's treatment of Moscote as a minor presence in Macondo also corresponds to the writer's general strategy with respect to politics in the Macondo cycle: he communicates a powerful political statement by seemingly not highlighting matters political. The author's nuanced modernism often functions most effectively

---

[18] In this case, the modernist strategy seems to have its origins in the *greguería* of Ramón Gómez de la Serna.

in this way in *Cien años de soledad*. Moscote is never really accepted in the town and only allowed to remain after reaching a political compromise with the citizens of Macondo: the soldiers of his entourage leave the town and the citizens are allowed to pursue their own political traditions or customs. More specifically, they are to be allowed to paint their homes either the traditional color blue associated with the Conservative Party in Colombia or the traditional color red associated with the Liberal Party.

A plague of insomnia is one of the most discussed and memorable episodes in Chapter 3. Despite the imaginative methods the people of Macondo devise to overcome their shared insomnia, no one can find a way to sleep. As is typical of Macondo's maladies, the insomnia eventually dissipates of its own accord. This insomnia could well be understood as a metaphor for the shared trauma suffered with the Conquest and the establishment of the Spanish medieval and colonial order. The trauma is never forgotten or overcome, but its effects are slowly transformed: they are progressively less remembered as the people of Macondo are eventually able to sleep once again.

Thia plague of insomnia brings with it a growing memory problem. The citizens of Macondo eventually lack the ability to remember even the most basic things, as García Márquez satirizes the consistent lack of historical memory of the oligarchies that have ruled in Latin America. The local reaction to this monumental problem is entertaining: José Arcadio Buendía invents simplistic solutions. He places little signs on basic everyday objects, explaining their function. His signs include an identification of the town, 'Macondo'. This sign might seem ridiculous, even though cities and towns throughout the Americas usually have such signs today. His larger sign, 'Dios existe' ('God exists'), satirizes the pervasive influence of the Catholic church. In imitation of European medieval practices, José Arcadio even invents a 'memory machine' with thousands of entries on items to be remembered.[19] Eventually, in a further playing out of one scientific response, Melquíades gives the suffering residents of Macondo a magic potion that cures them of their illness.

The first artist to arrive in Macondo appears in Chapter 4. This handsome and elegant Italian, Pietro Crespi, teaches the art of the pianola, from the assembly to the playing of the instrument. In the context of this society,

---

[19] Carlos Fuentes has explored the idea of a character with a memory machine in *Terra nostra*, published eight years after *Cien años*. Both fictional versions of this machine are based on the real historical existence of such devices in Europe in the Middle Ages. See Raymond L. Williams, *The Writings of Carlos Fuentes*, Pan American Series (London & Austin TX: University of Texas Press, 1996).

Crespi is the artist who is basically frivolous in the sense that he has little impact on the flow of events, and eventually becomes the prototype of the frustrated artist in Latin America.

The people of Macondo seem to understand life in ways often associated with oral cultures, and not in ways accepted by Western science and rational middle-class society. Thus, in Chapter 3, the ubiquitous Melquíades dies again, for the second time, and José Arcadio Buendía has the task not only of overseeing his burial, but also of burying Prudencio Aguilar, who has also returned from the dead. Both of these seemingly inexplicable deaths allude to García Márquez's earlier fiction, for Melquíades's funeral is described as the best in Macondo since the burying of Mamá Grande (from 'Los funerales de la mamá grande'), and Prudencio Aguilar's 'death within death' is a phrase from García Márquez's early fiction of the 1948–52 period.

García Márquez's treatment of the growing love affair between Aureliano and Remedios la bella in Chapter 3 also contains allusions to his own earlier writings, as well as to works written by others. The obsessiveness of Aureliano's love is reminiscent of several other characters of the Macondo cycle whose actions are marked by their obsessiveness. Aureliano's seemingly endless writing of love poems about Remedios la bella represents a rewriting of a classic Romantic novel of Latin America, *María* (1867) by the Colombian Jorge Isaacs. (Later, in *El amor*, Florentino Ariza also writes love letters obsessively, a parody of the Romantic tradition and re-enactment of the Aureliano figure in *Cien años*.) At the end of Chapter 9, García Márquez carries out another memorable parody of the Romantic literary tradition. A young military commander dies 'of love' next to Remedios's window ('amaneció muerto de amor junto a su ventana', 158). Since the melodramatic affair of Efraín and María in *María* is centered around the flower-laden window of María's home, the parody of this novel is obvious to a Colombian reader, as well as to other readers familiar with the Latin American literary tradition. In the English translation, the chapter ends as follows: 'On New Year's Day, driven mad by rebuffs from Remedios the Beauty, the young commander of the guard was found dead under the window' (*One Hundred Years*, 180).

Beginning with Chapter 5, *Cien años* deals with social and political realities less directly associated with the colonial legacy. From this point onwards, there are direct parallels between events in Macondo and the history of nineteenth- and twentieth-century Latin America; the novel becomes increasingly less metaphorical and more historical.

Colombia's crisis-laden history since independence in the early nineteenth century is unique in so far as political institutions are concerned: Colombia is the only Latin American nation with its two major traditional parties, the

Liberal Party and the Conservative Party, still intact in the twenty-first century as the two major political entities in the nation. Party allegiances have been passed along family lines for two centuries, with political life often played out not only as class conflicts, but also as century-long family feuds. Chapter 5 narrates the emergence of these two political parties in the mid-nineteenth century, when they still represented political ideas and economic interests that they do not represent in precisely the same way today. In general, the Liberal Party of the nineteenth century favored a federal concept of state government, and many of their proponents were committed to a radical model of semi-autonomous states loosely associated with a central government. The Liberal Party also tended to be more generally supported by the emerging merchant class and by the business interests of a new middle class that arose in Colombia after the nation's independence from Spain. It tended to oppose the old landed elites. As the two parties and the new national economy developed, a new creole aristocracy of the landed elites took over the old agricultural plantation economy of the new nation. These groups tended to be supporters of the Conservative Party and of the authority of the Catholic church. Consequently, the Spanish medieval legacy was generally more promoted by the Conservative Party than by the Liberal Party.

Given the depth of family identity with political parties in Colombia, there were many exceptions to the tendencies outlined above, and enough ambiguity among the general uneducated populace about these two political parties for García Márquez to ridicule the politics and values of both. Aureliano's understanding of the Liberal Party, as articulated by his father-in-law, is as follows:

> Los liberales, le decía, eran masones; gente de mala índole, partidaria de ahorcar a los curas, de implantar el matrimonio civil y el divorcio, de reconocer iguales derechos a los hijos naturales que a los legítimos, y de despedazar al país en un sistema federal que despojara de poderes a la autoridad suprema. (*Cien años*, 88)

> The Liberals, he said, were Freemasons, bad people, wanting to hang priests, to institute civil marriage and divorce, to recognize the rights of illegitimate children as equal to those of legitimate ones, and to cut the country up into a federal system that would take power away from the supreme authority. (*One Hundred Years*, 97)

As ridiculous as this lightly burlesque description of the Liberal Party may seem, the divisions between the two traditional parties in Colombia were intense enough to lead to a number of civil wars; the history of many Latin American nations was the struggle among forces similar to those in conflict in Colombia. Thus, in Chapter 5, Aureliano becomes Colonel Aureliano Buendía and he fights thirty-two battles in these civil wars, losing them all.

In the Colombian case, two constitutions were the basis for political ideas and the political conflict described in Chapter 5. A political convention in the town of Rionegro (Department of Antioquia), in 1862, resulted in the approval of an exceptionally progressive constitution that embodied many of the more lofty liberal ideals circulating at the time in Europe and Latin America. The Constitution of 1862 was in effect for two decades and was the cause of ongoing conflict. The Liberal President Rafael Núñez designed a reformed constitution, which resulted in a split of the Liberal Party into two factions – the Independents and the Radicals. The Independents, as well as the Conservatives, sided with Núñez. He was unable to unify the party, however, and as in *Cien años*, the dissidents (Radicals) staged an armed revolt in 1885.

The historical figure who was the model for Colonel Aureliano Buendía was General Rafael Uribe Uribe. After he suffered numerous losses on the battlefield, a second constitution was signed in 1886; this document embodied conservative principles returning significant powers to the central government and the Catholic church. Liberals such as General Uribe Uribe reacted against this constitution with an uprising, but met with as little success in war as does Colonel Buendía in the novel. Uribe failed repeatedly in his attempt to defend Liberal ideals and ended a lifetime of conflict by signing the Treaty of Neerlandia in 1902, signaling an end to the War of a Thousand Days, which lasted from 1899 to 1902. Without entering into such historical detail, the characters do make references to this war.

Beyond their heroic and spontaneous personalities, the fictional Aureliano Buendía and the historical General Rafael Uribe Uribe share many similarities. When faced with death, both of them attempted to flee from the immediate situation and from government forces. García Márquez himself never met General Rafael Uribe Uribe, but one of his grandfathers did fight at Uribe Uribe's side, and the author, as a child, heard stories of the battles involved. Both the fictional and the historical characters attempted to gain support from abroad. (Not mentioned in the novel is a group that campaigned to annex the Department of Antioquia to the United States of America.) By the end of his life, General Uribe Uribe had become a legend which lived on throughout the twentieth century; Colonel Aureliano Buendía embodies much of this legendary quality. Both lives represent one faction of the Liberal Party in Colombia in the nineteenth century. In the novel, once peace is established, Colonel Aureliano Buendía retires and devotes his last years to making and remaking little goldfish ornaments. This activity seems to suggest the futility of the characters' activity in Macondo and the ultimate defeat of both the real General Uribe Uribe and the fictional Colonel Aureliano Buendía.

Of the second half of the novel, Chapter 16 is one of the most remarkable, for rain inundates Macondo and does not stop for four years, eleven months, and two days. Biblical in content and tone, this chapter underlines once again the cyclical nature of many events in Macondo, suggesting the futility of any attempt to escape from the colonial past and the seemingly permanent dominance of the Spanish medieval order. With this flooding of Macondo, the materialistic and corrupt society temporarily vanishes. The lost innocence and simplicity of the town are reborn; soon all the elements that had characterized civilized society return, and the cyclical nature of life in Macondo is reborn. The last four chapters recount the impossibility of returning to a prehistoric innocence as well as the inevitable growth of modern society. At the end of the novel, an increased series of references to literature bring a sense of closure. Characters from other novels of the Boom, such as Cortázar's *Rayuela* and Fuentes's *La muerte de Artemio Cruz*, appear in the novel, as do real people from García Márquez's literary life, such as his old friends from the Group of Barranquilla: the *sabio catalán* of the novel is his father-figure Ramón Vinyes, and, as we have seen, Álvaro, Alfonso and Germán are based on old friends of the author.[20] At the very end, Aureliano Babilonia manages to decipher some manuscripts that had left generations of the family perplexed. As it turns out, the manuscripts had been written in Sanskrit and had already told the story of the Buendía family, thus closing another of the numerous circles of the novel. As García Márquez's 'total' novel, it not only displays a metaphorical version of the history of Latin America and the West, but also offers the reader clues of how to read it. The complexities of the reading process and the following of an engaging plot make *Cien años* communicate experience so directly to the reader that the act of reading seems to parallel real life experience. The process of reading is as important as the intellectualization that follows it.

The appearance of the Sanskrit language in the last pages of the novel is a culmination of numerous instances of translation in the novel, as Aníbal

---

[20] The presence of these writers in *Cien años*, as well as the critical work of Germán Vargas and Jacques Gilard, are the main reasons why the Group of Barranquilla has been far more recognized in the literary formation of García Márquez than the more recently recognized group of mentors in Cartagena. I believe the primary reasons that García Márquez himself chose to recognize his friends in Barranquilla in *Cien años* was that Cepeda Samudio, Vargas, and José Félix Fuenmayor were more peers and friends than strictly mentors. The group in Cartagena was senior in age and they were all primarily mentors.

González has pointed out.[21] González has explored the multiple implications of translation in *Cien años*, and concludes that this novel suggests the importance of translation in Latin American literature, as well as serving as a reminder of Latin American literature's 'impure', contradictory, and conflicted origins.

Melquíades's use of Sanskrit, I would argue, is only another guise, yet another translation; the unspoken, unwritten, prohibited, and most feared language in *Cien años* is Arabic. The greatest fear of Christian and Spanish Macondo is to encounter and accept its deeply semitic origins from the Hebrew and Arabic peoples on the Iberian Peninsula. The history of these peoples from the eighth to the fifteenth centuries in the Iberian Peninsula has not been fully and widely recognized in recent centuries as it might have been. On the other hand, the diverse origins of the 'Spanish' people who settled in such places as Macondo were systematically obscured by the Spanish Crown. The Sanskrit language, then, can be seen as a disguise for Arabic.

*Cien años* contains the basic affirmation of humanity and respect for the plight of the common person that can be observed in much of García Márquez's Macondo fiction, and in particular in the story 'La siesta del martes'. As cyclical, deterministic, and dismal as the depiction of the social context is, the reader might well think of García Márquez as a pessimist, a social conservative, or perhaps both. A basic faith that the spirit of the common man will prevail with dignity, however, implies that social change is possible. That basic affirmation is the conclusion of his later Nobel Laureate address.

### The early construction of Macondo: *La hojarasca*

García Márquez's first novel of the Macondo cycle of fiction, *La hojarasca* (*Leafstorm*) is one of his most socially and historically based texts, for it refers directly to the human toll of the United Fruit Company's activities in the Caribbean region of Colombia in the first quarter of the twentieth century. The action of *La hojarasca* ostensibly takes place from 1903 to 1928, although a more mythic reading of the text suggests the idea that the story covers a period from Macondo's foundation to 1928. The use of the word 'action' is

---

21 Aníbal González, 'Translation and genealogy: *One Hundred Years of Solitude*', in *Gabriel García Márquez: New Readings*, ed. Bernard McGuirk and Richard Cardwell, Cambridge Iberian and Latin American Studies (Cambridge: Cambridge University Press, 1987), 65–79.

perhaps not appropriate, in the sense that the social setting and its atmos-phere are more important than the actual events. As in *Cien años*, the lack of causality with respect to events makes these effects more important than their causes, historical or fictional. The integration of the characters and events of Macondo is evident not only in the novel's obvious references to *Cien años de soledad*, but also in the presence in *La hojarasca* of all the characters of the story 'Monólogo de Isabel viendo llover en Macondo' ('Monologue of Isabel watching it rain in Macondo'). Both *La hojarasca* and 'Monólogo de Isabel' were written in the early 1950s as part of the same rough draft, a manuscript that had been tentatively titled 'La casa'.

This early version of the Macondo story, as related in the printed version of *La hojarasca*, focuses on only four characters: three members of one family, who are narrators, and a doctor whose wake is the central circumstance of the novel. The work contains twenty-nine narrative segments. The initial segment is narrated from a collective 'we' point of view; a ten-year-old-boy is the first of three narrators who each tell the story in first person. The boy narrator is present at the wake and his narrative consists of his thoughts and perceptions at the time. The two other first-person narrators are Isabel (the boy's mother) and his grandfather.

The presence of an unnamed American banana company is García Márquez's first fictionalized reference to the United Fruit Company in Colombia. Rather than naming the company and the town of Aracataca, the company becomes novelized as a mythical 'leafstorm' and the town becomes Macondo. By doing this, García Márquez was seeking the universal reso-nances of his literary master Faulkner; this was his initial work in the 'tran-scendent regionalism' that characterizes the entire Macondo cycle of fiction; he uses a specific locale to create a universal experience.[22] In a general sense, the 'leafstorm' of the novel consists of the people and economic progress associated with the North American company. The simple and innocent life of Macondo is transformed by a 'leafstorm', as the modernization of the town by the foreigners changes the town dramatically. The title of the novel, which was previously going to be 'La casa', seems to have originated in a journalistic piece written by the mentor of García Márquez in Cartagena, Clemente Manuel Zabala, in which Zabala describes an *hojarasca* as a 'masa extraña o foránea que llega a agregir y arrinconar lo propio' ('a strange and foreign mass that eventually hurts and corners that which is its own').[23] In his

---

[22] Brushwood discusses the term 'transcendent regionalism' in *The Spanish American Novel* (see especially Chapter 12).
[23] García Usta, *García Márquez en Cartagena*, 39.

piece, Zabala was referring to foreign music (jazz and Cuban *guaracha*) as an *hojarasca*. The 'banana boom' results in a new prosperity – with scenes in which the wealthy used bills to light cigars – but the prosperity is fleeting. The *nouveaux riches* who arrive and take advantage of the new wealth, as well as the workers who follow them, are resented by those residents who have lived in Macondo for generations. The grandfather figure, for example, belongs to one of Macondo's established rural elite families. They preceded the arrival of the foreign banana company by several decades and not only resent its arrival, but particularly the subsequent arrival of masses of unknown outsiders.

The novel provides the reader with a minimal social and economic context for the events at hand, beginning with the central fact that the local elite of established families had arrived in Macondo in the late nineteenth century. Specific historical dates, such as the grandfather's participation in a civil war in 1885 and Colonel Aureliano Buendía's presence as a commander in the area in 1903, provide this basic historical context, and draw a contrast between the nineteenth-century life of the locals and the modernization imposed by the foreigners. The fictionalized account of this historical story has the Colonel in 1903 writing a letter of introduction on behalf of the doctor, who is then accepted by Isabel's father as a guest in his house. Once accepted in the household, he remains there for eight years. The text suggests that the apogee of economic prosperity came in around 1915, which would correspond to the most solid years of the United Fruit Company's presence in Colombia. In the novelistic version, the foreign company leaves the region in 1918, about ten years before the actual historical exodus of the United Fruit Company. In the fictionalized account, the last ten years (approximately 1918 to 1928) are years of postboom decadence.

García Márquez provides detailed external and internal descriptions of Macondo in 1928. In the more internal psychological descriptions, the town lives with a constant nostalgia for a distant past that the people of Macondo have idealized as a way of denying the brutality and suffering of the civil wars that were, in reality, the most traumatic experiences of their lives. By now exhausted, the people of Macondo disdain the more recent experience of the 'leafstorm'; that is, the inhumanity that comes with modernization. García Márquez might be considered a writer dealing with trauma that is not as much part of his personal experience as it is the common experience of his people in Aracataca.

García Márquez's methods for describing the fictional world in this first novel are early experiments with the methods of modernism that had been explored for several decades by modernist writers in Europe and the United

States, and for a decade (since the mid-1940s) in discrete sectors of Latin America.[24] One of García Márquez's strategies in *La hojarasca* was to imitate simultaneity: he chooses an exact moment in the present of 1928 at exactly 2.30 in the afternoon. He begins his description of 2.30 with the image of a woman whose physical and emotional body suggest the atmosphere in the town: 'Pienso en la señora Rebeca, flaca y apergaminada, con algo de fantasma doméstico en el mirar y el vestir, sentada junto al ventilador eléctrico y con el rostro sombreado por las alambreras de sus ventanas' ('I think about Señora Rebecca, thin and looking like parchment, with the touch of a family ghost in her look and dress, sitting beside her electric fan, her face shaded by the screen in her windows').[25] This scene is followed by another depressing scene, also at exactly 2.30 p.m., evoked this time by Isabel: a crippled man is observed saying goodbye at a train station, the cripple turns past a deserted corner, a mule arrives in a cloud of dust carrying a mailman, the town priest appears motionless, and then belches.

In 1982, some three decades after writing *La hojarasca*, a writer friend asked García Márquez what he thought, in retrospect, about the young writer who wrote that first novel. The now fifty-five-year-old writer said that he viewed the novice author of *La hojarasca* 'con un poco de compasión, porque lo escribió con prisa, pensando que no iba a escribir más en la vida, que aquélla era su única oportunidad, y entonces trataba de meter en aquel libro todo lo aprendido hasta entonces. En especial, recursos y trucos literarios tomados de los novelistas norteamericanos e ingleses que estaba leyendo' ('with a little compassion, because he wrote it quickly, thinking that he wasn't going to write anything else in his life, that that was his only opportunity, and so he tried to put into that book everything he had learned by then. Especially techniques and literary tricks taken from the American and English novels that he was reading').[26] Faulkner's *As I Lay Dying* was his most obvious literary model among those American novels, for García Márquez used a structure and shifting narrative point of view that were close imitations of the Faulkner novel. In response to some critics' claim that he was, in fact,

---

[24] I have discussed the interaction between García Márquez generation and the European modernists in *The Twentieth-century Spanish American Novel* (London & Austin TX: University of Texas Press, 2003).

[25] García Márquez, *Leafstorm and Other Stories*, tr. Gregory Tabassa (New York: Avon, 1973), 24. Subsequent quotations are from this edition.

[26] García Márquez and Plinio Apuleyo Mendoza, *Conversaciones con Plinio Apuleyo Mendoza: El olor de la guayaba* (Bogotá: La Oveja Negra, 1982), 58. The translation into English is mine.

basically copying Faulkner, García Márquez has claimed that his novel is not exactly the same as *As I Lay Dying*:

> Yo utilizo tres puntos de vista perfectamente identificables, sin ponerles nombres: el de un viejo, un niño y una mujer. Si te fijas bien, *La hojarasca* tiene la misma técnica y el mismo tema (puntos de vista alrededor de un muerto) de *El otoño del patriarca*. Sólo que en *La hojarasca* yo no me atrevía a soltarme, los monólogos están rigurosamente sistematizados.

> I utilize three perfectly identifiable points of view without giving them names: that of an old man, a boy and a woman. If you look carefully, *Leafstorm* has the same technique (points of view organized around a dead person) as *The Autumn of the Patriarch*. Only in *Leafstorm* I didn't dare let myself loose, the monologues are rigorously systematized.[27]

Technically, *La hojarasca* contains not three but four points of view. In the first section, there are the voices of a collective 'we', followed by three first-person singular voices. The function of these voices varies. The collective 'we' of the first section offers a broad, historical framework in a poetic discourse. The broadness of the historical context and the lyrical quality of the language produce effects that García Márquez would have had difficulty evoking without the use of this collective 'we'.

*La hojarasca* begins with the following sentence: 'De pronto, como si un remolino hubiera echado raíces en el centro del pueblo, llegó la compañía bananera perseguida por la hojarasca' ('Suddenly, as if a whirlwind had set down in the center of town, the banana company arrived, pursued by the leafstorm'). In this opening line, García Márquez establishes the novel's central metaphor, the *hojarasca*, or leafstorm. Without giving the banana company a name or providing any specific historical background, this metaphor begins a process of characterizing the invading foreign company in the unnamed invaded nation. The author's method in this opening line has two effects. On the one hand, the situation portrayed is general enough to be understood as a universal problem, rather than exclusively and specifically a conflict between the United Fruit Company and workers in Colombia. On the other, García Márquez credits his fictionalized reader with an implicit understanding that the historical events in the novel fit an historical pattern that an informed reader of Latin American literature and culture can recognize. Resonances of the invasion of all of Latin America by the Spanish conquerors are part of reading the book for anyone in any Latin American nation; these are reso-

---

[27]  *ibid.*

nances of the Spanish colonial empire. Finally, the reader has become aware of the historical meaning of an important visual image from the outset.

The modernity imposed by foreign neocolonial powers is the focus of the remainder of the first section. The narrator refers several times to the objects and people that have arrived from the outside as 'rubble'; these objects of rubble (electric plants, amusement parlors, hospitals) and those incomers are consistently associated with modernity. The individuals who arrive from outside are the 'dregs' because they do not fit comfortably into Macondo: the fact that they arrive unmarried and then rapidly purchase homes and military titles makes them suspect and undesirable.

The established and traditional society of Macondo, by contrast, is the collective 'we' of this first section:

> Hasta los desperdicios del amor triste de las ciudades nos llegaron en la hojarasca y construyeron pequeñas casas de madera, e hicieron primero un rincón donde medio catre era el sombrío hogar para una noche, y después una ruidosa calle clandestina, y después todo un pueblo de tolerancia dentro del pueblo.  (*La hojarasca*, 9)

> Even the dregs of the cities' sad love came to *us* in the whirlwind and built small wooden houses where at first a corner and a half-cot were a dismal home for one night, and then a noisy clandestine street, and then a whole inner village of tolerance within the town.  (*Leafstorm*, 10, my italics)

In this case, it is the collective 'we' that had resided in the town before the institutionalization of prostitution. The condemnation by the 'we' has an obvious moral overtone.

In addition to opposing the transformation heralded by the arrival of the outsiders, the voice of the collective 'we' feels it has been displaced by them. As the narrator says: 'los primeros éramos los últimos; nosotros éramos los forasteros, los advenedizos' (*La hojarasca*, 8) ('the first of us came to be the last; we were the outsiders, the newcomers', *Leafstorm*, 10). This is the only section of the work where this collective 'we' is directly voiced.

The reader finds three distinct narrative voices in the next four sections. Two segments are narrated by the boy, one by his grandfather, and one by his mother. The respective functions of these segments are very different. The boy's narrative contains the most limited framework of spatial and temporal boundaries. His most intimate thoughts and feelings are these boundaries, and the reader perceives nothing else from him. Even his references to the past involve only the immediate past of the day at the wake: 'Por primera vez he visto un cadáver. Es miércoles, pero siento como si fuera domingo porque no he ido a la escuela y me han puesto este vestido de pana verde que me aprieta en alguna parte' (*Hojarasca*, 11) ('I've seen a corpse for the first time. It's Wednesday but I feel as if it were Sunday because I didn't go to school and they dressed me up in a green corduroy suit that's tight in some places', *Leafstorm*, 15). The boy's voice and most of his narration are limited to the verb *ver* ('to see'). In this case, the brief reference to the past of being dressed up in a suit suggests only how uncomfortable he feels at the present moment. The boy also uses the present tense of the verb *sentir* ('to feel') when he does not use *ver*. As an indicator of the repetition involved with these verbs, seven of the nine sentences of the fourth paragraph begin with the phrase *Veo que* ('I can see that'). This phrase emphasizes the immediacy of the experience for both the reader and the narrator. The first narrative segment provides the young boy's perceptions and emotional reactions at his first wake and reveals a situation involving the three persons who are narrators and four Guajiro Indians at the wake.

## The tri-ethnic culture of the Costa

The presence of the Guajiro Indians is part of García Márquez's integration of a tri-ethnic cultural context into the entire Macondo cycle. The Caribbean region of northern Colombia is tri-ethnic in heritage and has both a popular and an oral culture. As we saw in our discussion of *Cien años*, this Costa region has its roots both in Spanish literary tradition and in a local primary oral culture based on African, indigenous, and Spanish oral traditions. The city of Cartagena was one center of Spanish bureaucracy during the colonial period, a *ciudad letrada* with a small lettered elite.[28] The Spaniards also brought with them an influential form of oral tradition, the *romance*, or ballad. Cartagena was also a center of slave traffic in the Caribbean; approximately 150,000 slaves passed through Cartagena destined for either the Vice-Royalty of New Granada or other areas in the Spanish colonies. (This period of the slave trade is most elaborately fictionalized in García Márquez's later *Del amor y otros demonios*.) Cartagena's economy declined drastically in the nineteenth century, as described in the later novel *El amor en los tiempos del cólera*. Nevertheless, a small writing elite remained in the ninenteenth and twentieth centuries: Dr Juvenal Urbino of *El amor* is the quintessential reader of the lettered elite, and Florentino Ariza is the quintessential writer who imitates

---

[28] For a history of Cartagena that describes the social classes in this city, see Theodore E. Nichols, *Tres puertos de Colombia: estudio sobre el desarrollo de Cartagena, Santa Marta y Barranquilla*, Biblioteca Banco Popular (Bogotá: Banco Popular, 1973).

the lettered elite. At the same time. the oral tradition remained, as inherited from the Spanish tradition of the *romance* and from the tri-ethnic and popular culture of the Costa, which was strongly influenced by Afro-Colombian culture. The African slaves eventually worked in the Magdalena River mining towns of Guamocó, Simití, Norosí, and Loba. The city of Mompox on the lower Magdalena River, a *ciudad letrada* of the colonial period, was an administrative center for the distribution of slaves to neighboring towns. Mompox and the surrounding area became a stronghold for Afro-Colombian culture and enjoyed a noteworthy presence of oral culture.

The African presence in this region relates directly to slave rebellions during the colonial period that led to the founding of villages of African rebels, some of which have survived for centuries. One such village is Palenque de San Basilio, an isolated village located inland from Cartagena, between Mompox and Cartagena. Palenque de San Basilio can be seen as the opposite of Cartagena's Spanish and lettered aristocracy: it consists entirely of runaway African slaves, virtually isolated for over three centuries from the writing culture of the region's cities. As for the four Guajiro Indians in *La hojarasca*, they are originally from the north-east region of Colombia, in the Department of La Guajira which borders Venezuela.

In addition to the tri-ethnic culture suggested by the presence of the four Guajiro Indians in *La hojarasca*, the modernization of the region is important in this novel, in much of the fiction in the Macondo cycle, and in *El amor*. The context for modernization has been cities larger than Macondo (or the real town of Aracataca), as well as the cities of Cartagena, Barranquilla, and Santa Marta. Barranquilla had been an insignificant village during the colonial period but grew rapidly throughout the nineteenth century, becoming the largest metropolitan center in the region by the beginning of the twentieth century. The first steamboats (of the type seen in *El amor*) connected Barranquilla to the interior of the country by the 1830s via the Magdalena River, and this turned Barranquilla into the major port city of Colombia when coffee from inland became Colombia's principal export beginning in the 1880s. By the 1920s, Barranquilla was rapidly assuming the identity of a modern city with an expanding middle class.

After the ending of the first section of *La hojarasca* with this allusion to this region's tri-ethnic culture, the boy's second narration functions in a similar fashion. His references to the past are limited to what the boy experienced on the Wednesday; his feelings and thoughts of the moment, however, are the main focus of this section. In the last paragraph, a series of sentences enumerate what the child sees, including his house, a boy, the town, and the house next door.

The mother's narration at first seems quite similar to the boy's, being another immediate reconstruction of the events at hand. This version, however, is quite different, for the boy's vision is limited to a very immediate reality, whereas the mother expands reality to broaden the boundaries of the fictionalized world. Like the boy, she reacts to the immediate situation of the wake. The boy's sense of the past includes only events immediately prior to the wake; for the mother, the past encompasses over two decades leading back to the day the doctor arrived in their home. In her first narrative segment, she also refers to a time when the doctor's concubine, Meme, disappeared. Not as limited by time as her son, the mother defines her boundaries by space rather than by time. She speaks of a personal world inhabited by the small group of characters who occupy a small space in Macondo: those in her immediate physical vicinity.

The grandfather is a voice of authority in this rigidly hierarchical society. His is a strong presence for both the past and the present of Macondo. He is the character who provides the first possible explanation for the doctor's being so disliked in Macondo: in a crisis situation, he had refused medical attention to a person in need. (The grandfather's personality is vaguely modeled on an historical figure of the region, General Rafael Uribe Uribe; he is probably a synthesis of that historical figure and García Márquez's own father.) The grandfather functions as the town's historian: the boy tells his own story, the mother relates the family story, and the grandfather narrates the town's story. As the voice of authority, the grandfather also occupies the most space in the novel, with twelve monologues; the mother has ten and the boy six.

García Márquez achieves several effects by using these multiple points of view. More than is usually the case with novels made up of small fragments, the work moves the reader back in time and into the underlying realities of the situation. This movement in time is caused primarily by the grandfather and secondarily by the mother. The interrogation of the subjective or underlying reality of the situation is narrated primarily by the boy and secondarily by the mother.

In the Macondo cycle of fiction, and even predating it in his first amateurish stories of the late 1940s, García Márquez was interested in exploring and possibly creating an 'other reality' beyond the norms of Western rational thought. When he went to Cartagena in 1948, he found a group of intellectuals – Clemente Manuel Zabala, Héctor Rojas Herazo, and Gustavo Ibarra Merlano – who were equally interested in exploring the outer limits of reality. In a few of his earliest stories from the late 1940s, this 'other reality' was a liminal state of existence located somehow between life and death. *La hojarasca* was García Márquez's first novelistic attempt at fictionalizing this 'other reality' in the Macondo setting. The reader can see a similarity between some of the procedures in *La hojarasca* and in the early stories: for example, a death functioning as the starting point for probing the underlying reality of a town. This is not a fictional world of causality. Several extraordinary occurrences or circumstances are never resolved; many are best left unexplained, for there is no rational explanation.

The language of *La hojarasca,* which features the frequent juxtaposition of objects from the empirical world with emotions from the psychological world of the characters, also contributes to the special quality of the novel. García Márquez's method for creating a special sense of reality – this 'other reality' – is to subvert the boundary between objects and either emotions or intellectual abstractions. For example, he personifies a clock that is caught between *parsimonia* ('parsimony') and *impaciencia* ('impatience'), and time is described as an object that drips as liquid. This type of language game is close to the illogical uses of language in the *greguerías* of Gómez de la Serna.

In *La hojarasca* and in the Macondo fiction in general, García Márquez pursues a mythic vision as part of his creation of this 'other reality'. As a Faulknerian modernist, he works toward creating a non-linear, non-traditional concept of time that some readers might perceive as a continuous, ongoing present, or as mythic time. This continuous present is staged in the half-hour duration of the novel, but it also includes an historical past covering twenty-five years (1903–28), and a vague past stretching back to the founding of Macondo, as well as the subjective time of the three narrators who remember the past. Other terms have been used to describe this mythic vision, such as 'neoregionalism' and 'transcendent regionalism'.[29]

The medieval legacy and neocolonial past of Colombia and Latin America are often evoked in *La hojarasca*; they are part of the very fabric of its textual organization. Beyond the ongoing conflict between the old elitism and the neocolonial modernity already discussed in this novel, the language often reveals a patently hierarchical society and deeply embedded medieval mentalities and social order. The key figure of the hierarchical society is the grandfather, the supreme authority as a narrative voice. In this, he pre-figures the pathetic authority figure in *El otoño*. The language of this medieval world is of prophesies, mysterious forces, and long-standing traditions. The mother employs this language when she explains how everything seemed to obey the natural fulfilment of a prophecy (*Leafstorm*, 107).

---

[29] For a discussion of the terms neo-regionalism and transcendent regionalism, see Brushwood, *The Spanish American Novel* and Williams, *The Twentieth-century Spanish American Novel.*

In *La hojarasca*, a profoundly medieval social order, a nascent capitalist society, and a neocolonial foreign capitalist society are all placed in uncomfortable juxtaposition. The multiple narrators and languages of this novel are used to convey this heterogeneity. Thus, García Márquez began his novelistic career and the cycle of Macondo by portraying an ancient society in decadence and a more modern but chaotic world of destruction. Some of García Márquez's more politically militant friends felt that *La hojarasca* had no political virtue because it does not explicitly denounce the military dictatorship of Gustavo Rojas Pinilla and the violence of the civil war. Nevertheless, the foundations of the political scenario are questioned in this novel.

## Later Macondo novels

The next two novels of the Macondo cycle, *El coronel no tiene quien le escriba* and *La mala hora*, are also political works and reflect further on the Caribbean region as a nascent capitalist society in conflict with a persistent neocolonial order. *El coronel* and *La mala hora* are short but important works in the Macondo cycle and are written in a minimalist style that contrasts with the style of *La hojarasca* and *Cien años*. In *El coronel* the political situation is the most important feature in the lives of all the people. Paradoxically, the protagonist, an elderly colonel, in common with Macondo's other inhabitants, avoids using political language at all costs. Thus, the silence of *El coronel* is a form of non-articulated political censorship.

In this work, García Márquez reduces language, structure, and plot to their bare essentials. This brief novel (ninety-two pages in the Spanish edition) tells the story of the colonel and his life in Macondo in a straightforward, simple style. As Gutiérrez Mouat has pointed out, García Márquez's measured language avoids being either excessive or insufficient.[30] The time-frame is the mid-1950s and the civil war of La Violencia during the dictatorship of Gustavo Rojas Pinilla. This civil war, the dictatorship, and the War of a Thousand Days (1899–1902) are minor elements in the political context of *Cien años* and *El amor*, but are major factors in *El coronel*: the seventy-five-year old protagonist was, at the age of twenty, a colonel in this most memorable of Colombia's numerous civil wars of the nineteenth century,

---

[30] Ricardo Gutiérrez Mouat, 'The Economy of the Narrative Sign in *No One Writes to the Colonel* and *In Evil Hour*', in *Gabriel García Márquez and the Powers of Fiction*, ed. Julio Ortega and Claudia Elliott (Austin TX & London: University of Texas Press, 1988), 17–33 (30).

the War of a Thousand Days. Colonel Aureliano Buendía, a warrior from *Cien años*, battles alongside the protagonist of this novel. In real history, the War of a Thousand Days ended with a peace treaty signed in the town of Neerlandia, and both this novel and *Cien años* make brief reference to it. The protagonist of *El coronel* goes to Neerlandia at the end of the war to turn over funds for his revolutionary cause to Colonel Buendía. Once the war ends, the defeated colonel takes up residence in Macondo. Once again, the legacy of the United Fruit Company is inserted into the Macondo story, for the colonel suffers from the decadence brought about by the arrival of the foreign banana company. Given the dismal situation, he leaves Macondo in 1906, gets married and fathers a son who is born in 1922. The colonel's entire postwar life, however, seems futile, for he dedicates the remainder of his life to waiting for the arrival of a check for his military pension. The check never arrives.

From the beginning of *El colonel*, the colonel is living this dismal life: something as basic as making a satisfactory cup of coffee is a struggle. His son Agustín is shot for circulating political literature against the regime. Agustín gives the colonel a fighting cock at the end of the story with the hope that the bird's victories in the ring will provide financial security. At the level of plot, the novel is a subtle critique of the oligarchies which have exploited the less privileged in Latin America as they perpetuate the elitist values of the Spanish medieval oligarchies well into the twentieth century. In summary, the novel presents a devastating representation of violence and depravity.

With the futile political situation and a citizenry reduced to silence through violent repression, the reader might conclude that the situation is depicted as hopeless. The kind of basic human dignity found in the stories from *Los funerales*, however, is also an essential component of *El coronel*. The colonel is a more fragile person than the mother in 'La siesta del martes'. Nevertheless, he exhibits a constant and firm dignity and never gives up hope that his heroic acts of war will be justly compensated. A fundamental optimism underpins the work. Its form and its textual economy seem to fit ideally with its political economy.[31] The work belongs to the Macondo cycle, even though the town is not actually named but simply referred to 'el pueblo' ('the town'); like Macondo, it is located in the northern Caribbean region of Colombia. Nevertheless, the characters of the story reappear in *Cien años*. Altogether, this work is part of the author's process of learning to tell the complete Macondo story.

[31] *ibid.*

*La mala hora* is a continuation of the Macondo saga of political repression and violence, but here the violence is less subtle. Yet the novel still avoids the explicit violence of much Colombian literature of this period. The fabric of Macondo becomes more complex, as more characters, themes, and anecdotes appear and reappear; some are thematic mainstays of the Macondo stories and others are gestures in style and language.[32] The dentist from the story 'Un día de éstos' appears in *La mala hora*, and his politically motivated actions involving the mayor are repeated. This novel also includes, among other characters, the Montiel family from the story 'La prodigiosa tarde de Balthazar', Mina and Trinidad from 'Rosas artificiales', and Don Roque from 'En este pueblo no hay ladrones'.

García Márquez presents a panoramic view of Macondo in this novel, which consists of ten unnumbered chapters and forty brief narrative segments. As a young Faulknerian modernist, García Márquez uses *montage* techniques and a series of narrative segments that do not follow a chronologically linear story. As the reader assembles these narrative segments, a story with subplots gradually emerges. A character named César Montero is the main focus of the first chapter. The first brief narrative segment, however, also deals with Father Ángel, busy with the trivial details of his everyday life and in conversation with his assistant, Trinidad. At the end of the chapter, Trinidad mentions something that will become key in the novel: some *pasquines* or lampoons of a political character that implicate members of the local elite in scandal. Soon thereafter, César Montero reads one of the lampoons and proceeds, coolly and methodically, to shoot Pastor, the person whom he associates with the posting of these lampoons. The mayor learns of the shooting and immediately puts into action a cover-up plan. In the final narrative segment of this first chapter, Father Ángel prohibits the showing of a film at the local movie house on the grounds that no entertainment is to be permitted during this period of mourning. This act serves as a metaphor for the historical role of institutional authority in suppressing artistic and literary expression in Latin America.

The remaining nine chapters contain similarly quick-moving events described in brief narrative segments, all of them dealing with an increasing number of lampoons appearing in public spaces and the intensely repressive measures taken to control their content. When the lampoons are accompanied by the appearance of a clandestine newspaper in Chapter 8, the repression mounts to such a degree that the subversives are forced into the mountains

---

[32] García Márquez has pointed out that 'Macondo' *per se* is never named in this novel. Nevertheless, the setting and characters make it part of the Macondo cycle.

to join the guerrilla movement operating there. The lampoons are a sign of resistance to the order imposed by the local elite. They are also a metaphor for literature as an effective form of resistance or political critique. The lampoons, like literature as García Márquez conceived of it in the 1950s and 1960s, are a form of subversion.

García Márquez had explored silence in *El coronel*, as he had in the story 'Un día de éstos'. Both are subtle works of silence that require the reader to interpret the stories as political on the basis of what is not stated. On the other hand, *La mala hora* is a novel of what is said; it demonstrates the real and objectively understandable effects of the spoken and written word. García Márquez's technical challenge in *La mala hora*, as an aspiring young modernist, is his new use of *montage*. Juxtaposing a multiplicity of scenes, he creates an experience of simultaneity. Now more sophisticated than in his stories of the late 1940s (in which play with reality is an end in itself), García Márquez employs his technical ability in *La mala hora* to offer the reader a broader canvas of social and political reality.

**Conclusion**

As the final and most accomplished novel of his Macondo cycle of fiction, *Cien años* is one of García Márquez's three major novels, along with *El otoño* and *El amor*. Widely read, it is arguably one of the most important novels ever written in the Spanish language. García Márquez's 'total' novel, the synthesis of all his Macondo writing, is the final product of a process that began in 1948 when the twenty-one-year-old law student and journalist went to the Caribbean coastal town of Cartagena to pursue his real passion: writing. When he arrived in Cartagena, he was soon to experience the fortunate marriage between the oral tradition of the Costa (which he had heard most significantly in the voices of his grandmother and aunts) and the written tradition of not only Faulkner and other modernists, but also of the *greguería* of Ramón Gómez de la Serna. This marriage of his grandmother's stories and Gómez de la Serna's *greguería* took place in the home of the young García Márquez's mentor in Cartagena, Clemente Manuel Zabala.

As his most elaborate metaphor for Latin America, *Cien años* is a metaphorical compendium of Latin American history, culture, and society. It is his major statement about solitude, which is a predominant theme in all his work. In the Macondo cycle, García Márquez constructs Macondo as a powerful metaphor for the center of the universe and the history of Macondo as a metaphor for the history of Latin America. The depth and breadth of these metaphors enhance the mythic qualities that García Márquez first developed in *La hojarasca* and 'La siesta del martes' and later perfected in *Cien años*. While *Cien años* relates some actual events of Colombian history and while it is a metaphor for the broad patterns of Latin American and Western history, the function of history in the work and in the Macondo cycle more broadly is still elusive and problematic. Roberto González Echevarría has explained the phenomenon of history and what we learn from the novel about Latin American history lucidly: 'What we learn is that while writing may be mired in myth, it cannot be turned into myth, that its newness makes it impervious to timelessness, circularity or any such delusion'.[33]

The most unfortunate and exhausted concept attached to *Cien años*, used initially as a critical term and later as a cliché, is the tag 'magic realist'. In reality, the roots of much of what has been considered magic realism are to be found in García Márquez's synthesis of the oral tradition of the Costa; the *greguería* of Gómez de la Serna; the exotica of North-American journalist Ripley; the journalistic humor of Clemente Manuel Zabala; and the popular humor of the *costeño* poet Luis Carlos López. These sources and writers have in common a remarkable capacity to express *lo insólito* (the unexpected) that has always fascinated García Márquez; they have always served as his models as a writer. In *Cien años*, much of what has been called magic realism is more appropriately understood as a manifestation of the mindset of primary orality, the oral tradition that García Márquez learned from his aunts and grandmother.

*Cien años* in particular and the Macondo fiction in general have received a vast amount of critical commentary from a broad range of perspectives. Much of the interpretative process has involved the assigning of symbolic value to virtually every action, person, place, and thing in Macondo. The interpretative process does admittedly require some assignment of symbolic meaning to some things that appear in the Macondo fiction. Nevertheless, readers might be well advised to pay heed to Garcia Márquez's many warnings that symbolic meaning should only be assigned in *Cien años* with due care, for he has stated that critics have tried to find symbolic value when there is none: 'I maintain that in the entire book, there isn't a single conscious symbol'.[34]

---

[33] González Echevarría, '*One Hundred Years*', 94.

[34] Claudia Dreifus, 'Playboy Interview: Gabriel García Márquez', in *Conversations with Gabriel García Márquez*, ed. Gene H. Bell-Villada (Jackson MS: University of Mississippi Press, 2006), 93–132 (124); originally published in *Playboy* (February 1983), 65–77, 172–78.

The first two novels of the Macondo cycle, *La hojarasca* and *El coronel no tiene quién le escriba* are subtle and masterful political tales. As García Márquez has pointed out, they are also about old people.[35] In *La hojarasca*, an old man gives up on life and hangs himself. In *El coronel*, an old man waits forever for a letter that never arrives. In this sense, these two novels are the forerunners for García Márquez's later fiction about elderly people and ageing. The protagonist of his next novel after the Macondo cycle, *El otoño del patriarca*, is an elderly dictator.

---

[35] Marlise Simons, 'Love and Age: A Talk with García Márquez'. in *Conversations*, ed. Bell-Villada, 141–47 (142); originally published in *The New York Times Book Review*, 7 April 1985, 1, 18–19.

# 3

# *El otoño del patriarca*
# and the Political Writings

García Márquez has been a politically involved and politically motivated writer since the 1950s. Much of his writing has implicit or explicit political content; there is a continuity to be found in the political themes of *Los funerales de la mamá grande* (*Big Mama's funeral*, 1962), *El otoño del patriarca* (*The Autumn of the Patriarch*, 1975), and *El general en su laberinto* (*The General in his labyrinth*, 1989). This continuity can be seen as an outline of García Márquez's career as a political writer concerned with issues such as autocratic rule, the nature of power in general, and specific abuses of power in particular. He grew up in the one and only region of Colombia that has ever been dominated by foreign capitalists, and the young García Márquez heard stories about their presence from an early age.[1] Because of the poverty of this Caribbean region of Colombia, García Márquez witnessed and experienced social and economic inequity, some of the most dramatic in Latin America. Another key factor in the development of his political vision has been his age: he belongs to a generation of Latin American intellectuals who were markedly influenced by Marxist and neo-Marxist thought, as well as by the writings of Jean-Paul Sartre.

For many readers, the essence of García Márquez seems to be primarily that of a magic realist whose works are not significantly political or social in emphasis but rather offer an escape into the fantastic and the exotic. Nevertheless, he has spent a lifetime writing politically critical journalism and participating in a variety of political processes in Latin America. In addition to the several factors already mentioned, the broader life story behind the formation of his political vision includes: his 1955 book *Relato de un náufrago* (*Story of a shipwrecked sailor*); his travels in 1957 behind the 'Iron

---

[1]   For a more lengthy overview of the presence of oral tradition in Colombia, see Orlando Fals Borda, *Historia doble de la costa*, 4 vols (Bogotá: Carlos Valencia, 1979–86), and Raymond L. Williams, *The Colombian Novel, 1844–1987* (London & Austin TX: University of Texas Press, 1991).

Curtain' of Eastern Europe; his own direct experience; his work for Cuba's Prensa Latina news agency as a journalist posted to Bogotá, Cuba, and New York in the late 1950s and early 1960s; the publication of *La mala hora* and *Los funerales de la mamá grande* in 1962; his founding of the leftist magazine *Alternativa* in Bogotá in 1974; his publication of *El otoño del patriarca* in 1975; his publication of *Operación Carlota* (his essay on Cuba's role in Africa) in 1977; and the publication of *La aventura de Miguel Littín, clandestino en Chile* (*Clandestine in Chile: The Adventures of Miguel Littín*, 1986). The focus of this chapter is on several very different kinds of political writings: his masterpiece of political fiction, the novel *El otoño del patriarca* (*The Autumn of the Patriarch*, 1975); the short journalistic book *Relato de un náufrago* written early in his career (1955); the short stories 'Un día de éstos' ('One of these Days') and 'Los funerales de la mamá grande' ('Big Mama's funeral') from the volume *Los funerales de la mamá grande*; and a fictionalized account of the political life of Simón Bolívar published in 1989 under the title *El general en su laberinto* (*The General in his labyrinth*).

Scholarly publications and critical work on García Márquez the political writer are abundant. The early assessments of his work written by the other writers of the Boom, Carlos Fuentes and Mario Vargas Llosa, offered an insider's view of the political vision of this Colombian author. In his *Gabriel García Márquez: historia de un deicidio*, written before the publication of *El otoño*, Vargas Llosa did in-depth research on the Colombian sociopolitical context of the Macondo cycle. One of Vargas Llosa's basic theses was that the writer is a rebel and a substitute figure for God, and thus a symbolic God killer. More recently, Armando Estrada Villa has dedicated a lengthy book exclusively to the subject of politics in selected works of García Márquez.[2] Several scholars have pointed to political concerns in *El otoño*. In an early reading of the novel, Julio Ortega described it as a work not only about a Latin American dictator but also about the Latin American people who suffer under this paradigmatic tyrant.[3] Ortega points out that the political code in the novel emerges from Latin America's colonial and dependent condition; one of the sources of this dictatorial power is the colonial phase of Latin American history, and the other is its imperialistic phase. In a different approach, Jo Labanyi affirms that language and power are closely linked, and that *El*

[2] Armando Estrada Villa, *El poder político en la novelística de García Márquez* (Bogotá: Universidad Pontificia Boliviariana, Escuela de Derecho y Ciencias Políticas, 2006).

[3] See Julio Ortega, '*The Autumn of the Patriarch*: Text and Culture', in *Critical Essays on Gabriel García Márquez*, ed. George R. McMurray, Critical Essays on World Literature (Boston MA: G.K. Hall, 1987), 168–87.

*otoño* is concerned with the expression of power via language, particularly via the written word.[4] It is a novel that depicts a dictator who is not directly responsible for his commands, but nevertheless becomes their prisoner. García Márquez likes to portray characters and narrators who appear to be naive, and *El otoño* can initially appear to be politically naive. Rather than exonerating the dictators of their crimes, however, Labanyi contends that the novel is an exploration of the relationship between language and power.

### *El otoño del patriarca*: Politics and power

The contemporary background to the writing of *El otoño* was the dictatorships of Rojas Pinilla and Pérez Jiménez. Many of the maneuvers of the ageing dictator in *El otoño* are exactly the same mechanisms that were employed by Rojas Pinilla, Pérez Jiménez, or Fulgencio Batista in Cuba, as recounted later by his ex-military leader Sosa Blanco. All three of these dictators are, like the ageing patriarch in the novel, twentieth-century manifestations of the strong authority figure that has dominated in Latin America since the imposition of Spanish order in the sixteenth and seventeenth centuries. This novel is the story of a dictator in an unnamed country located vaguely in the Caribbean region but not limited to the Costa of Colombia. When García Márquez began to struggle with the creation of the physical setting for the book and was vaguely interested in a generically Caribbean location, he took a break from the construction of *El otoño* while he and his wife Mercedes visited in turn each of the Caribbean islands. Thus, the book is replete with images and people from all parts of the Spanish, English, and Dutch Caribbean, including some descriptions of the city of Cartagena in Colombia. Intrigued by what he has called the 'mystery of power', García Márquez wrote a novel in which the main theme is power itself. Indeed, while writing the book, García Márquez in an interview described it as a 'meditation on power'.[5]

The first chapter of *El otoño* begins with the discovery of the protagonist, a General, in his presidential palace. The narrator moves quickly to several anecdotes about the General's life. One of the most engaging anecdotes tells

[4]   Jo Labanyi, 'Language and Power in *The Autumn of the Patriarch*', in *Gabriel García Márquez: New Readings*, ed. Bernard McGuirk and Richard Cardwell, Cambridge Iberian and Latin American Studies (Cambridge: Cambridge University Press, 1987), 135–49.
[5]   Ernesto González Bermejo, 'And Now, Two Hundred Years of Solitude', tr. Gene H. Bell-Villada, in *Conversations with Gabriel García Márquez*, ed. Gene H. Bell-Villada (Jackson MS: University of Mississippi Press, 2006), 3–30 (24).

of his 'first death', when his government-appointed double, Patricio Aragonés, was assassinated. Following that 'death', the General is able to observe the enthusiastic celebrations of his own supposed demise. García Márquez has asserted that the seeds of this novel are not to be found in character or plot (as is the case for many novelists) but in visual images. In fact, the catalyst (what Genette calls the 'generator') for many of his novels is a central image around which he constructs the book. The central image in *El otoño* is the decadent presidential palace in the opening scene. Here is the first sentence:

> Durante el fin de semana los gallinazos se metieron por los balcones de la casa presidencial, destrozaron a picotazos las mallas de alambre de las ventanas y removieron con sus alas el tiempo estancado en el interior, y en la madrugada del lunes la ciudad despertó de su letargo de siglos con una tibia y tierna brisa de muerto grande y de podrida grandeza.
>
> *(El otoño*, 5)[6]
>
> Over the week-end the vultures got into the presidential palace by pecking through the screens on the balcony windows and the flapping of their wings stirred up the stagnant time inside, and at dawn on Monday the city awoke out of its lethargy of centuries with the warm, soft breeze of a great man dead and rotting grandeur.   (*The Autumn*, 7)

This visual image of vultures perched on a decaying palace is based on an image that García Márquez had seen in a drawing in a book of art dating back to the nineteenth century. Two French explorers traveled through Colombia in the nineteenth century and sent copious descriptions back to France. Then a French artist, who had never actually been in Colombia at all, used the written descriptions to produce a book of drawings.[7] In this post-Macondo period, when much of García Márquez's writing has been generated from visual images of drawings, seeing his work simply as magic realism is inappropriate; his writing is better perceived as a realist and sometimes modernist description of drawings containing elements that some may consider to belong to the realm of the fantastic.[8] The key visual image of the palace in *El otoño* emphasizes the decadence of the physical setting, with the vultures

---

    [6]  García Márquez, *El otoño del patriarca* (Buenos Aires: Sudamericana, 1975), 5. All quotations are taken from this edition.

    [7]  *Fabulous Colombia's Geography: The New Grenade as Seen by Two French Travelers of the XIX Century, Charles Saffray and Édouard André*, ed. Eduardo Acevedo Latorre (Bogotá: Litografía Arco, 1984). This volume is a reproduction of a nineteenth-century text originally published in French in a magazine entitled *Le Tour du Monde*.

    [8]  Having studied these drawings, I find some of them closer to the realm of the fantastic than to realist descriptions of nature in Colombia.

exploiting the rotten decadence of the palace. The physicality of the description is blatant, with vultures overwhelming both the exterior and the interior of the building. García Márquez often relishes the opportunity to exploit the possibilities of physical detail; he thus joins the vultures in their joint plunder of the palace. However, García Márquez the modernist takes this setting to another level, beyond mere realism, by evoking the abstract and conceptual ideas not found in the physical description of the objects destroyed by the vultures. First, the vultures remove 'time' ('el tiempo') that seems to have frozen ('el tiempo estancado en el interior'; 'the stagnant time inside'), suggesting not only the length of time the dictator's rule had lasted, but also pointing back to the authoritarian rule of the colonial period.

Consequently, this novel is not only about the dictatorships of the 1970s, but also about the continuity of historical authoritarian regimes in Latin America. In addition, the first sentence ends with the evocative words 'podrida grandeza' ('rotten grandeur'). The key word *grandeza* is found in many texts, legitimizing the legacy of power; it was a word that often appears in texts of the colonial period, such as Bernardo de Balbuena's *Grandeza mexicana*.[9]

The visual image in this opening scene is the structural device for the entire novel. *El otoño* consists of six chapters; the narrator begins each with an allusion to this opening image, and the dictator's story is told, using this as the point of departure. The second chapter begins as follows:

> La segunda vez que lo encontraron carcomido por los gallinazos en la misma oficina, con la misma ropa y en la misma posición, ninguno de nosotros era bastante viejo para recorder lo que ocurrió la primera vez, pero sabíamos que ninguna evidencia de su muerte era terminante, pues siempre había otra verdad detrás de la verdad. (*El otoño*, 47)

> The second time he was found chewed away by vultures in the same office, wearing the same clothes in the same position, none of us was old enough to remember what had happened the first time, but we knew that no evidence of his death was final, because there was always another truth behind the truth. (*The Autumn*, 45)

In this sentence, the narrator evokes the image of the vulture having eaten at the rotting body of the dictator, the body that corresponds to a decadent, rotting nation. The last part of the sentence is noteworthy both politically and aesthetically. In political terms, the end of the sentence underscores how authoritarian rule, after decades of individual despotism or centuries of this

---

[9]  Bernardo de Balbuena, *Grandeza mexicana* (1604). Balbuena was born in 1561 or 1562 and died in 1627.

type of regime, seems endless. The phrase that there is always another truth behind the truth ('siempre había otra verdad detrás de la verdad') is noteworthy as García Márquez's aesthetic manifesto: the aesthetics of modernism provide for an ongoing revelation, with varying perspectives, that things are often not what they appear to be.

The third chapter begins with a reference to the General's cadaver:

> Así lo encontraron en las vísperas de su otoño, cuando el cadaver era en realidad el de Patricio Aragonés, así volvimos a encontrarlo muchos años más tarde en una época de tantas incertidumbres que nadie podía rendirse a la evidencia de que fuera suyo aquel cuerpo senil carcomido de gallinazos plagado de parásitos de fondo de mar.   (*El otoño*, 89)

> That was how they found him on the evening of his autumn, when the corpse was really that of Patricio Aragonés, and that was how we found him again many years later during a moment of such uncertainty that no one could give in to the evidence that the senile body there gouged by vultures and infested with parasites from the depth of the sea was his.
> (*The Autumn*, 83)

In this sentence there is one reference with a scope that goes beyond the original situation (the death scene): 'en una época de tantas incertidumbres'. The second sentence refers to the physical (his hand) and from this point the sentence moves towards the past. By the third sentence of this chapter there are no references to the immediate physical surroundings present at the outset and the chapter has opened into a narration of the General's story. In what follows, the corpse is mentioned only as a device for relating the story. Thus, the original situation has become far less important than it was in the first two chapters.

In the fourth chapter of *El otoño*, the narrator makes no reference to the original situation graphically shown at the outset of the novel but instead relates popular opinion concerning the General:

> Sin embargo, mientras se adelantaban los trámites para componer y embalsamar el cuerpo, hasta los menos cándidos esperábamos sin confesarlo el cumplimiento de predicciones antiguas, como que el día de su muerte el lodo de los cenegales había de regresar por sus afluentes hasta a las cabeceras, que había de llover sangre.   (*El otoño*, 129)

> Yet, while the plans for reassembling and embalming the body went forward, even the most candid among us waited without so confessing for the fulfilment of ancient predictions, such as the one that said that on the day of his death the mud from the swamps would go back upriver to its source, that it would rain blood.   (*The Autumn*, 120)

These rumors from the streets represent the only recourse left to the general populace if they are to understand their circumstances in the context of a hierarchical power structure. The third sentence does not refer to the General's physical environment. Instead, it continues with the various rumors about his actions and false rumors about his life. The narrative now opens into the broader story of the General's past, taking the reader from the immediate personal tragedy to the wider story of power and national politics.

The first sentence of Chapter 5 refers specifically to the original situation:

> Poco antes del anochecer, cuando acabamos de sacar los cascarones podridos de las vacas pusimos un poco de arreglo en aquel desorden de fábula, aun no habíamos conseguido que el cádaver se pareciera a la imagen de su leyenda. (*El otoño*, 169)

> Shortly before nightfall, when we finished taking out the rotten husks of cows and putting a little order into that fabulous disarray, we were still unable to tell if the corpse looked like its legendary image.
>
> (*The Autumn*, 157)

In this chapter, García Márquez's ongoing modernist agenda is exhibited in a subtle way. In the Spanish, the narrator speaks of putting 'arreglo' to the 'desorden'; the English translation has him bringing 'a little order' into 'that fabulous disarray'. In both versions, the narrator expresses the general modernist tendency to build a narrative by moving from initial disorder or chaos to a final state of order or harmony. In this way, the general movement of *El otoño*, as in many modernist texts and particularly those of the Faulknerian mode, is from chaos to order.

The second sentence continues with a description of the original scene and deals with the attempts made, in the immediate present, to prepare the General's corpse. The third sentence is a transition between the original situation and the opening to the past. It also extends to the immediate present by narrating the meeting of the officers in a nearby room where they discuss the new distribution of power now that the central power has been eliminated.

Chapter 4 opens the narrative beyond the original situation in the fourth sentence:

> Nos encontrábamos inermes ante esa evidencia, comprometidos con un cuerpo pestilente que no éramos capaces de sustituir en el mundo porque él se había negado en sus instancias seniles a tomar ninguna determinación sobre el destino de la patria después de él, había resistido con una terquedad de viejo a cuantas sugerencias se le hicieron desde que el gobierno se trasladó a los edificios de vidrios solares de los ministerios y él quedó viviendo en la casa desierta de su poder absoluto. (*El otoño*, 170)

> We were defenseless against that evidence, compromised by a pestilential
> corpse that we were incapable of replacing in the world because he had
> refused in his senile insistence to take any decision concerning the destiny
> of the nation after he was gone, with the invincible stubbornness of an old
> man he had resisted all suggestions made to him ever since the government
> had been moved to the ministry buildings with their sundrenched glass and
> he had stayed behind living alone in the deserted palace of his absolute
> power. (*The Autumn*, 158)

The narrator makes note of the 'cuerpo pestilente' at the beginning of this
sentence. Thereafter, however, he describes the General's actions prior to
this state of affairs. From this point, the chapter continues as the story of the
General and there are no more references to his corpse. The first sentence is
also descriptive of how the general populace is 'defenseless' (or 'inerme'),
even with the prospect of assuming power.

In the sixth and last chapter of *El otoño*, the broadening out to the wider
story occurs on the very first page. There are several references to the original
situation in the first sentence. The author culls images from the gruesome
deaths of several historical Latin American dictators to provide the images
of the corpse. Very soon after that, by the end of the first page, the narrative
opens to past history.

Often writing like a modernist who seems to be a realist, García Márquez
is both an innovator and a traditionalist in his deft handling of these opening
sentences describing the situation in each of the six chapters. The way physical space functions in *El otoño* is a wink at the realist-naturalist tradition:
the beginning of the novel focuses primarily on descriptions of the physical
space. After the physical setting has been amply described in the early chapters of the novel, the narrator then expands the narrative to tell the General's
story without such elaborate descriptions of the physical setting. But García
Márquez does not use physical space in exactly the same way as would a
traditional nineteenth-century novelist; he manipulates it in such a way that
the reader is progressively more limited with respect to physical space and
setting. Yet, at the same time, the reader is progressively more involved in the
complete story of the General's life.

The repeated gradation in each chapter from the situation to the General's story is supported technically by the use of a progressive lengthening
of the sentences.[10] This is the second feature of each chapter opening. The
sentences lengthen at the same point in each chapter: at the very moment that

---

[10] José Miguel Oviedo has noted the progression in sentence length. See 'García
Márquez: la novela como taumaturgia', *Americanist Hispanist*, 1/ii (1975), 7. I have

the focus shifts from the basic situation to the General's story. The opening sentences of each chapter are of a moderate or normal length; the sentences expand in length as the chapter continues. Each chapter has fewer sentences than the previous one, a further indication of this progressive development toward employing longer and longer sentences.

The first and only sentence of the last chapter begins 'Ahí estaba, pues como si hubiera' (El otoño, 219) ('There he was, then, as if it had been', The Autumn, 203). This reference to the corpse at the palace is the briefest of all the references in any chapter to the situation. On the very first page of this chapter, the sentence already moves to matters relating to the General's story. The sentence length is now expanded to its maximum: a total of one thousand, eight hundred and twenty-five lines in the original Spanish.

A third feature of this 'opening out' we find in each chapter of El otoño, is a widening of focus. Each chapter begins with a relatively limited narrative focus, and then pans out to take in other points of view. This shift of narrative focus creates various effects. The beginning of the first chapter is recounted by an unidentified narrator. That narrator and other unidentified characters enter the presidential palace where they come across the rotting corpse. The narrator, then, can be seen as a 'narrator-discoverer'. From the beginning of the next sentence the position of the narrator is placed firmly within the story ('nos atrevimos' or 'we dared'). In the next three pages, the narrative is voiced by this narrator who enters the palace with his accomplices. The narrative begins to open out to include other speakers by the fourth page, where the narrative focus moves from the original situation to the General's story. Lengthy sections articulated by other speakers appear later in the chapter.

Following what is by now an established pattern, the second chapter begins with the narrow focus of the narrator-discoverer. The expansion beyond the limits of this narrator occurs on the fourth and fifth pages of the chapter, which is the same place we have already seen as the point at which other chapters broaden out. The narrative shifts from general knowledge to the specific words of the General. Soon after this, other voices appear in the text. The widening of the focus in the third chapter occurs at an earlier point than in the first two. The narrator-discoverer has control of the narrative on the first page only. It is in the fourth sentence (the same place as in the other chapter openings) that the narrative involves speakers other than the narrator-discoverer.

<hr>

studied sentence length and the novel's structure in more detail in 'The Dynamic Structure of El otoño del patriarca', Symposium 32/i (1978), 56–73.

The structure of the fourth chapter is similar to that of the third and it contains approximately the same number of sentences. The lengthening of the sentences begins in the third sentence, which has forty-nine lines in Spanish. In the fourth, of forty lines, the focus expands to encompass a variety of speakers. From this point in the chapter, a multiplicity of voices is heard, including that of the narrator-discoverer, but the story has opened well beyond his individual story.

The progressive nature of the structure is carried to an extreme in the sixth and last chapter. It moves to the General's story on the first page and the sentence length extends to include the entire chapter. The presence of a variety of speakers occurs earlier here than in the first five chapters, beginning immediately after the first page. The differing narrative voices of this one-sentence chapter make it the most elaborate and complex of the entire novel. The different voices speak more frequently and at greater length than in the first five. The beginning of this, the last chapter is exceptional: the first extensive change in focus consists of the words of an adolescent girl, a monologue of twenty-seven lines describing how she was seduced by the General. Another of his lovers narrates a monologue on the second page, describing the General's sexual desires in detail.

The changing narrative focus not only creates a more complete characterization of the General, but is also the source of much of the novel's humor. By placing the external focus on the General's supposed omnipotence and contrasting this with his basic simplicity in the internal focus, humorous effects are produced. This is a novel about political power, and power appears from the first page as a subject of analysis. The narrator-discoverer communicates the generalized perception of the General's power by apparently believing in his power to command trees to bear fruit.

García Márquez also creates humor in *El otoño* by showing the pettiness of the General's own understanding of power (the inside view in contrast with the grandiosity of the God figure) and his paranoia and puerility (again, the inside view). Once the chapter has opened out beyond the immediate situation, the omniscient narrator proceeds to describe the General's understanding of his godlike capacity to 'decide' destiny.

The inside view of the General regularly emphasizes his puerility and pettiness in contrast with the God-like power that he wields. His paranoia is extended throughout the novel by the way he repetitively locks an elaborate combination of 'las tres aldabas, los tres cerrojos, los tres pestillos' ('the three crossbars, the three locks, the three bolts') in his room. An aspect of his character not described by the narrator-discoverer is his simplicity. After the narrative focus has broadened to include other speakers, his simplicity becomes evident. An omniscient narrator explains in the first chapter, for example, that the General oversees the milking of the cows each day, offering a humorous contrast with the grandiose figure seen by the citizenry.

Right from the beginning of the novel, the General is described as a child-like figure. He plays with toys intended for children, and his relationship with his mother tends to be a mother-child one. His mother reprimands him, for example, about his health and instructs him to stay home for dinner. With this characterization, García Márquez debunks the real innate power of classic figures of authority who have ruled with dictatorial power in many Latin American nations.

The fourth, and final, level of 'opening' in the structure of this novel is the opening of each chapter onto a 'seen' reality. Each begins with clearly delineated boundaries of reality: that which can be seen. This handling of the visible and the invisible reality works in conjunction with the three other features of chapter openings in *El otoño*. The narrator portrays vultures entering the presidential palace in the first scene of the novel. The first sign that the General may finally have died is, then, provided by means of the visual. For the remainder of the novel, it becomes increasingly evident that only that which is seen may possibly be believed: the General, the citizenry, and the reader learn to believe only what they can see. The matter of visible and invisible reality becomes central to the main theme of the novel: power. After the initial description of the first sign of death, the vultures, the narrator-discoverer places emphasis on what can be seen: 'y las cosas eran arduamente visibles en la luz decrépita' (*El otoño*, 5) ('and things were hard to see in the decrepit light', *The Autumn*, 7). The narrator-discoverer continues with a detailed elaboration of his realm of the visible, employing the verb *ver* ('to see') throughout. The verb *ver* appears for the final time when they actually find the corpse. At this point in the narrative (the opening), the story moves beyond what is seen, and verbs such as *comprender* (to understand) and *saber* (to know) are used. Thus, the narrative changes from exclusively what can be seen to what is understood and what is known.

A central theme – the problem of the visible and real versus the illusory – is established in the first sentence of the second chapter where the narrator-discoverer begins a description of what he sees. When he and his companions enter the General's bedroom, the emphasis is placed on the tangible, on what is 'found' rather than what is 'seen'. At this point in the chapter, corresponding to the opening of the other three features discussed, the narration deals with what is said rather than what is seen. This move away from seeing takes place on the first page of the third chapter. Rather than the verb *ver* ('to see') the verb *encontrar* ('to find') is used, emphasizing the tangible. The second sentence also describes what is visible, albeit that the next sentence moves beyond the visible to what it *seemed* like, as well as what those involved thought and were doubtful about.

In Chapter 5, the first sentence refers to the matter of the visible versus the invisible General. The latter is the figure that had been imagined, created by popular legend of the '*se dice*' ('it is said'). In this section, the narrator-discoverer is in the presence of the visible General but makes an attempt to make the figure correspond more to the legend than the reality. The second sentence deals with a physical process in which the narrator-discoverer attempts to reconcile the two conflicting images of the General. By the third sentence, the theme of visible versus invisible reality is abandoned; the chapter moves to problems beyond the visible, such as the meeting between officers after the General's death.

The sixth and last chapter, just like the previous ones, begins with the theme of the visible General versus the popular legend. His visual image is emphasized in the first words of the first sentence: 'Ahí estaba, pues como hubiera sido él aunque no lo fuera' (*El otoño*, 203) ('There he was, then, as if it had been he even though it might not be, lying on the banquet table', *The Autumn*, 203). Now, at this point, the visible and the invisible as a theme has again become a matter of consideration: at times actions that appear to have been the General's actually are not, and the matter is never crystal clear. There is another reference to the problem of the visible versus the invisible General later on the first page, reaffirming the importance of the visible in this novel. By the time we reach the final chapter, the characterization of the General confirms the observation made earlier concerning the reiteration of the verb *ver* ('to see') in the opening chapters of the novel: the visible can offer the possibility of being believable, even though it does not assure credibility.

This fourth feature of the chapter openings in the novel is important in several ways, all of them related to power. On the one hand, there is the manipulation of the visible and the invisible. On the other, the General controls power by controlling what is visible and invisible. Consequently, *El otoño* develops a correlation between character and characterization, as well as between theme and technique. The General is profoundly changed after having seen his own death (that of his double) in the first chapter. The description of this scene involves the repetition of the verb *ver* ('to see'). The fact that he actually sees 'his' death intensifies the experience for him. He learns to believe in reality only when he can see it, and eventually becomes a victim of the circumstances he has created through his power. Once he falls in love with Manuela Sánchez, he uses visible manifestations of his power to attempt to attract her. Given his logic, the most impressive gift for her is a visual spectacle: his gift for her is a comet.

The General maintains his power by manipulating the visible and the invisible. After an assassin attempts to murder him, the General orders the man to be put to death; however, even more important in the context of the visible, the General orders that the assassin's body parts be exhibited throughout the nation, thus providing a visible sign of the consequences of threatening his power, as well as one that recalls medieval and colonial practise. When he feels the need to exert power effectively, he visibly observes its operation. When his power is threatened by the Church's refusal of sainthood to his mother, the General assumes direct control of the situation, declaring 'civil sainthood' for her; he then visibly oversees the fulfilment of his orders. In a key description, the General is most content when he views his country through his window. Along the same lines, he considers himself less responsible for what he does not see. For example, he suffers no compunction about ordering the massacre of two thousand children because he does not observe the actual killing; similarly, the violent political operations of Sáenz de la Barra are of little consequence to him because they are not visible. Well aware of the significance of the visible in this regime, one of the General's officers suggests that Sáenz might be eliminated from the government if the General could actually see the atrocities taking place.

The matter of the visible and the invisible and its relationship to the main theme of *El otoño*, power, is also well developed through the presence of the sea in the novel. As the most visible object in the General's daily life, the sea is his most valued possession. In the first chapter, the sea is first mentioned when, after a reiteration of the verb *ver* ('to see'), the narrator-discoverer states the following: 'vimos los cráteres muertos de ásperas cenizas de luna de llanura sin término donde había estado el mar' (*El otoño*, 7) ('we saw the dead craters of harsh moon ash on the endless plain where the sea had been', *The Autumn*, 9). It is understood that, since the General believes his sea is lost, the people, indoctrinated by him, also believe that to be the case. The sea also becomes closely associated with his window from the first chapter; from this point his window and his sea are inseparable throughout the entire novel. This association is established through the use of the preposition 'de' ('of'): 'oyó por la ventana abierta del mar los tambores lejanos' (*El otoño*, 25) ('through the open windows facing the sea he could hear the distant drums' (*The Autumn*, 25–26). The General condemns some political prisoners to death, but international pressure forces him to annul the order. When facing such moments of pressure, he contemplates the situation from his window. He turns to his window more frequently as he gradually loses his power. At the end of Chapter 5, by now decrepit and in his hundredth year of power, he goes to his window and contemplates the sea, seemingly observing the very loss of his power: 'iba viendo pasar el mismo mar por las ventanas' (*El otoño*, 216) ('he went along seeing as he passed the same sea through the windows') (*The Autumn*, 201).

The General's power, his sea, and his window, become so intimately connected that he insists on maintaining possession of his window and his sea as adamantly as he does his power. As he begins losing power, he is insistent about not losing his sea. He defends his connection with the sea in an extensive dialogue with an ambassador:

> tratando de explicarle que podía llevarse todo lo que quisiera menos el mar de mis ventanas, imagínese, qué haría yo solo en esta casa tan grande si no pudiera verlo ahora como siempre a esta hora como una ciénaga en llamas, qué haría sin los vientos de diciembre que se meten ladrando por los vidrios rotos, cómo podría vivir sin las ráfagas verdes del faro, yo que abandoné mis páramos de niebla y me enrolé agonizando de calenturas en el tumulto de la guerra federal, y no crea usted que lo hice por el patriotismo que dice el diccionario, ni por espíritu de aventura, ni menos porque me importaran un carajo los principios federalistas que Dios tenga en su santo reino, no mi querido Wilson, todo eso lo hice por conocer el mar.
>
> (*El Otoño*, 201–2)

> trying to explain to him that he could take anything he wanted except the sea of my windows, just imagine, what would I do all alone in this big building if I couldn't look out now as always at this time at what looks like a marsh in flames, what would I do without the December winds that sneak in barking through the broken windowpanes, how could I live without the green flashes of the lighthouse, I who abandoned my misty barrens and enlisted to the agony of fever in the tumult of the federalist war, and don't you think that I did it out of patriotism as the dictionary says, or from the spirit of adventure, or least of all because I gave a shit about federal principles which God keep in his holy kingdom, no my dear Wilson, I did it all so I could get to know the sea.    (*The Autumn*, 187–88)

The General responds in a similar manner when speaking with a foreign diplomat named Ambassador Stevenson. Another diplomat makes an attempt to negotiate a deal, and the General is equally negative with him. The indicator that the General has indeed finally lost his power is the fact that he sells his sea at the end of the novel:

> les concedí el derecho de disfrutar de nuestros mares territoriales en la forma en que lo consideren conveniente a los intereses de la humanidad y la paz entre los pueblos, en el entendimiento de que dicha cesión comprendía

no sólo las aguas físicas visibles desde la ventana de su dormitorio hasta el horizonte sino todo cuanto se entiende por mar en el sentido más amplio, o sea la fauna y la flora propias de dichas aguas    (El otoño, 249)

I granted them the right to make use of our territorial waters in the way they considered best for the interests of humanity and peace among peoples, with the understanding that said cessation not only included the physical waters visible from the window of his bedroom to the horizon but everything that is understood by sea in the broadest sense, or, the flora and fauna belonging to said waters    (*The Autumn*, 230–31)

At this point at the end of the novel the General has lost his view of the sea and, consequently, everything related to the power that was so important for him: 'se llevaron todo cuanto había sido la razón de mis guerras y el motivo de su poder' (*El otoño*, 249) ('they carried off everything that had been the reasons for my wars and the motive of his power', *The Autumn*, 231).

The four features of the structure of *El otoño*, as described above, are instrumental to the development of the work's themes. The opening out of the original situation of the novel at the presidential palace into the broader story of the General and his power provides an ample characterization of the General not subordinated to the traditional requirements of space and time. Space and time are subordinate, in this novel as in several García Márquez novels, to the very act of telling a story. The gradual increase in sentence length is the basis for a progressively more elaborate textual presentation of the story. The widening of the narrative focus allows for a variety of understandings of the General, and is important both for an ample characterization of him and for the novel's humor. On yet another level, the opening of a seen reality into a confluence of the visible and the invisible relates to the novel's central theme: the illusion of reality and power. With this work, García Márquez announced in the clearest possible way the end of the Macondo cycle. Many aspects of human experience, in this case related to the acquisition as well as to the uses and abuses of power, however, relate it to previous Macondo works, such as *Cien años* and stories from the volume *Los funerales,* as well as to his other political works. Of all his works, this is García Márquez's most elaborate and lengthy tour de force.

## Other political writings

After *El otoño*, García Márquez published two more intentionally political books, *La aventura de Miguel Littín, clandestino en Chile* (1986) and *El general en su laberinto* (1989). By the time he wrote *La aventura*, García

Márquez was an internationally recognized Nobel Laureate writer and this fact was part of the book's function: to use celebrity status to draw attention to a political situation. The Chilean leftist film director Miguel Littín had been in exile for several years when he dreamt up an elaborate plan to return surreptitiously to Chile and make a documentary film denouncing Pinochet. Littín carried out his plan by entering Chile disguised as a Uruguayan businessman and succeeded in making the film. After the film project was finished, García Márquez interviewed Littín at length and heard many of the details of this incredible political act of daring; once again, reality was more fantastic than realist fiction. Then, García Márquez took the tape recording of this interview, reworked it, and created his own story. Written in an assumed first-person voice (as he had done three decades earlier in the *Relato de un náufrago*), the story is in Littín's voice as reconstructed by the author. As is the case for all of García Márquez's fiction and non-fiction since the publication of the *Relato de un náufrago*, the Littín story is masterfully reconstructed to maintain reader interest with the riveting suspense of a spy novel.

In *La aventura*, García Márquez's approach to his political interests once again differs from what he had done before. Now, he is writing as García Márquez the Nobel Laureate, and he uses his status as a public intellectual to lend international support to a political cause. Littín's documentary film was a success within the genre of documentary political films, but the audience for such films is relatively limited compared to the worldwide readership commanded by García Márquez in the 1980s and 1990s. Thus, García Márquez's political work with this book was primarily an act of good will and political activism: by the very act of telling Littín's story, García Márquez was collaborating with him to raise international awareness of Pinochet's atrocities in Chile.

After *La aventura*, García Márquez's last book about a general does not portray a dictator such as the real one in Chile or the fictional one in his first dictator novel; like *El otoño*, it is not part of the fictional world of Macondo, but it does hark back to this work in the sense that it is set in the Caribbean region of Colombia in the 1950s. This book, *El general en su laberinto* (*The General in his labyrinth*), is about a general and portrays the historical figure of Simón Bolívar. In addition to the expected allusions to the General in *El otoño*, the author portrays a character who has much in common with Colonel Aureliano Buendía of the Macondo cycle and the retired colonel in *El coronel*. Once again, he was approaching a subject in vogue: *El otoño* was written at a time when several Latin American writers were publishing books about dictators; a little over a decade later, three Colombian writers wrote books about Simón Bolívar. *El otoño* begins with the death of the General; *El general* also deals with the end of the protagonist's life, for this novel focuses on the final months of Bolívar's life in the 1830s, as his ageing and crumbling body travels down the Magdalena River to his death. Occasional flashbacks relate more fully the story of the Bolívar's life, which García Márquez presents as a tragic march toward nothing. This is also one of several novels dealing with ageing bodies; the central focus on this subject appears in the latter part of the writer's career, particularly in *El amor* and *Memoria*.

With the story of the striking banana workers in *Cien años* and the history of many Latin American dictatorships in *El otoño*, in addition to others fictions that are more intuitively historical than professionally historiographical, García Márquez has demonstrated more than once that fiction can be more powerful than official records as a way of recording the forgotten past of Latin America. In *El general*, he suggests that one of the supposedly best known of Latin America's political heroes is actually one of the least known. The author defies many of the sterile legends about Bolívar and depicts a character who, in the end, is far more engaging than the political legend. Like his predecessors in the Macondo cycle, particularly Colonel Aureliano Buendía, Bolívar is an august and tired warrior who recognizes the stench of his military victories as much as he acknowledges the glory. In accordance with most of the legends constructed around Bolívar, García Márquez's character is a brave and democratic visionary. In contrast to these popular legends, however, he is also constructed in this novel as an egotistical, vulgar, and authoritarian philanderer. By the time he reaches the end of his life, the contemporary myths around him are as weakened as is his physical body.

García Márquez has dedicated a lifetime to analyzing and exposing the contradictions of political human beings; what stands out in *El otoño* is not the General's bad character as such but his contradictory personality: his innocence in the face of the perversion of all human values. What characterizes Bolívar, above all, is a similar contradiction. His dream and his memories, interspersed throughout the novel, reveal his enormous contradictions and ambiguities. Bolívar had already been viewed by some scholars as a victim of the nation he inherited after he led the populace to independence; in this novel, however, he is also seen as an active agent in creating the political system that failed both him and the recently created nation. His obsessive dream of a unified continent seems to be a forerunner of those entertained by many other visionary idealists and, like Colonel Aureliano Buendía and General Rafael Uribe Uribe of Colombia's War of a Thousand Days, he dreams, right to the end of his days, of one last war to reverse his fortunes. When he imagines creating the greatest nation of the world ('la nación más grande del mundo'), extending from Mexico to Argentina, the reader recalls the drunken dreams of Baltazar in the bar in the story 'La prodigiosa tarde de Baltazar'. When the novel appeared, many intellectuals in Latin America were reluctant to abandon their idealized version of Bolívar in favor of a García Márquez portrayal that suggested that the Emancipator's failure was due to his own defects of character.

Like many of the most attractive characters in García Márquez's fiction, the Simón Bolívar that García Márquez fictionalizes is most admirable simply because of his deep humanity. He is robust with energy for life, with a passion for learning everything from law to dance. As part of García Márquez's progressive recovery of African culture in Latin America, he here discovers traces of an African bloodline in Bolívar, giving his protagonist a truly Caribbean, tri-ethnic identity. This tri-ethnic cultural identity, in addition to the multiple contradictions in his politics, made Bolívar a character few of Latin America's elite were willing to embrace as their hero. On the contrary, the fictionalized Bolívar constructed by García Márquez and the novel *El general* were rejected by many of the intellectual elite and the polemical work was widely debated throughout Latin America when it appeared in print in 1989. Whatever one's political understanding of Bolívar may be, García Márquez's accomplishment is unquestionable: he has captured at least some of the quintessential Bolívar.

Well before publishing *El otoño* in 1975 and *El general* in 1989, García Márquez had written a series of shorter texts with explicit political content. Three very different types of explicitly political stories that were forerunners of *El otoño* were the novelette *Relato de un náufrago* (*Tale of a shipwrecked sailor,* 1955) and the stories 'Un día de éstos' ('One of These Days') and 'Los funerales de la mamá grande' ('Big Mama's funeral'). All three are the work of a young writer acutely aware of his colonial and neocolonial past as it survived into the twentieth century. They shed further light on the different ways in which García Márquez has assumed the role of a political writer and taken on the political questions that interest him most.

García Márquez's journalistic account, *Relato de un náufrago*, was initially serialized in a newspaper before appearing as a short book. Having been recently employed by the newspaper *El Espectador* in 1955, he and many of his colleagues there were well aware of the journalistic potential of a human interest feature story when on 28 February the news broke that sailors on a Colombian navy destroyer called the *Caldas* had fallen from the ship during a storm and drowned. The *Caldas* was on route to Cartagena from Mobile, Alabama, where it had been docked for four months for repairs. The directors at *El Espectador* and García Márquez the journalist saw the potential for an eye-catching and polemical feature story when, a week later, the Colombian navy revealed that the one sailor, Velasco, had survived on a raft for ten days. Velasco arrived on a beach in Colombia exhausted but alive. García Márquez, however, could not gain access to Velasco, for the navy carefully isolated him from any questioning by any journalist keen to learn anything beyond the official government version of what had happened. (This whole series of events has many parallels with the government cover-up of the banana workers strike in 1928 that was not revealed in writing until Alvaro Cepeda Samudio published *La casa grande* in 1962 and García Márquez came out with *Cien años* in 1967.) Once García Márquez the journalist failed to get the story direct from the sailor, he gave up and has since confessed that he even felt humiliated by this dismal failure, which he clearly took very personally. The Director of *El Espectador*, however, saved the cause by paying the sailor for the rights to his story, and then reassigning it to the recently disappointed García Márquez. Given his overwhelming sense of failure, however, the young journalist accepted the assignment on the condition that his name did not appear on the story. That decision turned out to be fortuitous, for it meant that he had to write it in the first-person voice of the protagonist, in his words and under his name. Consequently, as García Márquez has himself put it, 'sería el monólogo interior de una aventura solitaria, al pie de la letra, como la había hecho la vida' ('it would be the internal monologue of a solitary adventure, just as it had happened and just as life had made it').[11] García Márquez and Velasco originally agreed on a story in fourteen instalments, hoping to maintain ongoing suspense for the readers of *El Espectador* for a period of two weeks. The first instalment was published on 5 April 1955, and from this date forward, daily sales of *El Espectador* skyrocketed. As García Márquez listened to Velasco tell his story, he discovered an incredible truth: there had been no storm at all, and the navy had fabricated a huge lie to protect itself from a potential scandal. The actual truth was that the sailors had purchased a number of household appliances (refrigerators and the like) in the United States, and the ship was grossly overloaded to such an extent that the inside of the ship was full and there were even appliances on deck. In addition, the ship was not carrying the required number of life rafts and those that were available did not carry the necessary supplies for survival. Velasco had been pressured by the navy into not revealing any of these facts in his official public interviews upon his return to Colombia. Once García Márquez began elaborating this story, its success in *El Espectador* was so overwhelming that the newspaper's editorial committee recommended that

---

[11] *Vivir para contarla* (Bogotá: Norma, 2002), 564–65; *Living to Tell the Tale*, tr. Edith Grossman (New York: Knopf, 2003), 520.

the planned fourteen instalments be extended to twenty. Eventually, the military let García Márquez know that they considered him a traitor to the nation.

The politics and aesthetics of García Márquez's early political writing are noteworthy. *Relato de un náufrago* was an early example of his using political storytelling to seek truth. In terms of storytelling, this was an important exercise in how to write with a well-developed awareness of the reader. Reader interest corresponded directly with newspaper sales, so this was an important early lesson in creating chapter-by-chapter suspense for the reader. Reflecting on *Relato de un náufrago* years later, García Márquez offered his own summary of the multiple interests he created for readers: 'Pienso que el interés de los lectores empezó por motivos humanitarios, siguió por razones literarias, y al final por consideraciones políticas, pero sostenido siempre por la tensión interna del relato' ('I think the interest of readers began for humanitarian reasons, continued for literary reasons, and in the end for political considerations, but it was always sustained by the internal tension of the account').[12]

*Relato de un náufrago* is an explicitly political exposé in which the author directly questions the legitimacy of institutional truth. A very different approach to political subject-matter appears in some of his own fiction of this same period. On the advice of his superiors at the newspaper *El Espectador*, García Márquez left Colombia to distance himself from the military establishment that he had challenged (and directly criticized) with his *Relato*: he was to remain in Europe from 1955 to 1958. He was far away not only from the threat of bodily harm at the hands of disgruntled elements of the military, but also from the day-to-day experience of living under the military dictatorship of Rojas Pinilla and the civil war known as La Violencia. In Europe, he began some of stories that appeared later in the volume entitled *Los funerales de la mamá grande.*

One of his most subtle and nuanced political stories is 'Un día de éstos', a brief work that tells the story of a small-town mayor suffering from a toothache and the consequences of his visit to a humble dentist. A key to understanding the full political dimension of the story is the fact that during that period (and for most of the twentieth century in Colombia), Colombians did not hold local elections to elect the mayors of towns and cities. Thus, the mayors were basically representatives of the central power or, in the 1950s, of the military dictator Gustavo Rojas Pinilla, and knowing this fact is essen-

---

12  *Vivir para contarla*, 571: *Living to Tell the Tale*, 525.

tial for grasping the full political meaning of the story 'Un día de éstos'.[13]
The other key element of the social context is that being a dentist in rural
Colombia is not by any means the upper-middle-class profession that it is in
the United States or in Europe; a rural dentist in Colombia occupies a modest
position that would barely qualify one to be considered part of the middle
class in a rural area, and produces such a modest income that the lifestyle of
a dentist would be more comparable to that of a working-class person in the
United States. Generally speaking, a dentist would not necessarily be aligned
or associated by profession with the oligarchy.

The story 'Un día de éstos' begins with a description of the setting, the
surgery of Don Aurelio Escovar, a practising dentist without a degree. This
assures that the reader is aware of the character's modest standing, for the
underclass of the dental profession in Colombia is the rural dentist who has
not actually completed all the requirements for a degree. In the first dialogue,
his son asks the dentist, as he is working in his surgery, if he can pull out the
tooth of the suffering mayor, who is in the waiting room. The dentist requests
that the boy inform the mayor that the dentist is not present. The mayor hears
the dentist's voice, however, and raises the level of the confrontation: he tells
the boy that if the dentist does not oblige him, he will shoot him. The dentist
does not budge and instructs the boy to tell him to go ahead and shoot. This
is the dentist's own power play, since a dead dentist obviously cannot pull out
a tooth. When the mayor sits down with his swollen jaw, the tension between
the two is evident from their short initial exchange. The dentist's workplace
is described as 'pobre' ('poor'), clearly aligning the dentist with the working
poor. After inspecting the tooth, the dentist announces to the mayor that the
tooth must be removed without the use of anesthesia, and the reason the
dentist offers seems suspicious: because the mayor has an abscess. The interaction between the two remains brief and tense. The dentist then puts the
mayor through extreme pain, a pain that the mayor feels to the depths of his
kidneys. Following the rituals of the power-game in play, however, the mayor
shows no external sign of his pain, lest he give the dentist the pleasure of
knowing how successfully he has inflicted it. After this act is finished, the
quiet and methodical dentist makes a statement that raises the story to a political level, saying to the mayor that he is now paying for twenty deaths ('Aquí
nos paga veinte muertos, teniente', *Los funerales*, 22). With this statement,
the reason for the dentist's initial indifference and later aggression is finally

---

[13] For a broader and more detailed reading of this story, see Robin Fiddian, *García
Márquez, Los funerales de la mamá grande*, Critical Guides to Spanish Texts 70 (London:
Grant & Cutler, 2006), Chapter 3.

revealed: the mayor is an active repressor and killer, a true ally of the military dictator who is invisibly present in the background and who has indirectly appointed him as mayor. At the end of the story, the power relations shift once again, however: the dentist asks if he should charge the mayor's office for his services, and the mayor responds 'Es la misma vaina' (*Los funerales*, 23). With this cynical response – using a Colombian colloquialism that means 'it makes no difference' – the mayor both reasserts his power and alludes to the corruption of political practices in Colombia.

In this early story, García Márquez found a new method for writing about politics, and one at the opposite end of the spectrum from the direct denunciation found in the *Relato de un náufrago*. Metaphorical situations and indirect allusion were his new methods for communicating a political message that was no longer limited just to Colombia, but could be read (and has been read) as a story about political repression and authoritarian regimes in many societies. As a modernist, García Márquez was searching for methods of telling specifically Colombian stories that could be read and understood as universal.

The story 'Los funerales de la mamá grande' is about a powerful matriarch, probably based on a legendary real-life matriarch in La Sierpe, a town of the Costa region. She is literally larger than life. The hyperbole of this story provides the groundwork for a particular kind of hyperbole that García Márquez develops and fully exploits in *Cien años*, and is more fully developed in terms of power in *El otoño*. The narrator begins by taking everyday objects, situations, and actions and describing them in hyperbolic terms. In the first chapter, the hyperbolic treatment of an everyday object – ice – as the great invention of our time ('gran invento de nuestro tiempo') is the beginning of this procedure in *Cien años*. Later, characters do prodigious things, such as engender an extraordinary number of children, and these seemingly fantastic matters are treated as common and even banal events.

'Los funerales de la mamá grande' was a foundational story in the evolution of Macondo as the center of the universe. In *Cien años*, Macondo is portrayed early in the novel as the primordial cradle of civilization, the village where human society arises out of a Biblical Garden of Eden. He was well aware, of course, of the numerous precedents for using a small rural space, such as Faulkner's Yoknapatawpha County, as a metaphor for the universe. 'Los funerales' is García Márquez's pioneer work in portraying Macondo as universe, while at the same time he mocks the very idea of this town as a 'center'. This use of modernist narrative strategies at the same time that he parodies them is trademark García Márquez.

As a precursor to *El otoño*, this story is a hyperbolic treatment of the autocrat whose power seemingly has no limits, for the protagonist who rules over her town claims to possess all the moral virtues ('bienes morales') that she enumerates on her deathbed. In addition, she claims an invisible patrimony ('patrimonio invisible') that involves a humorous juxtaposition of the material, the institutional, the political, and the philosophical. As Robin Fiddian has pointed out, this passage listing all her possessions abounds in humor deriving from incongruous juxtapositions and satire, especially of the rhetoric and ideology of the oligarchy.[14]

**Conclusion**

García Márquez's major piece of political writing and most successful political novel was *El otoño*. Along with *Cien años* and *El amor*, this is also one of his three major novels. García Márquez wrote the book asking himself what is the spark that generates power and what is the nature of power.[15] For readers interested in political fiction, this was his novelistic masterpiece. Nevertheless, García Márquez's entire writing career has been essentially political, with some writings treating the political dimension more directly (or less metaphorically) than others. For him, the act of constructing his stories always depends upon a central visual image (such as the decaying palace in *El otoño*), and the context in which the action is developed is often a remnant of Spanish medieval order. Thus, the authoritarian regimes operating behind the scenes in the *Relato de un náufrago* and in 'Un día de éstos' are fundamentally the same type of regimes operating in Pinochet's Chile or the colonial regime of Philip II in Latin America. These works – a novel, a journalistic 'tale', two short stories, and a documentary 'adventure' – are just five representative examples from a writing career as closely associated with political commitment as it has been with telling a good story. García Márquez is a deeply political person.

*El otoño* was the culmination of a two-decade long meditation on power. This story-based meditation began in Paris when he started writing drafts during the dictatorship of Rojas Pinilla for the stories of *Los funerales*, *La mala hora*, and *El coronel*. His first exploration of power was his satire of the excesses of autocratic rule in the story 'Los funerales de la mamá grande'. In *El otoño*, he combined the two most constant interests of all his writing, modernist aesthetics and an interest in the workings of politics.

---

14  *ibid.*, 126.
15  González Bermejo, 'And Now, Two Hundred Years', 17.

His two novels with generals as protagonists invite comparison. The expectations that the reader brings to these two novels tend to be different: the reader expects a critique of a dictator in *El otoño*, while many readers expect sympathy for the hero of the independence in *El general*. García Márquez's presentation of the uses and abuses of power by these two protagonists, however, is not as Manichaean as many readers might have expected: the dictator figure in *El otoño*, solitary and pathetic in the isolation of his power, has many moments that can well compel the reader to be momentarily sympathetic; the Bolívar figure in *El general* is so driven by ego and power, among other things, that he is doomed to failure and evokes little sympathy. In both novels, individual personalities and personality traits are perhaps less significant than ideology, political legacies, and social structures, but important enough to merit recognition in both García Márquez's act of writing and the reader's act of interpretation and analysis.

With these two works, García Márquez moves closer to human sentiment and matters of the body and heart than had been explicit in the Macondo cycle. In the Macondo cycle, the author and the reader are consistently distanced from details of the human body and from the intimacy of the heart. These intimate details are the core of García Márquez's next novel, *El amor en los tiempos del cólera*.

# Postmodern Gestures:
## *El amor en los tiempos del cólera, Crónica de una muerte anunciada,* and *La increíble y triste historia de la cándida Eréndira y de su abuela desalmada*

On completion of the work in the Macondo cycle that has come to be recognized as the best of them (his signature Macondo story), *Cien años de soledad,* and after its publication, García Márquez decided to change the direction of his work. In *Cien años* and his short novels *La hojarasca, La mala hora* and *El coronel no tiene quién le escriba,* as well as the short stories of *Los funerales de la mamá grande,* García Márquez had told the story of Macondo, and now he was ready to begin a new stage of his writing career. As a writer with cosmopolitan and modernist interests, he left behind the characters and the unique world of Macondo. He launched this new stage with the publication of *El otoño del patriarca* in 1975, the most explicitly political of his novels and also the most disassociated from Macondo. Scholars and critics immediately noted that the author of *El otoño* had abandoned not only Macondo and its characters, but also many of the trademark gestures (above all, the fantasy) previously associated with his supposed 'magic realism'.

In his next novels, *Crónica de una muerte anunciada* and *El amor en los tiempos del cólera,* García Márquez's writing seemed to take a postmodern turn, for these are what are sometimes called self-reflective texts (that is, they contain internal comment or allusions to fiction in general) and that is something we find in postmodern fiction. Indeed, they are a technical tour de force in the art of storytelling, both of them examples of a writer at the height of his powers as a novelist. The complexity of García Márquez's work, however, precludes the reduction of these texts to mere postmodern exercises. Though they are postmodern tours de force and what are often termed hermeneutic tales (stories, that is, that invite multiple interpretations), they are also a continuation of his modernist project of exploring the Hispanic and African historical roots of Latin American society, as well as a return to some of the now standard fare of his Macondo fiction. These two novels, *El amor* and

*Crónica,* as well as selected short stories of *La increíble triste historia de la cándida Eréndira y de su abuela desalmada,* will be the focus of this chapter.

By the time García Márquez and his cohort of the Boom, Carlos Fuentes, were writing their fictions of the 1980s, Faulkner was already *passé* and the two novelists were living in an increasingly globalized world of postmodern culture. The postmodern fiction of such writers as John Barth and William Gass was as much in vogue as had been the novels of the 1960s Latin American Boom. For García Márquez and Fuentes, and more so for many younger novelists in the 1980s, it was increasingly appropriate to think of their recent fiction as 'postmodern'. Indeed, by the late 1980s, the idea of a postmodern fiction in Latin America was broadly recognized. Some of the fiction published after the 1960s by writers of the Boom and the next generation already had characteristics that associated it with the postmodern fiction being produced in the United States and Europe. The rise of postmodern fiction in Latin America was particularly evident from 1968 – a year after the self-reflective *Cien años de soledad* – with the novels of Manuel Puig and Severo Sarduy. Fuentes's fictional encyclopedia of postmodern motifs and strategies, *Terra nostra* (1975), was as important for the future of postmodern writing in Latin America as was Puig's *La traición de Rita Haworth* (*Betrayed by Rita Hayworth,* 1968) and Sarduy's *Cobra* (1972).[1] The culmination of García Márquez's modernist project with *Cien años* came during the period when the North American writer John Barth published his postmodern reflections on the literature of exhaustion and also during the period when the North American critic Leslie Fiedler popularized the term 'postmodern' in the United States. The term has been used too broadly to allow a precise definition, but common concepts associated with postmodern culture have included discontinuity, disruption, dislocation, decentering, indeterminacy, and antitotalization. These concepts represent ideas quite contrary to those that underlay the 'totalizing' modernist projects of García Márquez and the other writers of the Boom: the landmark novels, that is, that they wrote in the 1960s involving not only a set of characters but also a broad section of society and a sweeping overview of history. At the same time, as Linda Hutcheon has pointed out, postmodernism is contradictory, for it installs and then subverts the very concepts that it constructs and challenges.[2] Ihab

---

[1]   For an overview of the place of these novels in the context of the rise of postmodern fiction in Latin America, see Raymond L. Williams, *The Postmodern Novel in Latin America: Politics, Culture, and the Crisis of Truth* (New York: St Martin's, 1995), Chapter 1.

[2]   Linda Hutcheon, *A Poetics of Postmodernism: History, Theory, Fiction* (New York: Routledge, 1989), 16.

Hassan has developed some of the critical language and concepts for post-modernism, creating parallel columns that juxtapose characteristics of the modern and the postmodern. However, Hassan's 'either/or' thinking proposes a resolution of what should rather be seen as the unresolved contradictions of the postmodern.

Theorists such as Jean-François Lyotard, Jean Baudrillard, and Fredric Jameson have speculated about culture and society in postindustrial North Atlantic nations, with occasional remarks on Latin America, Africa, and Asia. Lyotard theorizes on the state of knowledge in post-industrial society, maintaining that we now live at the end of the 'grand narrative' or master narrative of science and the nation state that García Márquez, Fuentes, Cortázar, and other prominent Latin American intellectuals have also questioned in much of their writing.

Baudrillard shares some of Lyotard's ideas. For him, empirical reality was no longer real. García Márquez and many writers of his generation, such as Fuentes and Vargas Llosa, have dedicated a lifetime of writing to the search for truth. Baudrillard, however, rejects all discourses of truth and claims that we are in a logic of simulation which has nothing to do with the logic of facts.

In their discussions of the postmodern, theorists such as Jameson have spoken of postindustrial society in terms of a loss of history, the dissolution of the centered self, and the fading of individual style. For García Márquez and the writers of the 1960s Boom, the rewriting of history has been a major dimension of their work. Linda Hutcheon's arguments in favor of a postmodern novel that is historical helps us to see certain elements of García Márquez's writing as postmodern. Hutcheon proposes that the term 'postmodern' be used in the context of 'historiographic metafiction'. This fiction raises questions about the status of historical knowledge when rewriting history in the form of novelistic narrative. This historiographical metafiction – the postmodern novel that looks outward at real history and inward at its own textuality – reflects the view that only history can claim to be true, both by questioning the ground of that claim in historiography and in other human constructs. One function of historiographical metafiction like *Cien años* is to suggest that truth and falsity may not be the right terms; perhaps readers should be thinking of truths in plural. Paradoxically, *Cien años*, though the culmination of García Márquez's modernist (Faulknerian) project, is also an important precursor, as historiographical metafiction, of a more extreme postmodern fiction that would soon follow in Latin America in the 1970s and 1980s.

The most noteworthy precursor to the postmodern, however, was not *Cien años*, but selected fictions of Jorge Luis Borges. If stories such as 'Pierre

Menard, autor del Quijote', and 'La biblioteca de Babel' had set the stage for a modernist novel in Latin America, then important precursors for later postmodern fiction were the stories in the now classic volume *Ficciones* (1944) that suggested the concept of a universe as a centerless labyrinth. The blurring of the line between essay and fiction in texts such as 'Pierre Menard, autor del Quijote', and 'Las ruinas circulares' opened the gates for the fictionalized theoretical prose of the generation that followed the 1960s Boom, such as Ricardo Piglia and Severo Sarduy. The theorization in these specific stories interested García Márquez far less than Borges's more anecdotally oriented work.

After Borges, the next important predecessors for Latin American postmodern fiction of the 1980s were the postmodern tendencies noted in selected fiction of García Márquez, Fuentes (of *Terra nostra*), Vargas Llosa (of *La tía Julia y el escribidor/Aunt Julia and the Scriptwriter*, 1977), João Guimarães Rosa (*Grande Sertão: Veredas/The Devil to Pay in the Backlands*, 1956), and Julio Cortázar's *Rayuela/Hopscotch* (1963). Although still heavily endowed with the aesthetics of modernism and not really a postmodern work itself, *Rayuela* creates a writer named Morelli who proposes a radically postmodern type of fiction. After the publication of *Cien años* in 1967, the postmodern novel began to appear in Latin America, almost always inspired by either Borges or Cortázar: Guillermo Cabrera Infante's *Tres tristes tigres* (*Three Trapped Tigers*, 1967), Néstor Sanchez's *Siberia Blues* (1967), Puig's *La traición de Rita Rayworth* (1968), and Sarduy's *Cobra* (1972).

Some scholars have sensed a bridging of elite and popular art in postmodern culture. Since the 1960s, several Latin American writers who have been the object of academic study have, at the same time, been popular best-sellers, particularly García Márquez, Vargas Llosa, and Puig. Two post-1967 works that have been the object of academic study and have sold very well to the general public are García Márquez's *Crónica* (1981) and Vargas Llosa's *La tía Julia y el escribidor* (1977). These two novels can arguably be considered postmodern. The potential uses of popular art have interested García Márquez far more than the theories of postmodern culture.

Of García Márquez's work, the novel that is most closely associated with the postmodern is *El amor*. On the surface, this is a traditional, even classic love story: Florentino Ariza and Fermina Daza fall in love as adolescents, her father intervenes to break up the nascent relationship, and she marries the man chosen by her father: Dr Juvenal Urbino, a wealthy and highly respected doctor. The desperate lover, Florentino, spends a lifetime writing love letters to his lost lover. The novel's unlikely ending, however, breaks with the traditional, classic, realist love-story mode; it is also equally as unfitting for the ending of a nineteenth-century Romantic novel as it is for that of a modernist one: Fermina's husband dies an unpoetic and prosaic death from an accident while attempting to rescue his parrot; Fermina and Florentino are united; and the two of them make love on a poetic, even mythical cruise on a steamboat down the Magdalena River.

The central visual image for this novel, based on that same book of nineteenth-century drawings that provide the opening image for *El otoño*, is of a nineteenth-century river steamboat. A classic mode of transportation of nineteenth-century Romantic grandeur, the steamboat is the ideal central image for a novel about Florentino's love, which is more aesthetic than emotional or physical. This is not a love based on physical attraction, but a literary construct of Florentino's imagination. The story is basically about a triangular relationship between Florentino, Fermina and Juvenal, a relationship that involves several different kinds of love. After the original relationship between Florentino and Fermina begins with some brief encounters – and even more written notes – the affair is suspended by Fermina's father, who sends her out of town. Her physical absence, however, only promotes even more writing, for what were originally furtive notes now become full-length love letters. The father's intervention in the early stages of the relationship, then, not only makes the young Florentino a frustrated lover but transforms a scribbler of love notes into a writer of love letters.[3] The adolescent scribbler is forced to become a writer from an early age. From this point in the story, the relationship between Florentino and Fermina is developed almost entirely through writing. *El amor* is about writing itself both in the literal sense of using letters to move the plot and in the metaphoric sense of the self-reflective, postmodern novel.[4] This self-reflective element of the novel provides a metafictional quality that fits Hutcheon's concept of 'historiographic metafiction'.

Florentino's youthful letters of the scribbler in the process of becoming a writer are not the novel's only texts within the text. During the fifty-year period of Fermina's marriage with Urbino, Florentino produces many types of texts in the process of becoming a writer. He writes many love letters for those who need his services – primarily lovers in crisis lacking his gift for the

---

[3]   This situation recreates a common paradigm in modern Latin American literature: the repressive authority figure who is responsible for the creation of the oppositional writer. Vargas Llosa describes this paradigm as part of his theory of 'demons'. See Vargas Llosa: *García Márquez: historia de un deicidio* (Caracas: Monte Ávila, 1971). He also parodies this paradigm in his novel *La tía Julia y el escribidor*.

[4]   See Isabel Álvarez Borland, 'Interior Texts in *El amor en los tiempos del cólera*', *Hispanic Review*, 58 (1991), 175–86.

written language. Florentino eventually puts his writing experience to use by self-publishing a manual for lovestruck letter writers, a booklet that he titles *Secretario de los enamorados*. He also organizes a volume of his writings, under the title of *Ellas*, consisting of erotic descriptions of his numerous sexual encounters with a long series of women. His encounters encompass over six hundred women all of whom he uses as temporary substitutes for the woman he thinks he loves. Finally, Florentino as an older man writes other types of text: the mature love letters to Fermina are, in effect, the equivalent of the mature writing of Gabriel García Márquez in such novels as *El amor* itself. This is one of the novel's numerous self-reflective, metafictional qualities.

Other characters in *El amor* also produce texts within the text. Jeremiah de Saint-Amour writes a suicide letter that stands out as the first external text to enter the novel. It is also striking as a very peculiar type of suicide letter, for Saint-Amour does not make the decision to end his own life because he is broken-hearted over the loss of love but, rather, because, as a result of old age, he is suffering from the existential despair of losing his youth. This letter thus sets a direction for a novel that might appear, on the surface, to be primarily a love story, but which, in reality, has far more to do with ageing and writing than it has with love. Another set of texts consists of letters exchanged between Fermina and her husband Juvenal Urbino, which reveal to the reader the difference between their prosaic relationship and the highly poeticized and aestheticized version of love that Florentino articulates in all of his letters. A third set of external texts is provided by the letters that Fermina writes to Florentino. As Isabel Álvarez Borland has pointed out, *El amor* contains other types of embedded texts in addition to the texts written by the characters.[5] One of these is visual in nature and consists of a canvas portraying the death of Juvenal Urbino, which, as it turns out, is more the prosaic depiction of a man caught in a lamentably ridiculous situation than the idealized portrait of a beloved husband who has passed away. Thus, the prosaic visual image of Juvenal appears in stark contrast to the highly romantic image of Florentino. Once again, García Márquez uses a visual image as a key element of a story that is otherwise told as a narrative; in this case it is used to ridicule Juvenal Urbino as the rational and pro-European doctor. The other embedded text not written by a character is an article in *La Justicia*, a local newspaper.

---

5   *ibid*, 178.

In some ways, then, *El amor* can be associated with the motifs and devices of postmodern fiction. The ways in which the characters' actions and thoughts seem to be the playing out of textualities, give the novel self-reflexive qualities, and invite the reader to react to *El amor* as postmodern fiction. Indeed, as suggested earlier, this novel arguably has qualities of the historiographical metafiction that Hutcheon considers the virtual paradigm of the postmodern novel. Nevertheless, an in-depth analysis of the text will demonstrate that, rather than being a postmodern love story, it is not exclusively a postmodern text on love as literary construct, but also a modernist novel focused primarily on ageing, death, and the human impact of the Spanish medieval and colonial legacy in Latin America. In the same way that *Cien años* is more about myths than it is the actual creation of a myth, *El amor* is more about the postmodern than it is the actual creation of a postmodern text.

*El amor* begins with a comment on love: 'Era inevitable: el olor de las almendras amargas le recordaba siempre el destino de los amores contrariados' (*El amor*, 178) ('It was inevitable: the scent of bitter almonds always reminded him of the fate of unrequited love', *Love*, 3). This opening line is not what it initially appears to be: it is not about Florentino Ariza's five-decade-long experience of unrequited love, but is actually Dr Juvenal Urbino's reflection on the supposedly unrequited love of his friend Jeremiah de Saint-Amour. With this opening, García Márquez misleads the reader twice. By evoking the concept of 'unrequited love' in a novel titled *El amor en los tiempos del cólera*, the reader is invited to believe that this novel is actually a love story. In addition, this language leads the reader into an opening scene that seems, inevitably, to be about love. The lengthy opening scene, however, is not really about the unrequited love of Florentino Ariza or of Jeremiah de Saint-Amour; rather, it deals with Saint-Amour's unique method for addressing issues of ageing and death, a method that denies the importance of love. When he was a young man in his twenties, Saint-Amour decided that he would never live life as an old person and that the way to accomplish this objective would be to take his own life at exactly the age of sixty. Thus, unlike many suicides, his suicide is unrelated to love. The opening scene of the novel, then, is not in any way related to a love story; instead, it is the novel's first anecdote on the topic of ageing.

After the opening chapter introducing the stories of Jeremiah de Saint-Amour and Dr Juvenal Urbino, *El amor* proceeds with the more lengthy, complex, and elaborate story of ageing. The characterization of Dr Juvenal Urbino emphasizes his close association with the advent of modernity as it was slowly being embraced in the cities of the Caribbean coast of Colombia: Cartagena and Barranquilla. This modernity meant the entrance into

Colombia of new Western science, specifically in the forms of European medicine and new practices of hygiene that led to the construction of the first sewage systems. Dr Urbino is not only the promoter and champion of these scientific and technological advances in Cartagena but also the direct connection to modern European science, for he brings to Colombia the knowledge that he acquired in France and keeps the Colombian locals informed of the latest scientific advances taking place in Paris. The advent of European modernity means not only the progress associated with this new European science, but also a new vision of time as ordered, linear, and teleological. Dr Juvenal Urbino is the very embodiment of these new concepts about science and time; he is the man with the most impressive credentials, thoughts, and actions in the world of the rational. His rational abilities and methodical ways make him the quintessential man of reason and, by the time he dies, one of the most respected citizens of Cartagena, both because of his accomplishments as a scientific doctor and his civic leadership in the promotion of European modernity. The first chapter, then, relates the story of Dr Juvenal Urbino's life as the educated, progressive, and rational doctor as he methodically organizes both the city and his life until his death. At the end of the novel, he dies an unceremonious death that seems to betray everything that he was and represented, for, in contrast to the grandiosity and rationality of his entire life, his death is trivial and irrational: he unexpectedly falls off a ladder attempting to rescue an ordinary household pet, a parrot that has escaped.

Florentino Ariza, on the other hand, embodies qualities that make him the antithesis of Dr Juvenal Urbino. A man who never embraces anything associated with modernity, he is an anachronism of the late nineteenth and early twentieth centuries, even in Colombia. He lives in the literary and poetic world he constructs by dedicating himself to reading Romantic literature and Spanish Golden-Age poetry, as well as composing a constant flow of love letters to Fermina Daza. To the extent that Dr Juvenal Urbino both embraces and eventually falls victim to linear, ordered time, Florentino negates time while he simultaneously negates modernity: for Florentino, attention to feeling can alter the flow of time and the experience of ageing. Florentino confronts and denies time and ageing by thinking of Fermina Daza 'every single moment' for fifty-one years, nine months, and four days. Ignoring the embrace of reason and progress by both Dr Juvenal Urbino and the new progressive upper middle class of Colombia, Florentino lives a life consistent with his pledge of eternal fidelity and everlasting love for his idealized love figure. Thus, the narrator describes him as a man who believed he had 'amado en silencio mucho más que nadie jamás en este mundo' (*El amor*, 80) ('loved in silence for much longer time than anyone else in this world ever had',

*Love*, 48). In contrast to Dr Juvenal Urbino's embrace of the linear paradigm of 'progress', Florentino Ariza's feeling and loving body projects a kind of atemporal movement of the heart that, in turn, embodies a read and written truth of emotional attachment altering the body's status (Urbino's body, that is) as a mechanical time piece.

At the end of the novel, at Dr Juvenal Urbino's funeral, Florentino Ariza appears before Fermina Daza to reiterate his vow of everlasting love, made five decades earlier. After an initial rejection of Florentino, Fermina eventually accepts him, and he realizes his lifelong dream of accompanying her in a romantic, albeit anachronistic trip down the Magdalena River in a vehicle that predates the modernity of the new science of her deceased husband: a steamboat. In the end, Florentino profoundly humanizes not only time but also love and life in the face of a dehumanizing modernity and death.

## Colombian society, modernity, and the colonial legacy

In this novel, García Márquez weaves a story about ageing, love, and writing through a society fully aware of turn-of-the-century modernity and which attempts to participate in it at the same time that it is living the Spanish medieval and colonial legacy. In fact, *El amor, Crónica*, and *Del amor y otros demonios* are the three novels of García Márquez in which the medieval and colonial legacies are most prominent. In the latter half of his writing career, he has penetrated more deeply and intimately into the sociopolitical circumstances that had provided the backdrop to his previous work.

The physical space of *El amor* provides an ongoing reference to the Spanish colonial period, for much of the novel takes place within the city of Cartagena, surrounded by the protective defensive walls (now a historical monument) originally erected to guard the wealth and the inhabitants of the Spanish empire. García Márquez makes regular references to the streets and plazas built and named by the Spaniards during this period, and the names serve as a constant reminder that this is a city that still lives the reality of the colonial period. These allusions to the physical space of the Spanish empire are, moreover, supported by numerous more direct comments explaining the relationship of the city and its characters to the colonial period. The physical remnants of the Spanish colonial period enter into Florentino's mind as he experiences the following scene:

> Podía referir con sus pormenores menos pensados la historia de cada cascarón de buque carcomido por el óxido, sabía la edad de cada boya, el

origen de cualquier escombro, el número de eslabones de la cadena con que los españoles cerraban la entrada de la bahía. (*El amor*, 139)

He could recount the most unexpected detail of the history of each rusting hulk of a boat, he knew the age of each buoy, the origin of every piece of rubbish, the number of links in the chain with which the Spaniards closed off the entrance of the bay. (*Love*, 90)

The narrative continues with an explanation of Florentino's erudition on the question of the Spanish colonial presence. He knows the story of the treasure in a sunken galleon in the bay; he has learned that the *San José* was not the only ship in the coral depths; that it had been the flagship of the Tierra Firma fleet that arrived in Cartagena after May 1708; that, during the month it had remained there for the celebration of popular *fiestas*, the rest of the treasure intended to save the Kingdom of Spain from poverty had been taken aboard, including 116 trunks of emeralds and thirty million gold coins. He knows that the enormous Spanish colonial fortresses on the outer edges of Cartagena, called Boca Chica by the Spaniards and still carrying that name today, were where the *San José* left the bay, and that, after four hours at sea, it had sunk to the ocean floor. This is a novel in which the characters still live intimately with the colonial legacy.

The story of Florentino Ariza and Fermina Daza first connects to the story of the Spanish colonial empire when Florentino, in his voluminous love letters, includes all the details he knows about the sunken treasure destined for the Spanish crown. He does not realize that Fermina is, in fact, a much more informed recipient of his memoranda than he could imagine, for her father Lorenzo had dedicated much time and money to an effort to recover the treasure of the sunken *San José*. Thus, she is able rationally to evaluate Florentino's exaggerated claims of the proximity of the treasure; indeed, she fears that her bedazzled sweetheart must have 'perdido el juicio' (*El amor*, 143) ('lost his mind', *Love*, 93).

Inside the city, specific physical spaces such as the Portal de los Escribanos (Arcade of the Scribes), provide a link between Florentino's turn-of-the-century passion and the Spanish colonial legacy as it is still alive in *El amor*. The Portal de los Escribanos is the name of a place dating back to colonial times, a space where scribes wrote official public documents and private, personal letters, legal memoranda of petition or complaints, notes of condolence or congratulation, and, most importantly for Florentino Ariza and Fermina Daza, love letters appropriate for any stage of a relationship. For women who already had class credentials, or for women such as Fermina Daza, who aspired to the best class credentials, the Portal de los Escribanos had been a forbidden place; since colonial times, it had been a male commercial space, a busy and noisy area exclusively for the use of men. For Florintino Ariza, the Spanish writing tradition established in the colonial period and continued in the twentieth century is where he eventually practices professionally his art of writing love letters (for money) as a substitute for the writing of the real love letters he deeply desires to continue sending to Fermina Daza. For Fermina Daza, who is far less experienced and gifted in the art of writing love letters, the Portal de los Escribanos is the forbidden space that she transgresses in order to buy a bottle of golden-colored ink appropriate to write a love letter to Florentino. At different times, then, the two lovers occupy the same colonial space. Paradoxically, the colonial space that brings them together (at least for the act of writing love letters) is the same colonial space that keeps them apart for five decades: it is only because of their neocolonial mentality, their acceptance of the rigid rules of class difference inherited from the colonial past, that they believe and accept that they cannot marry.

The colonial city in which the characters live, then, seems to be a metaphor for the colonial and neocolonial mentalities that determine the characters' actions. Even the more progressive actors, such as Dr Juvenal Urbino, look to Europe to find their direction and to direct their followers. This now decaying city of former colonial splendor holds different meanings for the different characters of the novel; it is even a setting for renovation and rebirth for the character in the novel with the least connection to its colonial past and former glory, the father, Lorenzo Daza, who has no elite blood lines. An illiterate mule trader with a reputation in the nearby province of San Juan de la Ciénaga as a horse thief, Lorenzo Daza had accumulated wealth in land and cattle by a combination of hard work and cunning. His daughter, Fermina Daza, had learned to read at an early age. She not only performed well in school after the death of her mother, but had the ability to manage the operation of the household. With this background and this daughter, Lorenzo Daza moved to Cartagena, a place which the narrator describes as a 'ciudad en ruinas con sus glorias apolilladas, pero donde una mujer bella y educada a la antigua tenía aún la posibilidad de volver a nacer con un matrimonio de fortuna' (*El amor*, 126) ('a ruined city with its moth-eaten glories, where a beautiful woman with an old-fashioned upbringing still had the possibility of being reborn through a fortunate marriage', *Love*, 81). The past is mostly decadent, but the hierarchical social structure is still intact enough for Lorenzo Daza to consider his daughter as merchandise, much as he did the cattle he sold before moving from the country to the city.

This neocolonial mindset seems to be embedded in the decaying old walls surrounding the city to protect it against the attacks of pirates, in the white and gray colonial structures in which the citizenry of Cartagena reside, and, intangibly, in the tiny plazas and narrow streets that the Spaniards constructed to imitate urban spaces in medieval cities such as Toledo and Sevilla in the Iberian Peninsula. In this retrograde and decadent setting, all the human relationships focusing on the body and the heart – not only the one between Florentino Ariza and Fermina Daza – are doomed. While Fermina Daza and Dr Juvenal Urbino seem to possess all the individual personality traits to be good spouses and perform quite well the functions necessary for a good relationship, their marriage is predestined, in this anachronistic social organization, to be an unhappy one. When speaking of the marriage, the narrator establishes connections between the colonial space, the neocolonial mindset, and the modern body: 'Peor aún el de ellos, decía, surgido de dos clases antagónicas, en una ciudad que todavía seguía soñando con el regreso de los virreyes' (*El amor*, 306) ('And worst of all was theirs, arising out of two opposing classes, in a city that still dreamed of the return of the Viceroys', *Love*, 209). In this novel, neither the force of marriage (in the case of Fermina and Dr Juvenal Urbino), nor love (in the case of Florentino Ariza), nor modernity (in the case of Juvenal Urbino and other promoters of the modern) is able to reverse the repressive weight of medieval Spain that emanates from the walls and other structures that the characters inhabit.

In this decadent social milieu, an element of vitality is provided by the background presence of African people and culture throughout the story. Early in the novel, the narrator establishes the historical background to the African presence in Cartagena: 'su comercio había sido el más próspero del Caribe en el siglo XVIII, sobre todo por el privilegio ingrato de ser el más grande mercado de esclavos africanos en las Américas' (*El amor*, 35) ('In the eighteenth century, the commerce of the city had been the most prosperous in the Caribbean, owing in the main to the thankless privilege of its being the largest African slave market in the Americas', *Love*, 18). By the early twentieth century, where *El amor* ends chronologically, the enormous slave presence was largely ignored by social commentators, whose knowledge and research tended to concentrate on the slave market and the African presence in places such as Cuba and the United States. Indeed, the African presence in *El amor* is mostly in the background, even though the population of the region has been predominantly African since the eighteenth century. After the initial historical note about the slave trade in eighteenth-century Cartagena, no other African character appears in the novel until the mention of an African woman in the background, when the adolescent Fermina Daza goes to the Portal de los Escribanos to buy ink for the love letter. It is there that she has a seemingly trivial encounter with an African woman which turns out to be of life-changing importance. As Fermina Daza navigates her body through the lively open-air market at the Portal de los Escribanos, she is first overwhelmed by the noise and the visual imagery, and then by the Caribbean heat. In what appears to be an insignicant moment, she is drawn out of this momentary mental lapse of being overwhelmed by an African woman: 'La despertó del hechizo una negra feliz con un trapo de colores en la cabeza, redonda y hermosa, que le ofreció un triángulo de piña ensartado en la punta de un cuchillo de carnicero' (*El amor*, 155) ('She was awakened from the spell by a good-natured black woman with a colored cloth around her head who was round and handsome and offered her a triangle of pineapple speared on the tip of a butcher's knife', *Love*, 101). This tasting of a piece of pineapple is a typical scene on the streets of Cartagena, where African women have sold slices of pineapple for well over a century with the lure of an initial piece offered from the tip of a large knife. Because of this fortuitous encounter with the black woman and the pineapple, Fermina Daza experiences a type of epiphany that becomes the turning point in her life and the novel: 'Ella lo cogió, se lo metió entero en la boca, lo saboreó, estaba saboreándolo con la visita errante de la muchedumbre, cuando una conmoción la sembró en su sitio' (*El amor*, 151) ('She took it, she put it whole into her mouth, she tasted it, and was chewing it as her eyes wandered over the crowd, when a shock rooted her on the spot', *Love*, 102). She is 'shocked' to see the face of Florentino Ariza in the busy crowd, who questions why this 'diosa coronada' ('crowned goddess') is in such a place. With the African woman's pineapple in her mouth, she reaches a life-changing understanding about her relationship with Florentino Ariza: the love she feels for him is an 'engaño' (an 'illusion'). Somehow, it is the contact with the African woman that not only breaks the 'spell' in the busy Portal de los Escribanos, but also breaks her loose from the spell of love. This key moment is never further explained, but the African presence here seems to connect not only with Fermina Daza's purely rational capacity but also with the intuition and 'magic' associated with some non-Western ways of understanding. This intuitive way of understanding, often called 'irrational' by post-Enlightenment science, is a constant in García Márquez's work.

It is an African woman who shakes Fermina Daza from the 'illusion' of her adolescent fantasy about a relationship with a man whom, in the real world in which she lives, she cannot marry. The African woman lives close to the human lifeworld that Ong describes as typical of primary oral cultures. It is also an African woman who is the true woman of Florentino Ariza's life as he actually lives it in the empirical, everyday world (as opposed to his fantasies). The adolescent fantasy that he lives daily in his imagined life, of course, is to become Fermina Daza's lover and spouse. He does play out the fantasy of physical love by having sex with 622 women before his most important fantasy is fulfilled after five decades. As an adult living his daily life, he meets, by chance, an African woman named Leona Cassiani whom the narrator describes as the true woman in Florentino's life although neither of them ever knew it and they never make love (*Love*, 182). His first impression of Leona Cassiani is that she is 'negra, joven y bonita, pero puta sin lugar a dudas' (*El amor*, 267) ('black, young, pretty, but a whore beyond the shadow of doubt', *Love*, 182). This initial impression of attraction and rejection keeps him emotionally distant from her: 'La descartó de su vida, porque no podía concebir nada más indigno que pagar el amor: no lo hizo nunca' (*El amor*, 268) ('He rejected her from his life, because he could not conceive of anything more contemptible than paying for love; he had never done it', *Love*, 182). He also makes a mental connection, from the outset, between Cassiani's sexual body and the colonial past of slavery. He observes her: 'vestida como las esclavas de los grabados, con una pollera de volantes que se levantaba con un ademán de baile para pasar sobre los charcos de las calles, un descote que le dejaba los hombros descubiertos, un mazo de collares de colores y un turbante blanco' (*El amor*, 268) ('dressed like the slave girls in engravings, with a skirt of veils that that was raised with the gesture of a dancer when she stepped over the puddles in the streets, a low-cut top that left her shoulders bare, a handful of colored necklaces, and a white turban', *Love*, 182). (This is the one occasion in García Márquez's work in which he acknowledges the nineteenth-century French drawings, or engravings, that he used to describe the scenes from the period.) With his rejection of Leona Cassiani, Florentino is doubly imprisoned in his neocolonial mentality: he is imprisoned for fifty-one years in the fantasy of playing out an adolescent romance because he does not accept social class as a factor in marriage; he is imprisoned most of his adult life by the inability to make love with the one true woman in his life because, for him, she is too impure. Her impurity seems to be based on at least three factors: (*i*) the fact that in Florentino's mind no woman can be as pure as the (fantasy) purity of Fermina Daza, since she is a construct of his literary imagination; (*ii*) Leona Cassiani's possible background as a former sex worker; and (*iii*) Cassiani's ethnic status as a black woman of lower-class background, as well as her historical association with slavery.

Dr Juvenal Urbino and Fermina Daza also have telling relationships with Colombia's African past and with women. In old age, as Fermina Daza's body is showing visible signs of decay and Juvenal Urbino enters a crisis over both of their ageing bodies, Urbino has an affair with a black woman.

Thus, Juvenal Urbino manages to do what Florentino Ariza cannot: make love with a lower-class black woman. Juvenal Urbino confesses to Fermina Daza what he has done and she becomes intensely enraged. She even fears, in fact, that she will be 'ciega de rabia' ('go blind with rage'). The narrator paraphrases the central reason for the depth of her rage: 'Y lo peor de todo, carajo: con una negra' (*El amor*, 365) ('And worst of all, damn it: with a black woman', *Love*, 250). With this phrase and Fermina's other reactions, it becomes evident that she has indeed become a member of the elite to which she aspired and has assimilated its values, including its racism. She has become a true self-conscious 'soberana' (*Del amor*, 323) ('monarch', *Love*, 221) who lives in her self-designed medieval castle that she referred to as her 'villa'.

The most significant features of García Márquez's representation of medieval and neocolonial Spanish and African tradition in the Americas are the ones we have mentioned. Nevertheless, there are minor details in the text that support a reading of this novel as a critique of the neocolonial presence in Latin America and that legitimize the claim of the strength of African culture in the region. The ways in which the local oligarchy in Cartagena organizes and promotes its 'poetic festivals' are a reproduction of elite cultural rituals, centered on poetry and oratory, organized by the Spanish oligarchy during the colonial period. Dr Juvenal Urbino and Fermina Daza are at the center of these 'poetic festivals', a demonstration that, even though they do not have aristocratic blood lines, they have successfully learned to imitate the modes and ways of the elite both have spent a lifetime attempting to join.

For readers who have downplayed or ignored the social and political content of García Márquez's fiction in favor of 'magic realist' interpretations, the author offers winks at his Macondo fiction and insights into the 'magic realism' of his writing. The exotic parrot from Paramaibo in *El amor* affords the reader insights into what often seems to be an exotic fictional world. On the one hand, for the characters in *El amor*, the parrot from Paramaibo is not really exotic at all, but an everyday presence as parrots have been for well over a century. On the patios of the homes of Colombia, particularly in the Caribbean and other lowland regions, they are no more exotic than the household pets to be found in the homes of Europeans and North Americans. On the other hand, the death of Dr Juvenal Urbino is trivialized by the fact that he dies simply attempting to fetch this household pet from a tree in the patio. Related to all this, Dr Juvenal Urbino makes an unequivocal statement before his death about the role of parrots in these Caribbean households: 'las guacamayas no eran más que estorbos ornamentales' (*El amor*, 40) ('macaws were simply decorative annoyances' *Love*, 21). The parrot does at least enjoy a special status in the household, being the only domestic animal other than a land turtle to live inside the home. As an 'estorbo ornamental', however, the bird is defined by Dr Juvenal Urbino exactly as it actually functions in the corpus of García Márquez's work: he often uses exotic scenery as just such a decorative device. Such devices, from the butterflies in *Cien años* to the parrot in *El amor*, have often invited overinterpretation and led to frequent comments about García Márquez's 'magic realism'.

García Márquez himself has explained why the reader should proceed with caution when tempted to ascribe symbolic meaning to 'estorbos ornamentales' in the nineteenth-century setting of his fiction. Many of the details in the descriptions of scenes, such as cockfights, colonial plazas and churches, palm trees, and other descriptions of the flora and fauna of the region, do not have their origins in a desire to communicate symbolic meaning but rather are verbal representations of a particular book of drawings from the period that García Márquez used extensively in the writing of *El amor*.[6]

### *Crónica de una muerte anunciada* and the dangers of overinterpretation

*Crónica de una muerte anunciada* is a postmodern tour-de-force. As in *El amor*, García Márquez calls upon traditional, modern, and postmodern strategies to write his version of a detective story. He had been interested in detective novels since his youth in Cartagena and Barranquilla where he and his fellow writers read detective fiction of every kind. In the late 1970s, his cohorts from the Boom were interested in writing detective novels (or at least playing with the genre), as witness Carlos Fuentes's *La cabeza de la hidra* (*The Hydra Head,* 1978), and, later, Vargas Llosa's *¿Quién mató a Palomino Molero?* (*Who killed Palomino Molero?*, 1986). Following an established pattern in his fiction, the first line is arresting: 'El día en que lo iban a matar, Santiago Nasar se levantó a las 5.30 de la mañana para esperar el buque en que llegaba el obispo' ('On the day they were going to kill him, Santiago Nassar got up at 5.30 in the morning to wait for the boat the bishop was coming on'). By noting the death in the first line, García Márquez was announcing that he was playing with the detective fiction genre, too, but with everything in reverse. Though fully aware of the novel's denouement from the first line, the reader continues reading as if it were some kind of

---

[6] The two French travelers in Colombia were Charles Saffray and Édouard André. For further discussion of the drawings connected with their travels, see Chapters 1 and 2, above.

'whodunnit', but primarily to see exactly how the death comes about. Exactly how the killing will take place is as important as the death itself. The general situation and exact details of Santiago Nasar's death are gradually revealed, and they lead to one undeniable fact, incredible as it might seem: everyone in the town knew that he was going to be assassinated except Santiago himself. Many critics have insisted how 'incredible' or even 'magical' such events as Santiago Nasar's death are. García Márquez, on the other hand, has often claimed that he is actually a realist who copies down faithfully his experiences in Colombia (however incredible and magical these people, places, and things might seem). In defence of his contention that he is actually a realist, García Márquez can point to the fact that the Colombian magazine *Al Día* reported the following story:

> In the municipality of Sucre (of the department of the same name), the elders still remember with horror the rainy morning of 22 January 1951, in which a young man from Sucre, Cayetano Gentile Chimento, twenty-two years old, a medical student at the Javeriana University of Bogotá and heir to the town's largest fortune, fell butchered by Machete, the innocent victim of a confused duel of honor, and without knowing for sure why he was dying. Cayetano was killed by Víctor and Joaquín Chica Calas, whose sister Margarita married the previous day Miguel Reyes Palencia and was returned to her family by her husband the same night of her marriage. They accused Cayetano of being the author of the disgrace that had prevented her being a virgin at the night of her marriage.[7]

This factual record of events, based on an actual assassination in Sucre, Colombia, in 1951, was the source for the 'incredible' basic anecdote of *Crónica*. The five-chapter work is not an attempt at a documentary or a *testimonio* like *Relato de un náufrago* and *Noticia de un secuestro*. Rather, García Márquez appropriated the basic facts for a fictionalized version. The first chapter tells of the morning of the assassination carried out by the two brothers, Pedro and Pablo Vicario. The second chapter recounts the background of the relationship between Bayardo San Román and Ángela Vicario, the couple planning to marry. In this chapter, the story is taken up to the evening of the wedding ceremony, which is the focus of the third chapter. The narrative jumps forward in the fourth chapter, telling what happened after the assassination, including the autopsy and Ángela Vicario's life after the failed marriage. The fifth and last chapter delivers what was promised in the

---

7    Julio Roca and Camilo Calderón, *Al Día* (Bogotá), 1 (28 April 1981), 51–60 (my translation).

novel's first sentence: a graphic description of Santiago Nasar's assassination, accompanied by a detailed chronology of exactly how it transpired, creating the illusion of a *testimonio*, a documentary, or a chronicle. (The chronicle form is reminiscent of the first writings of the Spanish colonial period.)

Once again, García Márquez constructs a novel that is replete with details about the objective world, yet contains several elements woven into its texture that modify objective reality. These elements include premonitions and dreams that the characters interpret incorrectly, the ambiguous and ever-changing difference between how things occur and how they are remembered, and events that seem to carry symbolic meaning, such as rains, insomnia, dreams, and smells, but in reality do not have any symbolic meaning at all. As in *El amor* and *La increíble*, García Márquez cautions the reader not to over-interpret by assuming that all these elements are necessarily meaningful in a symbolic way. With fictions such as these and with a number of comments García Márquez has made in interview, the reader may conclude that García Márquez tends to reject broad, symbolic interpretations of *El amor*, such as the claim that the work is a metaphor for today's world.

The reader of *Crónica* may be tempted to reconstruct an underlying system that could provide a coherent, logical and in-depth understanding of things. This goal, however, is doomed to fail, for there is no such underlying system. As is often the case in García Márquez's fiction, the events and lives that the characters experience are determined by inexplicable forces that the rational mind cannot explain. The narrator even states directly that attempts at entirely rational explanations have not proven successful, even though a judge assigned to the Nasar case was committed to finding a rational explanation: 'Nadie podía entender tantas coincidencias funestas. El juez instructor que vino de Riohacha debió sentirlas sin atreverse a admitirlas, pues su interés de darles una explicación racional era evidente en el sumario' ('No one could understand such fatal coincidences. The investigating judge who came from Riohacha must have sensed them without daring to admit it, for his impulse to give a rational explanation was obvious in his report').[8] With this statement, the narrator establishes his skepticism about the possibility of resolving the mystery of this event with the rational. The narrator resists the temptation to offer his own explanation or speculation about how the story's events happened as they did.

---

[8]  *Crónica de una muerte anunciada* (Bogotá: Tercer Mundo, 1981), 20; *Chronicle of a Death Foretold*, tr. Gregory Rabassa (New York: Knopf, 1982), 83. All quotations are from these editions.

García Márquez uses journalistic techniques that he learned from his early days as a journalist in Barranquilla in the late 1940s and early 1950s. One of his techniques in *Crónica* for the creation of ambiguity is to use detailed observations about irrelevant matters, while being imprecise and vague about points of real importance. As in journalistic writing, the text abounds in detailed fact, but fails to provide a broad panoramic view of events. Consequently, there are questions that cannot be answered with certainty. Who really raped Ángela? Did Victoria Guzmán (the cook) and her daughter know of the assassination plan or not? Did the narrator's sister, Margot, know of the plot? Several other less important questions are also left unresolved.

The exact situation of the narrator and of the narrative situation creates more ambiguities. A narrator-investigator figure tells the story in the first person. After the assassination, this narrator-investigator returns to the town to tell the story in retrospect. Given that he does not know the whole story, however, his interpretation is replete with problems and doubts from the outset. He did not actually witness any of the events, so his job is to relate the story after having collected the facts and anecdotes, as well as to organize them. The narrator operates very much like an investigative reporter; he keeps the reader informed about this process as he writes, thus providing a postmodern touch to the book. In postmodern fashion, the procedure of writing often overshadows the story, for the account of the writing process frequently obscures the fact that important facts are never revealed. Some of the details here return the reader to the *greguería* of Gómez de la Serna and the fiction of the Macondo cycle. The narrator-investigator's mother recommends to the women of the house that they not comb their hair before going to bed or the sailors will arrive late. This humorous but illogical non sequitur, now classic García Márquez, follows the logic of the *greguería*.

*Crónica* includes several versions of what happened to the young engaged couple and to Santiago Nasar. In their entirety, these versions produce the 'dizque' ('it is said') of popular knowledge or legend. A total of thirty-seven characters contribute stories to the narrator-investigator's 'chronicle'. The 'record' for this supposed 'chronicle' consists of nine quotations from written sources and 102 quotations from the thirty-seven characters. Thus, the narrator-investigator relies far more on oral than written sources to construct his chronicle.

Contrary to its title, this work, of course, is not really a chronicle at all. The narrative situation contradicts and subverts the book's title and also any pretence that *Crónica* is anything but an imaginative verbal construct in the form of a narrative. The predominant and most authoritative voice in the novel, technically speaking, is that of Ángela Vicario, for she is quoted twelve times. Ironically, the narrator gives priority to the very person being investigated. In the end, the concept of authority itself becomes enigmatic, for there are no authoritative voices or figures in this text.

Besides questioning authority, *Crónica* reflects on the medieval legacy in Latin America.[9] The language and limits of the predominant mindset in the town are determined and defined by a medieval sense of honor. The bride's rejection, the idea of the assassination, and the execution of the act all take place as a continuity of medieval practices in the town, even though everyone knows exactly what is going to happen. The playing out of these predetermined actions as the town's citizenry witnesses them reveals a society with a hierarchical and static vision.

Class difference clearly is a central factor in the development of the tragic plot in *El amor en los tiempos del cólera*; social class is a more subtle and ambiguous factor in the development of the tragic plot in *Crónica*. The Nasar family belongs to the wealthy elite in the town, and this sets them apart them from most of the other characters in the novel. The family had become affluent while most of the others in the town had languished in poverty or were trapped within the limited confines of Colombia's working class. There is textual evidence of class resentment against Santiago Nasar. He is also physically attractive, making him the cause of jealousy for reasons beyond his class credentials, and the narrator-investigator is well aware of both of these potential motives for his assassination. In addition, Nasar's own fiancée, Flora Miguel, has the same class credentials as he does. The narrator-investigator's sister offers one woman's view of Nasar: 'Me di cuenta de pronto de que no podía haber un partido mejor que él, me dijo. Imagínate: bello, formal, y con una fortuna propia a los 21 años' (*Crónica*, 28–29) ('I suddenly realized that there couldn't have been a better catch than him. Just imagine: handsome, a man of his word, and with a fortune of his own at the age of twenty-one', *Chronicle*, 18). Given the economic, personal, and possibly even political interests underlying Santiago Nasar's assassination, this death involves not only the ambiguities common to modernist novels but some of the unresolved contradictions more typical of postmodern fiction.

Postmodern North-American writer William H. Gass, in an enthusiastic review of this book, suggested that *Crónica* is not so much told as pieced

---

[9]  As mentioned earlier, Christopher Little provides insight into the medieval mindset in '*Eréndira* in the Middle Ages: The Medievalness of Gabriel García Márquez', in *García Márquez*, ed. Robin Fiddian, Modern Literatures in Perspective (London: Longman, 1995), 204–13.

together.[10] Rather than being a novel about the protagonist's death (which is established in the first sentence), the real focus is on the very process of these pieces coming together: the story's coming into being. As in *El otoño del patriarca* and *El amor en los tiempos del cólera*, the act of writing takes precedence over the anecdotal material. In fact, *Crónica* shares many of the postmodern qualities found in *El amor* and *El otoño*.

As a postmodern text, *Crónica* subverts the conventions of the genre of detective fiction.[11] At the same time that García Márquez parodies these conventions, he takes advantage of the genre's inherent traits. The detective novel has been called the hermeneutic tale par excellence, for it contains a concern with interpretation at the expense of depth, an ambiguity of clues, and a turbulent flow of time.[12] By writing something closer to a parody of the hermeneutic tale than a real detective novel, and more a parody of a chronicle than a real chronicle, García Márquez attains an impressive symbiosis of the writer-as-novelist (of detective fiction) and writer-as-journalist (of a chronicle). This synthesis is achieved by using the techniques of the novel and of journalism as models. The confluence of reality and fiction becomes patently ambiguous when the narrator-investigator, who is a García Márquez alter ego, actually becomes García Márquez when he names his wife, Mercedes Barcha, as an actual player in the events (*Chronicle*, 43).

In some postmodern fiction, the use of the author's real name in the text operates as a reminder of the work's fictionality; in *Crónica*, the mention of Mercedes Barcha and her marriage to García Márquez contributes to an opposite kind of postmodern effect: the events and characters of this fictionalized 'chronicle' are part of the real world. In an activity more like reading a newspaper than a novel, the reader must carefully select the few significant details from among the mass of details that are unimportant. As with the macaw in *El amor*, the reader must discern carefully between substance and 'estorbos ornamentales' ('decorative annoyances'). He or she eventually learns that most of the details are irrelevant. As in *El amor* and *La increíble*

---

[10] William H. Gass, review of *Chronicle of a Death Foretold*, New York, 11 April 1983, 83.

[11] Isabel Álvarez Borland has offered perceptive insights into the subversion of the genre of detective fiction in 'From Mystery to Parody: (Re)reading of García Márquez's *Crónica de una muerte anunciada*', *Symposium*, 38 (1984–85), 278–86; repr. in *Gabriel García Márquez*, ed. Harold Bloom (New York: Chelsea House, 2007), 219–27.

[12] Frank Kermode has theorized about the hermeneutic tale in 'Novel and Narrative', in *The Poetics of Murder: Detective Fiction and Literary Theory*, ed. Glenn W. Most and William Stowe (San Diego CA: Harcourt Brace Jovanovich, 1983), 175–96.

*y triste historia de la cándida Eréndira*, *Crónica* is a postmodern work about storytelling that entertains the reader more than it explores the depths of Latin American society.

## *La increíble y triste historia de la cándida Eréndira y de su abuela desalmada* and the limits of intepretation

'Un señor muy viejo con unas alas enormes' ('A very old man with enormous wings', 1968), the first of seven short stories in this volume, is a hermeneutic tale that begins with an enigma: an old man appears on the beach with enormous wings protruding from his body. Different characters carry out their respective hermeneutic exercises, each offering their explanation of who the man might be. In reality, none of these explanations seems likely. This leads the reader to conclude that there is no rational explanation for the appearance on the beach of an old man with wings. In a dialogue with Mario Vargas Llosa, García Márquez himself made a number of assertions about the limits of rational thought in the interpretative process and about the constant search for explanations generally. In the year he published this story he wrote: 'Lo que tenemos que hacer es, creo yo, aceptar las cosas tal y como las percibimos, sin estar buscando continuamente explicaciones' ('What we have to do, I believe, is to accept things as they are, without continuously looking for explanations').[13] 'A very old man with enormous wings' and most of the other tales in this volume were originally written as children's stories, providing even more reason for handling the interpretative process with care.

The situation at the beginning of the story 'El ahogado más hermoso del mundo' ('The handsomest drowned man in the world') is identical to the first tale: an outsider arrives inexplicably and functions as a possible threat, or an interruption at the least, to the norms of everyday life. The outsider is actually a corpse that some children find on the beach – a corpse covered with a heavy crust of mud. In this case, the women are the interpreters of the foreigner, and they have sexual fantasies after observing that he is handsome, strong, and well endowed. After organizing a spectacular burial ceremony for the deceased man, the people are left to face how truly empty their lives actually are. Somehow, however, they believe their lives will improve, as will

13 Gabriel García Márquez & Mario Vargas Llosa, *La novela en América Latina* (Lima: Diálogo, 1968), 13. The translation is mine.

things in general in the town. 'The handsomest drowned man in the world' expresses and confirms the book's skepticism concerning the possibilities of interpretation. This theme was García Márquez's early statement about the 'estorbos ornamentales' ('decorative annoyances') in *El amor*.

The remaining stories in the volume, for the most part, are best read as entertainments. The one exception is the title story, 'La increíble y triste historia de la cándida Eréndira y su abuela desalmada' ('The incredible and sad tale of innocent Eréndira and her heartless grandmother'). Here, an adolescent girl is sexually exploited by her grandmother after serving, at the beginning of the story, as the grandmother's housekeeper and de facto slave. The girl seems to perform her duties as housekeeper well until she commits a serious error: she allows the candelabrum in her room to be blown over by the wind, and as a result the house burns down. The grandmother decides that Eréndira must pay for her error by working as a prostititute. Eréndira's life as a sex worker takes on a hyperbolic dimension typical of much of García Márquez's work. She works for six months, at which point the grandmother calculates that the repayment for household losses will require a total of eight years, seven months, and eleven days of sex labor. Eréndira's life begins to change when she meets Ulisis, the son of a Dutch farmer and an indigenous woman. The farmer and his son come upon Eréndira by chance when they see her tent with a line of soldiers waiting for her services. The young girl is allowed to rest one night, Ulisis visits her, and they fall in love. Consequently, she begins to imagine a life beyond exploitation. In a scene reminiscent of Vargas Llosa's *La casa verde* (*The Green House*), Eréndira is kidnapped by some nuns and placed in a convent. She seems to be happy for the first time, but the grandmother manages to exert control once again by paying an indigenous boy to marry her. Thus, when she gets out of the convent, she returns to the grandmother. The next escape is orchestrated by the lovestruck Ulisis, who flees to the border with the young girl but is arrested by soldiers who are informed by the grandmother of her political connections. After this setback, Eréndira is returned to her former life as a sex worker in the tent. Then the grandmother begins to teach her how to be an exploiter as an adult, but Ulisis once again appears on the scene to save her from this cycle of exploited and exploiter. At Eréndira's request, Ulisis attempts to kill the grandmother, who proves to be very difficult to kill, for he fails even with a prodigious amount of arsenic. When he places dynamite in the grandmother's piano, he destroys everything but her. He finally achieves his goal, killing her and watching her die in a puddle of green blood, an image that recalls the novels of chivalry.

Christopher Little has noticed various connections between this story and the novels of chivalry, as well as with the medieval period in general. Little reads this story in the tradition of historico-political allegories.[14] He reads the story persuasively as an allegory of exploitation in which the grandmother represents gluttonous Spain during the colonial period. The medieval literary order appears in 'La cándida Eréndira' in the use of romance, folktale techniques, proverbs, and the fantastic. Taken together, these augment the basic message of the allegory. García Márquez subverts these and other medieval elements or, as Little argues, he 'prostitutes' the Spanish medieval.


**Conclusion**

The novels discussed in this chapter, *El amor* and *Crónica*, are hermeneutic tales that warn the reader about the dangers of interpretative excess. The volume of short stories *La increíble* also contains some tales that offer similar warnings to the reader about interpretation. The novel *Crónica* and the stories in *La increíble* are hermeneutic tales that emphasize concerns about the interpretative process in itself, taking over at the expense of thematic depth. *El amor* is another tale that reminds the reader, given the abundance of 'decorative annoyances' (such as parrots) in García Márquez's work, to proceed with caution in the interpretative process.

  *El amor* is one of the three major works by the Nobel Laureate. What is exceptional in this novel is its bridging of popular and elite culture, with gestures toward both traditional storytelling and the postmodern. Once again, García Márquez constructs his tale around a central visual image: in this case, the image of a river steamboat. It is the first of several novels to address medieval and colonial legacies in a time and space closer to the colonial period than the fiction of the Macondo cycle: by placing the novel in the colonial city of Cartagena and in the nineteenth century, the author has the characters act out the behavior of a neocolonial society. The later novel *Del amor y otros demonios* is another step beyond *El amor* in evoking the colonial period. The African presence in *El amor* (as later in *Del amor y otros demonios*) is associated with the irrational and the emotional that García Márquez privileges.

  Beyond constructing a story around colonial legacies concerning class, courtship rituals, and marriage, García Márquez explores the theme of ageing and the nature of our feelings (and of love, in particular) as we age. Inasmuch as love is primarily a literary construct in *El amor*, ageing is more significant as a theme. In the Macondo cycle of fiction, the author affirms human poten-

---

[14]  Little, '*Eréndira* in the Middle Ages', 206.

tial; the romantic love associated with youth survives into old age. But the literary world of García Márquez rarely involves rigid dichotomies (unless he is parodying such dichotomies), and the reader finds several other manifestations of love in the novel to be as questionable as the literarily generated love of Florentino Ariza.

García Márquez's recent writing centers on this reflection on ageing, writing and love, particularly his most recent novel, *Memoria de mis putas tristes*.

# 5

# Recent Writing

García Márquez has continued writing fiction and essays well into his senior years as a distinguished public intellectual among Latin America's writers and as a spokesperson for them on a broad range of political, social, and cultural issues. His recent fiction both hearkens back to many of his lifetime interests since the early Macondo stories and also suggests new approaches and new emphases on previously worked themes. As in *El amor en los tiempos del cólera* and *Crónica de una muerte anunciada*, he fictionalizes his critique of medieval and feudal structures and attitudes in modern Latin America. In his recent work, he has taken the liberty of exploring once again several genres that have been integral to his creative efforts since the 1950s: the novel, in the form of *Del amor y otros demonios* (*Of Love and Other Demons*, 1994) and *Memoria de mis putas tristes* (*Memories of my Melancholy Whores*, 2004); the *testimonio*, in *Noticia de un secuestro* (*News of a Kidnapping*, 1996), and the short story, in *Doce cuentos peregrinos* (*Strange Pilgrims*, 1992).

His two most recent novels, *Memoria* and *Del amor*, refer most directly to *El amor* and *Crónica* in their consideration of themes, topics, and attitudes related to the old structures inherited from Spain. These four works address these particular matters more explicitly than does any other of his works, making the concluding chapter of his writing career the most definitive in terms of his political and related thematic interests. Like *El amor*, *Memoria* offers a focus on ageing and love, and includes some of the signature García Márquez language and gestures from his Macondo cycle.

## Ageing and love: *Memoria de mis putas tristes*

*Memoria de mis putas tristes* is the story of a ninety-year-old man, a retired journalist, who seemingly falls in love with a fourteen-year-old prostitute. He is the narrator of the story, so the matter of 'love' is always a question mark, as the reader is left to speculate about what 'love' might mean for him and in what ways a fourteen-year-old prostitute can 'love' her ninety-year-old client. The old man is a respected journalist with refined tastes, such as a passion for classical music. After abandoning his fiancée at the altar on the day of his marriage, he lives a lonely life in relative isolation. He confesses that he has never slept with a woman without paying her. Having rejected several offers from the *grande dame* of the local call girls, Rosa, he decides on his ninetieth birthday, to respond affirmatively – 'hoy sí' – to her phone call. After a series of events that lead the reader through the requisite description of Colombia's corruption, crime, and deaths, he receives the girl, Delgadina, as his permanent possession. The novel ends on an optimistic note about his life 'Era por fin la vida real, con mi corazón a salvo, y condenado a morir de buen amor en la agonía feliz de cualquier día después de mis cien años' ('It was, at last, real life, with my heart safe and condemned to die of happy love in the joyful agony of any other day after my hundredth birthday').[1]

Like *El amor*, this is a novel not just about love, but about love in the context of ageing. The Nobel Laureate thus takes upon himself a formidable challenge, engaging the reader in a series of highly improbable propositions, among them that a ninety-year-old-man can fall in love with a fourteen-year-old virgin prostitute, and that a fourteen-year-old virgin prostitute can fall in love with a ninety-year-old man in the process of receiving payment for her sexual services. As he has done since his first stories, García Márquez pushes the limits of the rational and the credible, but tells the story with such naturalness and craft that the reader more often responds in collusion with the author's numerous winks, as both reader and implied author enjoy a playful spoof on the human condition rather than rejecting the entire premise of the book which, on the surface, is absurd. Interestingly, the use of a first-person narrator makes any definitive judgment of this matter difficult. In the end, the reader wonders about issues such as the following: Is the old journalist entering a state of dementia? Could the child prostitute just be seeking an exit from the bordello? Such questions are inevitable, but never fully answered.

This novel is replete with signature García Márquez gestures, including the arresting opening line: 'El año de mis noventa años quise regalarme una noche de amor loco con una adolescente virgen' (*Memoria*, 9; 'The year I turned ninety, I wanted to give myself the gift of a night of wild love with an adolescent virgin'). With this opening, he deftly transgresses the moral codes of all institutional religions of the West, and leaves the reader intrigued with the term *amor loco* ('crazy love') in the context of old age, prostitution, and child abuse. In classic García Márquez mode, the author summarily

---

[1]  *Memoria de mis putas tristes* (Barcelona: Mondadori, 2004), 9; *Memories of my Melancholy Whores*, tr. Edith Grossman (New York: Knopf, 2004), 3. All quotations are from these editions.

bypasses these questions to proceed quickly with the plot. When the protagonist responds 'hoy sí' to Rosa, this is the first of several pronouncements
typical of García Márquez characters who, like Úrsula from *Cien años*, seem
to have an instinctive wisdom that leads them to swift and definitive deci-
sions. All such characters, including the old man in this novel and Úrsula
from *Cien años*, speak as wise old storytellers in the oral tradition. Most of
their comments are humorous, such as the protagonist's understatement near
the end of the novel, the 'Es que me estoy volviendo viejo' (*Memoria*, 95),
('The truth is, I'm getting old', *Memories*, 98).

With *Memoria*, García Márquez constructs another short masterpiece in
his comfortable environment of the Caribbean coast of Colombia, now using
the city of Barranquilla, where he lived his early adult years interacting with
the young, ambitious intellectuals of the Group of Barranquilla. Interestingly,
during these years in Barranquilla, his own place of residence was a cheap
bordello, so he does know, from his own experience, the world of prostitutes
and bordellos. Apart from passing references to the War of a Thousand Days,
this novel seems, on a first reading, to be devoid of any political or historical significance. As in all of his writing, however, the author invites several
possible metaphorical readings. Most importantly, this is a novel in which
the basic premise of the entire plot is a transgression of social and religious
mores. In a world of growing fanaticism among those holding conservative,
fundamentalist values in a broad range of institutional religions, he constructs
a work that pushes the limits when it comes to questioning moral convention.
In the process, he convinces the reader, in the end, that the ageing protagonist
might well actually be in love with the young girl, and that she might share
these feelings. The author also validates the lives of a population that can
often be marginalized from mainline society: the ageing and the very old.

*Memoria* is also a reflection on ageing in which García Márquez offers
a series of insights into nuances of sexuality during the process of ageing,
beginning with the narrator-protagonist's sudden and unexpected interest in
*amor loco*. The reader might well ask: is this a fantasy of a deranged and
exceptional man or is it typical of old age and/or dementia? In other observations on ageing, the narrator notes that 'oí decir que el primer síntoma de
la vejez es que uno empieza a parecerse a su padre' (*Memoria*, 14) ('I heard
that the first symptom of old age is when you begin to resemble your father',
*Memories,* 9). The narrator-protagonist also observes that one of the attrac-
tions of being old is that young women allow him 'provocaciones' ('provoca-
tions') because they consider old men to be 'fuera de servicio' ('no longer a
threat'). He is also demoralized by being required to provide personal identification in a public park because this request is symptomatic of old age: he

appears to be an ageing man who is homeless, lost, or both. In addition, he claims that the desire to disrobe a woman piece by piece is typical of elderly men. For the most part, however, this novel offers a relatively affirmative representation of ageing: certain things definitely change, but the changes seem comfortably acceptable, and the protagonist, in the end, either finds love or manages to convince himself that he has found it.

At another level of reading – the social or political interpretation of the novel – the well-informed reader sees yet another of García Márquez's light satires of conventional Latin American social mores. The Colombian oligarchy has prided itself for well over a century on being the promoter of Greco-Roman culture in Latin America, as witness their designation of Bogotá as the 'Athens of South America', a self-characterization and identity that this oligarchy has constructed and promoted since the late nineteenth century.[2]

Support for the classical tradition has been strong in the highland region, centered on the Instituto Caro y Cuervo, an elite center for research and graduate studies in the humanities located near Bogotá. García Márquez ridicules this oligarchy's exaggerated sense of self-importance and hyper-elite attitudes by characterizing the elderly *costeño* journalist (the very antithesis of the elite intellectual from Bogotá or *bogotano culto*) as a lifetime student of the classics who even claims Latin to be his 'lengua natal' ('mother tongue'), a satire on Bogotá's lettered elite. By characterizing this often pathetic old man as an effete and obsessed disciple of classical music and literatures as well as a speaker of Latin, he creates a light satire on one of the venerable institutions dear to the upper crust of Colombian society, as well as those in the middle and upper-middle classes who wish to emulate them.

This is a novel which occasionally reminds the reader that we are once again, as in the Macondo cycle, in the comfortable setting of the Costa, where the characters eat a local fish, *lebranche*, as well as fried bananas and other foods associated with the Caribbean region. The particular focus on the theme of love (love in the context of ageing) hearkens back to not only *El amor*, but also refers to the more recent novel *Del amor y otros demonios*.

[2] For an introduction to the literary implications of the concept of Bogotá as the 'Athens of South America', see Raymond L. Williams, *The Colombian Novel, 1844–1987* (London & Austin TX: University of Texas Press, 1991); also Gilberto Gómez Ocampo, *Entre 'María' y 'La vorágine': la literatura colombiana finisecular (1886–1903)* (Bogotá: Fondo Cultural Cafetero, 1988).

## The African Caribbean: *Del amor y otros demonios*

In *Del amor y otros demonios*, García Márquez constructs another love affair between an ageing adult and a young girl, but with a yet more extreme transgression of social norms, for the adult is a Catholic priest and the girl is even younger than the adolescent prostitute, and much more innocent. This affair, however, is not the central focus of the entire novel, which is set in the colonial period and has the most explicit development of the African elements in Caribbean culture of any of García Márquez's novels. The main focus is on a young girl who, after being bitten by a potentially rabid dog, is then demonized, isolated, and eventually killed by those around her who should be caring for her: her blood family and her church family. This is one of the most direct critiques of the institution of the Catholic church in García Márquez's entire output.

*Del amor y otros demonios* uses as its point of departure the circumstance that has provided the opening for several of his fictions: a news item. *Noticia de un secuestro* was an outgrowth of the author's lifelong work as a journalist, and books such as *Relato de un náufrago* and *Crónica* were direct products of news items that García Márquez had by chance noticed, remembered, and later fictionalized. In the case of *Del amor*, García Márquez the journalist, on a day with less significant news to report than on some other days, had been assigned by his editor to the investigation of the excavation of bodies which was part of a renovation project at an old Colonial church. The young journalist working in Cartagena witnessed something extraordinary at the site of this old church: the excavation of the corpse of a young girl named Sierva María de Todos los Ángeles who had hair measuring twenty-two meters in length.[3]

The young girl in the novel, Sierva María, is the only daughter of a Marquis, the Marqués de Casalduero, who has bloodlines directly connecting him to the Spanish nobility that governed the region of 'New Granada' (today's Colombia) in the eighteenth century. The daughter of this Marquis and a local criolla, Bernarda, is a uniquely multicultural character for reasons other than her bloodlines: she is reared not so much by her parents as by the African slave of the household, Dominga de Adviento, the head housekeeper. Consequently, Sierva María speaks not only Spanish (including the elite Spanish of Spain that she studies in class), but also three African languages that she

---

[3]   This journalistic anecdote converted into a novel is an example of García Márquez's lifelong interest in the 'Believe it or not' writings of Ripley. For a discussion of this interest, see García Usta, *García Márquez en Cartagena: sus inicios literarios*, Los Tres Mundos (Bogotá: Planeta Colombiana, 2007).

learns from the servants with whom she lives. Sierva María also appropriates a full array of African culture as part of her daily life, including African dance. In addition, she chooses to sleep in the slave quarters.

Through a series of unlikely and irrational events, the young girl is taken to the convent after she is bitten by a dog. A priest, Cayetano Delaura, is assigned to care for her and, after the church authorities decide that she is possessed by devil, is then directed to perform an exorcism on her. As the priest becomes acquainted with her, however, his care of her takes a bizarre twist: he falls in love with the young girl in a way quite unlike the sexual relationship between the old journalist and the young prostitute in *Memoria*: the priest's love is more platonic than physical, for he reads love poetry to her, verses written by a distant relative of his, the sixteenth-century Spanish poet Garcilaso de la Vega.

The young girl's name, Sierva María de Todos los Santos, suggests the novel's thematic direction. On the one hand, the name evokes Mary Queen of all the Angels and has multiple resonances that hark back to medieval and Catholic Spain, for each of the five words of her name after 'sierva' (servant) is significant. The name refers to the totality of the church in the lives of colonial citizens: 'María' is the most widely used female name of the Catholic church; 'de' is the preposition used in marriages for the male to take possession of the female and thus reaffirms the patriarchal order; 'todos' emphasizes absolute and total devotion characteristic of the Catholic church; 'los' indicates the multiplicity of the Catholic saints to whom that devotion is directed; and 'Ángeles' refers to the angels of Catholic tradition.

*Del amor* is García Márquez's most explicit fictionalization of the medieval and African legacy, and his most direct fictionalization of the medieval, patriarchal order. The novelists of the 1960s Boom in general, and García Márquez in particular, create an anxiety in the characters' minds that that they are not really all that modern (but, rather, medieval), and not all that European (but, rather, African). For writers such as Vargas Llosa, the medieval legacy far overshadows the presence of African culture. This Peruvian writer has often written of the debts he owes to the medieval writer Joanot Martorell, the author of *Tirant lo Blanch*. For García Márquez, the African tradition is just as present as the medieval in this particular novel. The young girl's first name, 'Sierva', stands out not only as an unusual and uncommon name, but also as the opposite of the Spanish nobility of her father's bloodlines. Thus, rather than being titled 'Marquesa', she is named as a 'servant' and associated with the African servants in the household and with African servitude in the colonies.

García Márquez stated in his Nobel Address (see p. 26), that 'La interpretación de nuestra soledad con esquemas ajenos sólo contribuye a hacernos cada vez más desconocidos, cada vez menos libres, cada vez más solitarios' ('The interpretation of our reality through patterns not our own serves only to make us ever more unknown, ever less free, ever more solitary').[4] Many of the characters in this novel suffer from the 'patterns' of Spanish and colonial mentality, and these patterns are at the heart of the problems, conflicts, and plot of the novel. Ironically, Sierva María's grandfather accumulated wealth through his success in the slave trade and the black market, so his involvement with African slaves connects directly with the cultural formation of his eventual granddaughter, Sierva María. Whatever business savvy the grandfather may have possessed, however, has been lost by the generation of Sierva María's father, Ignacio, who seems to be an incompetent and incapable colonial oligarch in degeneration.

The characters' Spanish medieval and colonial mentality, beginning with the father, leads to the novel's tragic ending. The father lives, like the solitary Macondo characters, in deep solitude and experiences a servitude that makes a paradox of his colonial status, given that he is a marquis. He lives in an all-encompassing fear of living creatures, not only of humans and dogs, but even of cows and chickens. After his first marriage to a Spanish woman of nobility (who is struck by lightning and killed), he marries the *mestiza* Bernarda, but is as distant and isolated from her as he is from the rest of the world. He does not sleep well in the dark, fearing that his slaves will murder him in his bed, and since his daughter Sierva María has been relegated to the de facto status of slave, he is as isolated from her as he is from the slaves. Her parental figure becomes Dominga de Adviento, the housekeeper and slave mistress who not only has Sierva María baptized in a Catholic religious ceremony, but also has her consecrated to Olokum, a Yoruban deity.[5] The fact that Sierva María becomes a de facto African slave in her own *criollo* household becomes a metaphor for the larger, all-encompassing slavehood, servitude, and solitude in which many citizens of the Americas (in the fictional world of García Márquez) live, including the Marquis himself. His one act of goodwill

---

[4]  *La soledad de América Latina: Brindis por la poesía* (Cali: Corporación Editorial Universitaria de Colombia, 1983), 8–9; 'The Solitude of Latin America', tr. Marina Castañeda, *Granta*, 9 (1983), 56–60 (58). The speech is also avilable in *Gabriel García Márquez and the Powers of Fiction*, ed. Julio Ortega and Claudia Elliott (Austin TX & London: University of Texas Press, 1988), 88–91.

[5]  For additional information on the Yoruba god Olokum, see *Understanding Yoruba Life and Culture*, ed. Nike S. Lawal, Matthew N. Sadiku, and P. Ade Dopamu (Trenton NJ: Africa World Press, 2004).

– attempting to find a cure for his daughter's rabies bite – leads to a diagnosis of madness or possession, and also to further isolation and solitude.

The priest's role completes the picture of the Spanish medieval legacy in this novel. Here, the church's representative faces isolation and solitude by falling in love with the young girl who is, in effect, his prisoner. In this pathetic relationship, he reads to her love poems written by his great-great grandfather, Garcilaso de la Vega, rather than his own works. They are the poems of his bloodline, the poems of the marginalized and solitary other which is the identity of the colonial *mestizo* poet. By descent, the priest is the colonial other. The characters in *Del amor* are not capable of escaping the colonial status inherited from the Spanish legacy in New Granada; Delaura the priest also incarnates the central role of the institutional Catholic church in this legacy.

The antithesis to that negative legacy is African culture, which is here seen as affirmative. In none of García Márquez's previous novels does he develop the importance of Yoruba culture as explicitly as he does in *Del amor*. Sierva María speaks three African languages, she learns to drink rooster's blood before breakfast, and she knows how to 'deslizarse por entre los cristianos sin ser vista ni sentida, como un ser inmaterial' ('glide past Christians unseen and unheard, like an incorporeal being').[6] She is consecrated to the Yoruban deity Olokum, who is not described or explained, but who is generally considered to be the Yoruba goddess of the sea or of the river. Nevertheless, there is a vast literature to suggest that Olokum can be either a male (God) or a female (Goddess), depending on the cultural context. The Yoruba, Afro-Cuban, and Caribbean belief systems have blended several African traditions. All in all, it is impossible to know exactly what Olokun might have been understood to be among the African slaves in Colombia in the mid-eighteenth century, when this novel is set. Less important than the exact identity of this Yoruban deity (among the numerous identities under ongoing debate), however, is the fact that Olokum was important and associated with African cultural and religious practices and not Spanish Iberian ones.

In another key passage in this novel, when the priest Delaura Cayetano falls in love with Sierva María, African tradition is present once again. In one of the most exotic and memorable scenes, Delaura, in noteworthy contrast to the sexual relationship in *Memoria*, first reads some love poems written

---

[6]   *Del amor y otros demonios* (Buenos Aires: Sudamericana, 1994), 60; *Of Love and Other Demons*, tr. Edith Grossman (New York: Knopf, 1995), 42. All quotations are from these editions.

by Garcilaso to the young girl. This exotic love encounter is the recreation of a medieval ritual in which writing in itself becomes the equivalent of love. In exchange for the priest's reading of this love poetry, Sierva María gives him a necklace or, more specifically, an African 'precioso collar de Oddua' (*Del amor*, 172) ('beautiful Oddua necklace', *Of Love*, 125). Then, after this exchange of poetry for an African necklace, Delaura carries out the most sexually physical act of the novel: he kisses her. This is the full extent of physical contact they have. As often happens in the transculturation process, the name of an immigrant changes in the trans-Atlantic journey. In this case, the name of the Yoruba deity known in Yoruba as 'Oddudúa' becomes 'Oddua' in Spanish in the novel. Oddua, the Yoruban deity married to Obataláa, is one of the five principal Orishas in Yoruba religious practices. An encounter, which could have involved Catholic religious practices and sexual intercourse is actually a remarkable exchange of a love poem for a piece of Yoruban jewelry and a kiss.

In this passage and others, it becomes evident that the world of mid-eighteenth-century Cartagena, despite the drive of its leaders to make it a purely Spanish and Catholic social construct, is significantly non-Christian and African. The characters speak Yoruba, Yoruba cultural practices abound in their world, and even the members of the church covertly and sometimes overtly recognize that the predominant cultural paradigm is African and *mestizo*, not Spanish and white. A priest involved with the Spanish Inquisition, in fact, learns Yoruba and says to Sierva María that he brings *collares* to her that contain images of Changó ('rojo y blanco del amor', 'red and black with love'), Eleggua ('rojo y negro de la vida y la muerte'. 'red and black with life and death') and Yemaya ('las siete cuentas de agua y azul pálido', 'seven beads of water and light blue').

In summary, *Del amor* is the novel in which García Márquez not only develops the most robust representation of African culture, but also the one in which the decadence and degeneration of Spanish medieval society, culture, and values are seen from the beginning of the decline of colonial society. The actions of the characters in positions of power may seem irrational; more than irrational, the characters simply have little understanding of the culture of their colonial society, which is not really exclusively Spanish and Catholic in any significant way, but rather most significantly Yoruba and *mestizo*.

García Márquez's fiction often portrays institutional leaders who are dismally incompetent and unaware of the society in which they live and which they lead. In *Del amor*, García Márquez explores the colonial roots of their twentieth-century behavior. When he made his first trip to Africa, he reconfirmed in an interview his understanding of Latin America's cultural roots as African and *mestizo*.[7] Among his novels, *Del amor* is the one that most explicitly confirms the author's intuitive understanding of the African elements he had begun to show in his early work.

Both the medieval and the African traditions contain a strong storytelling element, and this is one aspect of their respective legacies in *Del amor*. One seminal storytelling tradition for García Márquez and the other writers of the 1960s Boom has its roots in the novel of chivalry. In *Del amor*, García Márquez once again embraces this novelistic tradition, undertaking the formidable challenge of transforming a tidbit from a newspaper anecdote into a novel-length, credible, and engaging story for the reader. In the process of realizing this daunting task, he even pays direct homage to the novel of chivalry. When the priest Delaura visits the doctor, the latter has an antique Spanish edition of the *Amadís de Gaula* and questions what the poor would read if it were not for the novels of chivalry: '¿Qué leerían los pobres de hoy si no leyeran a escondidas las novelas de caballería?' (*Del amor*, 156), 'What would the poor of our day read if they did not read the novels of chivalry in secret?', *Of Love*, 115).

## Colombia as Inferno: *Noticia de un secuestro*

*Noticia de un secuestro* is a political book in ways very different from *Del amor*, and can be best associated with *Memoria de mis putas tristes*. Inasmuch as *Memoria* can be read as a subtle challenge to middle- and upper- class social mores of Colombia, *Noticia* portrays the far more explicit and violent drama of a different kind of challenge for Colombia's oligarchy: the challenge posed by drug kingpin Pablo Escobar in the early 1990s. More of a *testimonio* than a novel, *Noticia* is García Márquez's fictionalized account of an actual kidnapping orchestrated by Escobar, a kidnapping that shook the foundations of Colombian society.[8] The central actions in this book, researched and written in the fashion of a documentary, are events from Colombian life in the early 1990s when the nation was virtually paralyzed by kidnappings and assassinations. Thus, public figures such as President César Gaviria and Pablo Escobar, a high visibility priest named Father García Herreros, the chief of the special police force (DAS) Miguel Maza Márquez, as well as a host of

---

[7] See García Márquez and Plinio Apuleyo Mendoza, *Conversaciones con Plinio Apuleyo Mendoza: El olor de la guayaba* (Bogotá: La Oveja Negra, 1982).

[8] For a discussion of the *testimonio* in Latin America, see Elzbieta Sklodowska, *El testimonio hispanoamericano: historia, teoría, poética* (New York: Peter Lang, 1992).

other prominent Colombian citizens, are the main characters of this work. The kidnapping of the public figure Maruja Pachón de Villamizar (Director of Focine, a state-funded institution supporting film production in Colombia) and her sister Beatriz Villamizar de Guerrero, of a prominent Colombian family, affords García Márquez the opportunity to divulge to the reader an 'inside Colombia' report. Most Colombians lived in intense fear and confusion during this period, and many foreigners became aware that this nation had one of the highest homicide rates in the Western hemisphere. García Márquez offers a month-by-month report, built around a plot, of exactly what was really happening in Colombia from November 1990 to May 1991, with occasional background information about the 1970s and 1980s in Colombia, as well as an epilogue that takes the story up to 1993. This was a period in which the nation lived an infernal life of daily kidnappings and an average of four homicides a day. As García Márquez states in his prefaratory comments, the nation lived an 'holocausto bíblico ('biblical holocaust').[9]

From the kidnapping that takes place in the first chapter through to the surrender of Pablo Escobar in the last, García Márquez maintains a high level of suspense by using his classic repertoire of storytelling devices. Employing some of the techniques from *Relato de un náufrago* and from *Crónica*, he weaves the plot through the eyes of a multiplicity of players, including the two kidnapped women, their kidnappers, different representatives of law enforcement and government, and even Pablo Escobar himself. In addition to the constantly changing vision or understanding of 'truth' and 'national life' that is modified as different characters speak, the reader has access to a variety of other real sources of information culled by García Márquez the investigative reporter: newspaper accounts, television and radio reports, personal interviews, and private letters. In addition, García Márquez the novelist includes occasional minute details more typical of fiction than of a *testimonio* or newspaper account. The plot involves the attempts of different groups (representing a range of political and economic interests) to negotiate with Escobar in order to obtain the release of the two women. As the plot thickens, three different groups, including the government, become increasingly more desperate about the situation, the two women sense the threat of a sexual assault by their captors, and other prominent Colombians, such as Diana Turbay and Marina Montoya, are actually assassinated.

García Márquez offers both the Colombian and the foreign reader an insight into the real events, experiences, politics, and power at play during

---

[9]   *Noticia de un secuestro* (Buenos Aires: Sudamericana, 1996), 8; *News of a Kidnapping*, tr. Edith Grossman (New York: Knopf, 1997), 3.

this period when the drug kingpins and the Colombian government were at war. As he had done with the Bolívar figure, the author systematically avoids the standard and most simplistic understandings of what was really taking place during this period of national crisis in Colombia. For example, *Noticia* is neither a moralistic tirade against the drug cartels nor a condemnation of the United States for providing a market for drugs, even though there were many institutional voices in Colombia, as well as voices on the streets, that were vigorously articulating those two arguments. The two arguments, in fact, predominated in Colombia in the early 1990s. Rather than directly challenging them (a comfortable solution to this narrative puzzle), García Márquez operates as a de facto 'narrator as reporter' who presents a series of well-informed scenarios and lets readers reach their own conclusions about the chaotic and dismal state of affairs in Colombia during the early 1990s.

This narrator as reporter offers a prologue of sorts under the title of 'Gratitudes' ('Acknowledgements') in which he explains some of his role as the author of *Noticia*. The former kidnap victim Maruja Pachón de Villamizar and her husband Alberto Villamizar proposed to García Márquez, in October 1993, that he write a book about her experiences during her six months of captivity. He took their story and elaborated it over a three-year period, using the personal anecdotes of Maruja and Alberto as the backbone of the book.

In his prologue, he also allows the reader a preview of what awaits: not a dry documentary account, but 'una narracion laberíntica' ('a complex story'), hearkening back to *El otoño,* and a work of Biblical proportions: 'un episodio del holocausto bíblico', that recalls *La hojarasca.* The reader soon experiences numerous twists in the plot, declarations by the characters, phrases and stylistic flashes that carry the trademark of the García Márquez who spun tales of Macondo. Like *El amor,* then, his book contains traces of what many readers now consider 'classic' García Márquez gestures.

The most noteworthy plot strategy is García Márquez's ability, even in the genre of the *testimonio,* to engage the reader in anecdote, from the first page, and to keep the reader intrigued until the last. The novel opens with the rapidity that characterizes much of his fiction: Maruja and Beatriz lead a chase through Bogotá as they leave from work; by the novel's fourth page the two are captured by Escobar's men. As in the Macondo fiction, García Márquez moves deftly back and forth in time with the use of key phrases, such as 'años después' ('years later'), and the characters sometimes foresee or predict the direction of things in ways reminiscent of some of the exceptionally intuitive people of Macondo.

As a writer who began as a journalist, García Márquez has developed a style characterized by a directness and simplicity atypical of the literary language of Latin American fiction when he began writing in the 1950s.[10] In *Noticia*, he remains faithful to that fictional style, even though this book is not really fiction, and he even comments on style when referring to the diary of a character named Azucena: 'En el libro que publicaría poco después, lo relató con una sencillez admirable' (*Noticia*, 132) ('In the book she would publish a short while later, she narrated this with admirable simplicity' (*News*, 106). García Márquez's comment on the speaking style of Escobar is one the reader will instinctively relate to the author himself: 'el estilo oral de Escobar, tan conciso y cortante como el de sus cartas' (*Noticia*, 296) ('Escobar's speaking style, as concise and to the point as in his letters', *News*, 248).[11]

The ending of *Noticia* points to the prologue and makes the book into a metafiction. Maruja breathes a sigh of relief at the end and comments that her experience has been like writing a book: 'Todo esto ha sido como para escribir un libro' (*Noticia*, 346) ('Somebody ought to write a book', *News*, 291). The last line not only refers to the prologue and the metafiction, but also reminds readers that they have read an elaborately constructed and highly fictionalized story. That is, *Noticia* is not only a set of real events, but also very much García Márquez's fictionalized version: his story of these events.

In addition to affording the reader an 'insider's' experience into the horrific daily life of Colombia in the early 1990s, García Márquez also invites the reader to speculate about issues of truth. Much of his fiction, while making no claim to be 'real', had questioned different kinds of historical and political truths. This book, even with the inclusion of many 'facts', does not promote the idea of 'truth'. On the contrary, the reader is constantly evaluating the multiplicity of supposed truths presented.

### Magical Europe: *Doce cuentos peregrinos*

The stories of *Doce cuentos peregrinos* (*Strange Pilgrims*, 1992) are generally distant from the main interests of García Márquez's recent fiction. Nevertheless, there are some superficial similarities, such as characters who know

---

[10] The predominant mode in Latin America at the time was the opposite of this simplicity of style. See John S. Brushwood, *The Spanish American Novel: A Twentieth-century Survey* (London & Austin TX: University of Texas Press, 1975); Jean Franco, *An Introduction to Spanish American Literature* (London: Cambridge University Press, 1969); Naomi Lindstrom, *The Social Conscience of Latin American Writing*, Pan American Series (Austin TX: University of Texas Press, 1998); and Raymond L. Williams, *The Twentieth-century Spanish American Novel* (London & Austin TX: University of Texas Press, 2003).

[11] In chapter 6, the Epilogue of this study, I note some of the ways in which García Márquez's verbal style is also similar to his writing.

Latin or African women of Yoruba origin. Although not set in Macondo, the stories often celebrate the magic of everyday life or else make magic out of the commonplace, taking very mundane animals, such as rats, and giving them special qualities or finding magical elements in them.

The twelve stories in this volume were originally created, in their early form (or first version) in the late 1970s and early 1980s (between 1976 and 1982). Years later, after reworking them along with many other stories from the same period (most of which were eventually discarded), he rewrote twelve of them yet again in order to publish them under one title, *Doce cuentos peregrinos*. In a preface written that same year, he explains the exact process by which the stories were conceived as early as the 1970s, written over a period of years, and then rewritten over the next eighteen (1974–1992). They share a basic scenario: they all deal with the experience of Latin Americans in Europe and they tend to involve some aspect of the magic of life, or, as García Márquez calls it, 'the strange things that happen to Latin Americans in Europe' (*Strange Pilgrims*, viii). In the end, he managed to construct a volume of fictions set in different European cities and a volume that represents, in the author's words, 'el libro de cuentas más próximo al que siempre quise escribir' ('the closest to the one I had always wanted to write').[12] Seen in the global context of García Márquez's work, these are, as well as fictions with interesting insights into topics such as ageing and time, among the most magical and sometimes most incredible anecdotes he has penned on topics such as power and colonial mentalities (as a part of the Spanish medieval and African legacy).

'Buen viaje, señor presidente' ('Bon voyage, Mr President') takes the reader back to the scenario of the ageing patriarch of *El otoño*. It is an exceptional, seemingly fantastic commentary on power and the colonial mentality. In this story, set in Geneva in Switzerland, a seventy-three-year-old former dictator of an unnamed Caribbean nation lives in solitude and faces little more than death: he spends a lot of his time contemplating his own end. He is a reader of classics in the original Latin and also a fervent reader of the work of the Caribbean poet Aimé Césaire. The other main character in the story, Homero Rey, is a former supporter of the dictator; Homero had actually worked for the dictator during his political campaigns. Now an ambulance driver in Geneva, Homero recognizes the dictator, approaches him in conversation, and soon thereafter invites him to a dinner prepared by his wife, Lázara Davis, in their modest apartment. (She is a Puerto Rican mulatta who

---

[12] Prologue to *Doce cuentos peregrinos* (Bogotá: Oveja Negra, 1992), 18; *Strange Pilgrims*, tr. Edith Grossman (New York: Knopf, 1995), xiii.

likes to fancy herself as a 'Yoruba princess'.) The original intent of Homero
and the shrewd Lázara is to gain a huge sum of money from the moribund
dictator by selling him an elaborate and very complete funeral, including
repatriation. The couple successfully befriend the dictator, only to discover
that his wealth is not what they had expected: his only possession of real
value is some of his wife's jewels, 'heredadas de una abuela colonial' (*Doce
cuentos*, 45) ('a legacy from a grandmother who had lived in Colonial times',
*Strange Pilgrims*, 27). After having reacted very negatively to the ex-dictator
at the outset, Lázara begins to sympathize with him when, after discovering
his jewels were fake, she realizes that he is an impoverished, lonely soul, as
pathetic as the generals in *El otoño* and *El general*. He eventually returns
to his homeland and undergoes a physical and psychological recovery in
the Americas. At the very end of the story, incredibly, he launches a reform
movement as a presidential candidate.

This is a story about a corrupt and degenerate legacy. Just as the 'legacy'
jewelry has degenerated in value over the years, with real jewels having been
replaced by fake ones, so the unnamed Latin American nation of the story has
degenerated, largely as a result of its colonial legacy. When the deposed and
decrepit ex-dictator decides to re-enter the public sphere in his homeland,
the story seemingly enters the realm of the fantastic, for it would seem to
be impossible for him to have even a remote chance of entering the political
arena again. For a repressive, cruel, and violent ex-dictator to be able to
launch a reform movement, however, is the ultimate expression of how a
colonial mentality works.

Less important in this particular story than the colonial legacy, however,
is the fact that the ex-dictator is of an advanced age. In other stories in the
volume, such as 'La Santa' ('The Saint'), 'El avión de la bella durmiente'
('Sleeping Beauty and the Airplane') and 'María dos Prazeres', ageing is a
more important topic. In 'La santa', an ageing compatriot of García Márquez
spends twenty-two years in Rome attempting to convince the Vatican to
canonize his deceased daughter, whose uncorrupted body has been found
intact after eleven years in the soil. The father, Margarito Duarte, dedicates over two decades of his life to this attempt to convince the Pope that
this supposed miracle makes her worthy of sainthood. The key images of
this story, nevertheless, are not those of the daughter. Rather, they are the
poignant portrayal of the ageing father at the outset and at the end of the
story. When the narrator first encounters Duarte in Rome at the beginning of
the story, he barely recognizes him because of the ex-dictator's now halting
use of the Spanish language and his appearance of being an 'old Roman'. At
the end of the story, he encounters Duarte in Rome again, and by now the

old man has the appearance of being old and tired. The ageing process is so visible, in fact, that even Rome seems to be ageing and decrepit. The narrator refers to the ex-dictator, once again, as he had on the first page, as a 'an old Roman'. The sense of ageing is also communicated by the narrator's mention of puddles of rain where the light was beginning to decay. The ending of the story offers yet another little surprise and a conclusion: the narrator claims in the last line that Duarte, and not his daughter, is the real candidate for canonization, and that Duarte had in reality dedicated twenty-two years to promoting his own case.

This special twist at the very end of 'La santa' invites the reader to question the motives behind religious campaigns. On the one hand, it could well be that Duarte is really just campaigning in his own cause. On the other, the reader is invited to question the real motive of all religious fanatics such as Duarte, who devote their entire lives to a cause. This story also has a potential political reading, for the reader is invited to question the motives behind absolute dedication to any cause, be it religious or political or the interests of a group, individual, or concept.

The remaining stories in the volume tend to deal with incredible and fantastic people, places, and things in Europe. In a way, García Márquez is ending his career, in these last books, by showing his readers that the supposed 'magic realism' of Latin America also transpires in Europe or, as some readers have preferred to think, in their nation, whether their nationality happens to be French, Mexican, or Canadian. In effect, France, Mexico, and Canada each have their own 'Macondo', as do all other nations. The story 'El avión de la bella durmiente' ('Sleeping Beauty and the Airplane') deals with a woman from Colombia who goes to Europe and does what she does best there: she dreams. García Márquez also describes magical moments in Catalonia, Italy, and Spain in 'Maria dos Prazeres', 'Espantos de agosto' ('The Ghost of August'), and 'Sólo vine para hablar por teléfono' ('I Only Came to Use the Phone'). In 'Maria dos Prazeres', an ageing prostitute, who was taken from Brazil to Europe after being sold by her mother in Manaus, experiences a special, magical moment at the end of the story. The protagonist in 'Sólo vine para hablar por teléfono' becomes involved in an eerie interaction revealing not only a special obsession with the telephone and a need for power, but also a mindset with overtones of medieval authority and fascism. In this story, as in 'Espantos de agosto', reality takes surprising twists into the spheres of the unknown, the inexplicable, and the magical.

In stories such as 'Tramontona', García Márquez takes a situation, person, or event that is autochtonous to Europe and this situation, person, or event then leads to a rational, post-Enlightenment understanding, explanation, or, in some cases, interpretation. García Márquez thus invites his European readers to open their eyes to the magic of their own everyday 'real' lives at the same time that he questions European post-Enlightenment rational methods of understanding. (This approach constitutes yet another rejection of Latin America as the home of 'magic realism'.) For his Latin American readers, the volume is not only an entertaining set of anecdotes about the special experiences that Latin Americans might have in Europe, but also a type of response to Europe from Latin Americans who, for well over half a century, have had their multiple and diverse cultures reduced to the facile term 'magic realism'.

## Conclusion

As we suggested at the beginning of this chapter, García Márquez's two most recent novels, *Memoria* and *Del amor*, hearken back to *El amor* and to *Crónica* with their consideration of themes, topics, and attitudes related to Spanish medieval order and feudal structures. The four works address these particular themes, topics, and attitudes more explicitly than does the rest of his fiction, making the concluding chapter of his writing career one in which these political and related interests are prominent. Thus, it is in the latter stages of his life that he sets forth most explicitly his exposé of the negative legacy of the Spanish medieval order in Latin America, as well as the positive legacy of African tradition in regions such as Colombia, the Caribbean, and Brazil, where this cultural tradition has been most pronounced. In *Doce cuentos,* it is a decrepit and decadent Spanish legacy, and the jewels are the metaphor for this circumstance. *Del amor* is the novel that recognizes and most robustly embraces African presence in Colombia, the Caribbean, and other parts of Latin America.

With *Noticia*, García Márquez uses a real-life story and quasi-*testimonio* format, but then transforms his *testimonio* into a typical piece of García Márquez fiction, using the concise, minimalist style of some of his Macondo fiction, such as *Los funerales* and *El coronel*, as well as the metafictional qualities we associate with *Cien años* and *El amor*. By fictionalizing events, he distances the reader from this national trauma, just as he had distanced the political fictions he wrote during the period of La Violencia, such as 'Un día de éstos' and *La mala hora*, from violence.

# 6

# Epilogue

In 1982 Gabriel García Márquez was internationally recognized as a world-class writer when he was awarded the Nobel Prize for Literature. From 1967 to 1982, during the fifteen-year period between the publication of *Cien años de soledad* and the award of the Nobel Prize, he received any number of awards. In 1972 he was recognized twice: with the Rómulo Gallegos Prize in Caracas (at the time the major literary prize for work in the Spanish language), and with the Neustadt Prize in the United States. During this period, he was often compared to the very writers who had been his main role models: William Faulkner, Franz Kafka, and Jorge Luis Borges. He was also compared to many of his contemporaries who were already international celebrities, such as Italo Calvino, William Styron, and John Barth.

In Latin America, García Márquez belongs to a generation of writers who felt an urgent need to modernize a Latin American literature that for them was far too embedded in the realist tradition, and all too often imprisoned in nationalisms or regionalisms that were, by the 1950s and 1960s, no longer viable. Thus, García Márquez, along with Carlos Fuentes, Mario Vargas Llosa, Julio Cortázar, José Donoso, and a host of others, made the case in his fiction, essays, and public stances that the time had arrived for a modern Latin American literature. García Márquez is a dedicated modernist who occasionally exhibits some postmodern gestures.

Of course, García Márquez, Fuentes, and Cortázar were not the first Latin American intellectuals to call for this modernization. The original impetus came in the 1920s when Borges, Huidobro, and the *vanguardistas* from Buenos Aires to Mexico City made their first modernist inroads in Latin America. Their work, however, was largely ignored for several decades.[1] In the 1940s, Borges, Asturias, Yáñez, Marechal, Carpentier, and others

---

[1]  For a general introduction to the reception of the writings of the *vanguardias* in Latin America, particularly fiction, see John S. Brushwood, *The Spanish American Novel: A Twentieth-century Survey* (London & Austin TX: University of Texas Press, 1975); also Raymond L. Williams, *The Twentieth-century Spanish American Novel* (London & Austin TX: University of Texas Press, 2003).

published fiction that indicated a major shift toward invention and moderni-zation. Rulfo's *Pedro Páramo* (1955) was an equally significant contribution to this shift, and that work was an important model for García Márquez in particular.

It was with the 1960s Boom, however, that the labors of three genera-tions of Latin American writers finally came to fruition, and Latin American literature was no longer viewed as the folkloric or provincial cultural vehicle that it was when the leading writers of Latin America were Rómulo Gallegos, Ricardo Güiraldes, José Eustacio Rivera, and Mariano Azuela.

As we have seen, García Márquez's work is a lifelong critique of old institutions, customs, habits, and ways of thinking, many of which have their origins in medieval Spain. Much of his fiction is also a critique of the social mores of old elites from Spain that have been in power since the sixteenth and seventeenth centuries. His three major novels are *Cien años de soledad*, *El otoño del patriarca*, and *El amor en los tiempos del cólera*; these are his novels of greatest depth and breadth, as well as the works in which he exhibits the widest range of technical mastery as a dedicated modernist who always writes with a keen awareness of his realist predecessors in Latin America and his postmodern contemporaries on the international scene.

García Márquez's work has stylistic and thematic consistencies that invite the reader to organize them as cycles. The Macondo cycle consists of *La hojarasca*, *La mala hora*, *El coronel no tiene quién le escriba*, *Los funerales de la mamá grande*, and *Cien años de soledad*. The set of works dealing most explicitly with power and related political contexts includes the short story 'Los funerales de la mamá grande' and continues with *El otoño del patriarca* and *El general en su laberinto*. The works that deal with the human dimenions of love, the sentiments, and ageing are *El amor en los tiempos del cólera*, *Doce cuentos peregrinos*, *Del amor y otros demonios*, and *Memoria de mis putas tristes*. The tales in which thematic depth is less important and which instead offer the reader hermeneutic concerns are *La increíble y triste historia de la cándida Eréndira y de su abuela desalmada* and *Crónica de una muerte anunciada*.

We have seen that here is a writer who, at times, thinks historically; his books often relate to the history of Colombia in particular and to Latin America in general. We have also discussed the texts of a writer who under-stands that his books are not exactly a history of Latin America but more a metaphor for the region. With his earliest writing, he began this self-conscious construction of metaphors to substitute for empirical history, actual events, and real people. These metaphorically constructed stories are often critical of the social customs and mores of Latin America's ruling elite and often deal with their most historically important institutions: the Catholic church, traditional political parties, and the military. Most of García Márquez's metaphors for Latin America derive from colonial legacies that have persisted for centuries.

García Márquez is an erudite man, far more erudite than this seemingly innate storyteller of informal Caribbean manners might initially appear. It has been evident to readers and critics alike, since the publication of *Cien años*, that he is not a literary innocent, and his in-depth knowledge of the work of William Faulkner, Franz Kafka, Jorge Luis Borges, John Dos Passos, Virginia Woolf, Ernest Hemingway, and the Greek classics has been amply documented in the scholarly work of Mario Vargas Llosa, Suzanne Jill Levine, and the host of others who followed through with additional scholarly research and who interviewed the author. The depth and breadth of his reading, however, go far beyond the major writers of the Western European and North American classics. By claiming that he is a truly erudite writer, I am thinking of the erudition that characterizes intellectuals such as Umberto Eco, Jorge Luis Borges, and William H. Gass. García Márquez's literary baggage includes major and minor writers of the Spanish language from the medieval period to the twentieth century, including, most prominently, Miguel de Cervantes, Ramón Gómez de la Serna, Rubén Darío, Miguel Hernández, Ramón del Valle-Inclán, Adolfo Bioy Casares, and Juan Rulfo.

It is that erudite writer who suggested in 1977 that 'If I write stories again, the model now is Somerset Maugham'.[2] The reference to Maugham, followed by a description of exactly what he admires about Maugham's stories, perfectly illustrates his erudition. He has judiciously and studiously built a literary relationship with the likes not only of the Faulkner and the Kafka to whom the critics constantly refer, but also with Stefan Zweig, A. J. Cronin, Graham Greene, Ray Bradbury, Erskine Caldwell, Fyodor Dostoevsky, Yasuni Kawabata, Daniel Defoe, Alessandro Manzoni, Herman Melville, François Rabelais, Honoré de Balzac, Simone de Beauvoir, Truman Capote, and Joseph Conrad.

In his public appearances, he tends to shy away from any semblance of erudition, primarily because he associates erudition with pretentiousness. It is not in García Márquez's modest and humble *costeño* character to be a

---

2   García Márquez, 'Journey Back to the Source', tr. Gene H, Bell-Villada, in *Conversations with Gabriel García Márquez*, ed. Bell-Villada (Jackson MS: University of Mississippi Press, 2006), 79–92 (91). The original Spanish text of this interview first appeared in *Triunfo*, 25/cdxli (1971), 12–18, and was reprinted in *García Márquez habla de García Márquez*, ed. Alfonso Rentería Mantilla (Bogotá: Rentería, 1979), 159–67.

pretentious public intellectual; he feels that his real being is antithetical to the image of the flashy intellectual. He has been consistently simple and modest when I have met him, but on two or three occasions when I have seen him put on his glasses and scrutinize written texts (such as an occasion at the Hotel María Cristina in Mexico City), I have had the sense of a human being who is studiously unpretentious but deeply erudite.

When I think of García Márquez, the erudite scholar (as opposed to the public intellectual and the gifted yet modest storyteller), I also think of one of the very few Colombians (fewer than six of them) who know well the entire corpus of Colombian literature.[3] Intellectuals and writers close to Colombian literature will invariably be familiar with a set of writings that begins in the colonial period with *El carnero*, continues with the nineteenth century classic *María*, and then follows with the likes of José Asunción Silva, Tomás Carrasquilla, José Eustacio Rivera, Eduardo Caballero Calderón, Manuel Mejía Vallejo, Héctor Rojas Herazo, Álvaro Cepeda Samudio, and a host of more contemporary writers. Beyond the same dozen or so basic texts that readers of Colombian literature all share, however, there tends to be a very large vacuum. García Márquez, a reader of a collection of Colombian literature known as Aldana from his days in high school, is an exception. I have spoken with him in very specific terms about some relatively obscure Colombian writers, such as Rafael Gómez Picón, Jaime Ardila Casamitjana, Domínguez Camargo, and Clímaco Soto Borda, and have found that his intimate knowledge of the writings of these authors cannot be described in any other way than deeply erudite.[4] When he began writing in the late 1940s and elected to go against this tradition, it was not part of an intellectual pose; in fact, it was an act of a deep visceral need and authentic intellectual commitment.

Non-readers of Spanish occasionally ask how good the English translations of García Márquez are. I often quote García Márquez himself. When asked

---

[3]  In the 1980s, I searched for sources on the Colombian novel in the process of writing *The Colombian Novel, 1844–1987*. After completing the project over the course of several years, I reached the conclusion that I could only identify three Colombians who had read the entire corpus of the Colombian novel: Antonio Curcio Altamar (an academic who wrote an exhaustive history of the Colombian novel in the early 1950s), Germán Vargas, and García Márquez. See Curcio Altamar, *Evolución de la novela en Colombia*, Biblioteca Básica Colombiana 8 (Bogotá: Instituto Colombiano de Cultura, 1975).

[4]  He may, for example, have read many relatively obscure and forgotten Colombian novelists of the 1930s and 1940s, such as Tomás Vargas Osorio and Jaime Ardila Casamitjana; see Raymond L. Williams, *The Colombian Novel, 1844–1987* (London & Austin TX: University of Texas Press, 1991).

this question, he once claimed that he likes the English translation of *Cien años* (by Gregory Rabassa) better than the original. One could think about the meditations of Benjamin on the task of the translator or one could think more about Aníbal González's invitation to consider all books as translations. But the non-reader of Spanish sometimes just wants to know, in a very basic way, if the translations seem 'good' or 'accurate', based on a reading of the original Spanish. I personally believe that it is difficult to imagine how a translation could be more accomplished than Gregory Rabassa's *One Hundred Years of Solitude*. Never has it crossed my mind, when reading this book, that it deserves a better translation, or that a better translation could be done. On the contrary, it has often occurred to me that García Márquez was fortunate not to have been translated early in his career by some of the less capable translators who published translations of Latin American literature into English in the 1950s and 1960s. Without Rabassa, the Boom might not have reached the coast of Great Britain or the rest of the anglophone world. The translations of the later fiction by Edith Grossman are also the work of an accomplished translator.

Those of us who work professionally in the 'original languages' of literary texts tend to believe as a matter of principle that all readings based on translations are deficient. Some scholars consider readings based on translations to be so deficient as to be actually irrelevant. But we might well think of ourselves as readers in the manner advocated by Borges and accept that all books are translations of previous books.

Readers wishing to probe further the matter of the translation of *One Hundred Years of Solitude* will probably come to believe that Rabassa's work is a work of genius in a general sense: it tells the story not just efficiently but brilliantly. Perhaps for this very reason, Rabassa is relatively inaccurate in respect of some details. I have touched on this in Chapter 2 in the discussion of *One Hundred Years*; the original can be read as a parody of a Colombian Romantic novel, while the translation glosses over the parody, as indeed it must.

'Every single line in *Cien años de soledad*, as in all my books, has a starting point in reality', García Márquez insisted in an interview published in 1982.[5] This is one of his standard responses to endless queries from readers and critics

5   Claudia Dreifus, 'Playboy Interview: Gabriel García Márquez'. in *Conversations with Gabriel García Márquez*, ed. Gene H. Bell-Villada (Jackson MS: University of Mississippi Press, 2006), 93–132 (112). Reprinted from *Playboy* (February 1983), 65–77, 172–78.

who understand what happens in his books as magic rather than empirical reality. For better or for worse, the trademark phrase associated with García Márquez has become 'magic realism'. García Márquez and I both think this turn of events (promoted nowadays primarily by book reviewers and professors of English) has been for the worse. I have expressed my dissatisfaction with the term magic realism in the first two chapters of this *Companion*. For García Márquez, the fact that all his books are based on reality is important, given his multiple social and political interests as a writer, as a public intellectual, and as a self-consciously political human being. For me, those political interests are part of the reason I consider the term 'magic realism' to be a way of naming, reducing, and then dismissing García Márquez. I am, of course, only too aware of the many forms of the irrational that we find in his work and the very different reasons why seemingly 'magical' things happen in his novels: he is steeped in the oral tradition, was influenced by the *greguería*, and has had a lifelong fascination with the unlikely as reported by Ripley in his *Believe it or not* pieces. When García Márquez has the character Ulises, in the story 'La increíble y triste historia', make glass change color every time he touches it, it is because so much has already been said about love that the author, as he himself has explained simply 'had to find a new way of saying that this boy was in love'.[6] García Márquez's final fictional response to the whole matter of the magic realism syndrome appears in *Doce cuentos*, where the magic takes place in Europe, not Macondo; a continent other than South America is now the home of magic realism. This amounts to a statement to the effect that the space of the irrational, the unlikely, or the 'magical' is not exclusively the region identified as 'Latin America', as it was named by the French in the nineteenth century, but includes Europe, too.

García Márquez has continually presented African and indigenous influences as part of Colombian culture; Macondo and the other Caribbean settings in his work are tri-ethnic. As we saw in the discussion of the first Macondo novel, *La hojarasca*, the cultural context is tri-ethnic. In most of García Márquez's work, African people and culture are present, even if only in traces of the oral culture that has such strong roots in the Costa region.

   In his later writings, the African presence has become more pronounced and explicit. The novel in which this is most evident is *Del amor*, in which the young girl, Sierva María, is reared more by an African slave than by her own parents and speaks three African languages. In *El amor*, the two main

---

6    *ibid.*, 112.

characters, Fermina Daza and Florentino Ariza, are dramatically affected by African characters: Fermina's life-changing epiphany takes place in the presence of an African woman (and seems intimately though inexplicably connected to her), and the real woman of Florentino's life is not Fermina but an African lover (see Chapter 4, above). In the 1970s, when García Márquez went to Africa for the first time, he felt a familiarity that reminded him of the strong African presence of the Costa region. It took him a decade to find ways to fictionalize African people and culture more visibly than he had his early work; *Del amor* and *El amor* represent a development of this constant presence in García Márquez's work.

I have known García Márquez for as long as I have been studying his work professionally: since 1975. Since then, I have followed his fiction, the body of critical work that has grown up around his writing, and the interviews he has given. I have spoken with him on a dozen different occasions, with three or four in-depth conversations among them, including the one I published as a formal interview.[7] I believe this ongoing dialogue with him and his work has afforded me some reasonably good insights into the fiction and the man behind the writing, and the key interactions between the writing and the man.

Our first conversation was in Bogotá in October of 1975. I was in Colombia with a Fulbright Grant in order to carry out research for a doctoral dissertation on the Colombian novel after *Cien años*, from 1968 to 1975 and culminating in *El otoño*, a novel that appeared in print just a few months before our first meeting. This conversation was arranged by literary critic and lawyer, Néstor Madrid-Malo, a *costeño* from Barranquilla who had known García Márquez from the days of their youth. (Years later, Néstor always claimed in conversations we had that the 'Group of Barranquilla' was mostly an invention of foreign critics. He was referring primarily, I think, to a French critic, Jacques Gilard, but also to some in the United States, including myself.) That first meeting was arranged as a morning chat in the now defunct Hotel Hilton on the Avenida Séptima in the heart of downtown Bogotá, where García Márquez was staying on a visit from Europe. I was dressed in the classic Colombian style of that time for a meeting such as this: dark sports coat and tie. The lobby was filled with Colombian and foreign businessmen wearing dark three-piece suits. As I observed this scene, García Márquez came out of the elevator wearing blue jeans and a casual shirt. His attire was

---

[7]   See Raymond L. Williams, 'The Visual Arts, the Poetization of Space and Writing: An Interview with Gabriel García Márquez', *Publications of the Modern Language Association of America*, 104/ii (1989), 131–40.

quite an anomaly for Bogotá in the mid-1970s, when intellectuals and profes-
sionals alike still tended to dress in dark and formal wear. He invited me up
to his room, and we went up in the elevator in silence. Once there, we sat
on opposite sides of the small room. He sat on an easy chair and threw one
leg over its arm; I remember being unable to avoid looking at his leg when
I was not looking at his relaxed, self-assured face. By the time we met that
morning in October, a hardline Colombian Marxist intellectual named Jaime
Mejía Duque had already published an aggressive short attack, in a book of
some 80 pages, on *El otoño del patriarca*, in which he claimed that García
Márquez was unconsciously supporting and perpetuating the very structures
that he was claiming to question. During our conversation, I made no references at all to Mejía Duque's diatribe, but rather asked García Márquez a set
of very specific and mostly technical questions about *El otoño* (the questions
were based on the close reading that I had just completed in the first draft
of my dissertation chapter on that novel). I did not know exactly how self-
conscious García Márquez might be when it came to talking about narrative
technique; I had little idea, as I embarked on the interview, of how he might
respond to my queries. I was very pleasantly surprised: he was very interested in the questions of technique and narrative strategy that I probed. In a
way (perhaps as the innocent graduate student that I was), I felt that García
Márquez was validating my own reading of *El otoño*. That reading, eventually published in *Symposium*, has also been one of my most frequently cited
pieces on García Márquez. In it, I make no reference to the conversation I
had with him in Bogotá in October 1975. Two decades later, at a seminar in
Guadalajara, he confirmed my suspicion that he always had appreciated this
kind of work more than he ever admitted, since he generally claimed he did
not even read literary criticism at all: he stated at this seminar that foreign
critics had saved *El otoño*.[8] Whether we had 'saved' or 'salvaged' *El otoño*
or not, it is true that North-American critics in general have not seen it as a
paradigm for reactionary thought, and I do not believe that it is what it is.

Perhaps more important than my sporadic encounters with García Márquez
was the regular dialogue I enjoyed with Germán Vargas, a literary critic, journalist, and the mentor of García Márquez. Germán was the person who knew
García Márquez the best. I saw Vargas regularly from the early 1980s until his
death in 1993. During that period, I went to Colombia on an ongoing series of

---

[8]   In the mid-1990s, García Márquez invited a group of scholars to the Univesity of
Guadalajara, in Mexico, for a three-day seminar about his work. Behind closed doors with
two dozen of us, he fielded questions for several hours each day. He made this statement
about foreign critics in a number of interviews.

research trips, two or three times a year, usually spending my time in libraries in Bogotá, but always with a stopover of two or three days in Barranquilla to speak first and foremost with Vargas. My sense of García Márquez as a young writer, as an intellectual in formation, and, later, as an adult public intellectual came as much from those marathon conversations with Germán Vargas as they did from any other source. I usually stayed at the apartment in which Vargas and his wife Susie de Vargas resided; our chats frequently began before lunch and did not end until well after midnight. The role played by the Group of Barranquilla, as it has appeared in subsequent publications (including this one), was informed by these conversations. We did not ever record our ongoing dialogue, but I did often take notes.

Germán was a godfather figure for many young Colombian writers, beginning with the generation of García Márquez and Álvaro Cepeda Samudio, and ending with the generation that began writing in the early 1990s. Germán lived through the early years of frequent self-doubt and occasional setbacks that García Márquez experienced. Perhaps this was one of the reasons why he took so seriously the struggles of the young writers whom he spent a lifetime supporting by reading their manuscripts, encouraging their efforts, and even providing contacts with publishers. If Gabriel García Márquez was the creative genius in Colombia of the century, Germán was the nation's literary heart of the century.

In one of my informal encounters with Germán and García Márquez, we talked briefly about the dilemma facing young writers in Colombia. García Márquez had lent a helping hand to several promising young writers, none of whom ever enjoyed much success. He explained the situation to me in the following way, To become a world-class novelist, a young aspiring writer needs to make a conscientious decision to write well, to publish only the best of that writing, and to be determined never to be anything less than a world-class writer.

The anecdotes about the Group of Barranquilla, given a wider readership primarily by Germán Vargas and Jacques Gilard (and to some extent by myself), have overshadowed the role played by the group of Cartagena in 1947 and 1948. Consequently, the history of the intellectuals in García Márquez's life in this period has been slightly inaccurate. Of that group in Cartagena, Clemente Manuel Zabala died in 1963, before García Márquez's career had consolidated (and also well before my own first trip to Colombia in 1970). I did meet Héctor Rojas Herazo on two occasions. In October 1975, I interviewed him in a semi-formal manner, and he spoke of his interactions with García Márquez in both Cartagena and Barranquilla. The second time was more memorable: Rojas Herazo and I enjoyed a four-hour lunch conversation within the walls of the old colonial part of Cartagena with the young Colombian writer Gustavo Álvarez Gardeazábal.[9] During this chat, Rojas Herazo spoke eloquently and in great depth of every major piece of Colombian literature ever written, the role García Márquez's friends within the group of Cartagena played in his development, and the subsequent role of the Group of Barranquilla. I cannot imagine a more informed and competent literary interlocutor for García Márquez at age twenty than Rojas Herazo: he was a brilliant and exceptionally well-read novelist, poet, painter, and intellectual.

Of the old 'Group of Barranquilla', Germán Vargas was the senior living member at the time. Álvaro Cepeda Samudio had died young of cancer in the 1960s. The fourth member of the group, Alfonso Fuenmayor (son of novelist José Félix Fuenmayor), was still living in Barranquilla during those years and remained semi-active as a journalist. Vargas and I visited with Fuenmayor on a few occasions, and we met once with Cepeda Samudio's widow and daughter (the latter married to a North American and living in the United States). When we met with Alfonso Fuenmayor, the topic was always the same: the youthful days of the Group of Barranquilla in the cafés and bars of Barranquilla in 1949 and 1950, their readings of Faulkner, and their other reading and activities. As young journalists and aspiring writers, they lived the fantasy of becoming famous poets and fiction writers, a fantasy far more common among the youth of Colombia than among the young in Britain or the United States. García Márquez is one of the few Colombians actually to live that fantasy.

On the basis of my experience as a student of Colombian literature, as someone who has talked occasionally with García Márquez and in more detail with his closest friend Germán Vargas, the picture I have of García Márquez is of an exceptionally private person who describes himself as shy and extremely private, despite his vigorous writing and often bold public pronouncements. Unlike Fuentes and Vargas Llosa, who have lived much of their lives in academic environments, first as students, then in a variety of lecturing roles, García Márquez is fundamentally uncomfortable and often

---

[9] Gustavo Álvarez Gardeazábal was a leading Colombian novelist of the 1970s who seemed at one time likely to become the one writer in Colombia with the potential to compete with García Márquez, but his popularity was short-lived. Rojas Herazo wrote a set of three Faulknerian novels of remarkable quality, but they have been little recognized outside Colombia. Both knew the history of Colombian literature quite well. This kind of conversation is typical in nations such as Colombia, Argentina, and Chile, where literary culture is taken relatively seriously, but the opportunities for professional success are relatively limited.

suspicious of academics as people and of academic scholarship, particularly when it is of a theoretical nature. There are several reasons for his long-standing aloofness from things academic. First, when García Márquez burst on to the literary scene in the 1960s, very few Colombian scholars or critics (besides Germán Vargas and Ernesto Volkening) were trained to read modern literature, and their response to García Márquez's early production was often ill-conceived. Additionally, very few foreign critics (whether in Europe, the United States, or other parts of Latin America) were sufficiently informed about the writer and his nation to suggest reasonably sound readings. Exceptions to this generalization were critics and writers such as Ángel Rama, Emir Rodríguez Monegal, Mario Vargas Llosa, and Carlos Fuentes, but so much of the massive initial explosion of critical work on García Márquez was ill-informed or ill-conceived, and García Márquez was entirely justified in distancing himself from it. In addition, he was not himself the product of a university: he became a world-class writer despite his two years of law studies, not because of them.

The second time that I met with García Márquez was with Germán Vargas in Cartagena in May 1984. I flew from the U.S. to Barranquilla, where Germán and I met, and from there we travelled to Cartagena to see García Márquez with a specific mission in mind: to invite the writer to two academic conferences I was organizing at the time. One was to be in Colombia (in the town of Rionegro in the Department of Antioquia) and the other was scheduled for the following year in the United States, at Washington University in St Louis, where I was on the faculty. When we arrived in Cartagena, we went to a condominium building in the Bocagrande section, outside the colonial walls of the city. This modern building, called La Máquina de Escribir, was where García Márquez was residing temporarily in the condo of his good friend the painter Alejandro Obregón. It was an ideal location to finish writing *El amor*. His wife Mercedes arrived, and the four of us went to a nearby small, informal seafood restaurant with outdoor seating. We dined amidst the palm trees in the sultry Caribbean air. Nothing significant transpired at this gathering: García Márquez showed some interest in the two conferences without really committing himself to attend them, but also without discounting the possibility that he might participate. We also chatted informally about the usual subjects, such as Faulkner, but without anything being said that had not already been stated in published interviews. Mercedes was very reserved and said virtually nothing.

Many critics have commented on the special role of women in García Márquez's work. In general, his women tend to be more wise and powerful than their men. In García Márquez's life, he has purposely surrounded himself with women, and his staff, many of whom work in part of his house, are all women. Why this confidence in women? I believe men have been the source of his childhood trauma and women to have been the healers. He was abandoned by his father and reared by his grandparents, but the adults who had the most impact on him were women: his grandmother and his aunts. When he was in Barranquilla, working as a journalist and writing his first novel, he lived with women in a bordello. He has shared some anecdotes about his experiences with these prostitutes. One of them actually was writing about her own experience as a sex worker. When García Márquez was living in poverty in Paris in the mid-1950s, he eventually found himself unable to pay the rent, and struggling to survive economically while at the same time struggling with his early fiction. It was a kind and sympathetic woman at the hotel, probably the manager, who allowed him to stay in the hotel without ever having to pay his bill, and so facilitated the writing of *Los funerales*. The writing of *Cien años* was facilitated by another woman, his wife Mercedes, who found ways to manage the family budget while her seemingly crazed husband pounded away at his typewriter.

After the success and the celebrity associated with *Cien años*, García Márquez attempted to stay away from the public spotlight and did much of his research for his next novel, *El otoño*, while traveling with Mercedes throughout the Caribbean.

After the initial trauma of abandonment by his father, the next major trauma in his life was a letter written by a very prominent literary critic, Guillermo de Torre, rejecting his first novel. These two men, together with the dictator figures in Colombia and Latin America of the 1950s, have made García Márquez more of a comfortable ally and friend of women than of men.

That same summer of 1984, I was in Colombia for the months of May and June, and even though García Márquez did not attend the academic conference that I organized in Rionegro (the First Annual Meeting of North American Colombianists), the conference did draw national attention by virtue of the participation of several writers and the President of Colombia, Belisario Betancur. After the conference, in late June, Vargas and I returned to Cartagena. This time we went to dinner with García Márquez and Mercedes at his favorite restaurant, a small and unpretentious seafood establishment called El Calderito. With a successful conference in Colombia attended by many Colombians, we talked a little more about the coming conference in the United States, but nothing of significance was discussed at that dinner. Nevertheless, it was memorable for me because it was there that I saw García Márquez in his true social form, seeing the world and speaking exactly the way he writes. In the back part of El Calderito, where we were sitting around our table, there was a simple, amateurish painting that included a rooster, but in an odd location (I do not remember the exact location of the rooster). García Márquez pointed out the anomaly of the dislocated rooster soon after we sat down, and he was so fascinated by the painting that he mentioned it several more times during the dinner. By the end of the dinner, he had invented a phrase for a piece of fiction to describe the rooster and was offering up ideas about what might be done with this phrase in a piece of fiction (I cannot remember if he was thinking of the fiction he was currently writing or was thinking of writing a new piece of fiction with this rooster, but I believe he was not specific about exactly where he might use the rooster). Here was classic García Márquez doing exactly what he claimed was his creative process: taking something relatively mundane from his everyday life and creating a special effect around it. At dinner, he was struggling to figure out exactly what might be done with this bizarre image. He had other reactions and words at the dinner (particularly concerning a *lebranche*, a local Caribbean fish that was served to him). These reactions and words can only be described as 'classic' García Márquez for those who have read many of his books.

With the exception of two other substantive conversations, most of our meetings were like being in El Calderito: they were an opportunity to watch García Márquez seeing and speaking of the world in the way he often does in his writing, with the same unhesitant self-assuredness and brilliant simplicity of his grandmother (or the Úrsula figure of the Macondo cycle).

'I am not inclined to theorizing. I do not want to turn any of my experiences into theory and I also read very little literary theory', García Márquez stated in an interview in 1985.[10] He thinks in different ways from his contemporaries Cortázar, Fuentes, and Vargas Llosa. Cortázar's *Rayuela* presented a theoretical model for a new, postmodern-type fiction, and García Márquez has never written a theoretical novel comparable to this or similar to Borges's theorizing story/essay 'Pierre Menard, autor del *Quijote*'. Fuentes has written several theoretical reflections on fiction that have been informed by literary theory, such as *Terra nostra* and *Cervantes o la crítica de la lectura* (*Cervantes or the critique of reading*, 1976). Fuentes's book *La nueva*

---

[10] Marlise Simons, 'Love and Age: A Talk with García Márquez', in *Conversations with Gabriel García Márquez*, ed. Gene H. Bell-Villada, 141–47 (143); reprinted from *The New York Times Book Review*, 7 April 1985, 1, 18–19.

*narrativa hispanoamericana* was not only his introduction to the new novel in Latin America, but also his theory about how to read it. Vargas Llosa's *Gabriel García Márquez: Historia de un deicidio* and his book *La orgía perpetua: Flaubert y Madame Bovary*, are, like other essays, theories about reading and writing fiction. This type of abstract thinking and reflection has never interested García Márquez. His thinking is a response to individual and collective reactions to social circumstances, and he conceptualizes these matters anecdotally. The anecdotes are generated by visual images, and often structured around visual images.

The most substantive of our conversations since the initial meeting in the Hilton Hotel in 1975 took place in Mexico City and Cartagena, respectively. In 1987, I was in Colombia for several months with a Fulbright Grant when I was approached by the then editor of the journal *PMLA*, the late John Kronik, requesting assistance in recruiting García Márquez to write a lead article for *PMLA*. The journal was experimenting with a new format of beginning each issue with an essay by a creative writer, rather than the traditional scholarly article. From Colombia, I made arrangements through Germán Vargas to meet with García Márquez in Mexico City as part of a trip I had already planned. In our meeting at his home in the Calle del Fuego in the Pedregal area of Mexico City, he quickly discarded the possibility of writing anything for *PMLA* on the basis that it would represent too much of an interruption to his work.[11] He then went over to a nearby bookshelf and picked up a large coffee table book with old drawings, leafed through it, and explained that critics often got it wrong when they discussed his books because they were unaware of these drawings, which were the basis for many of the scenes in his novels. He offered the possibility of my interviewing him about these drawings for the piece that *PMLA* needed. We agreed that the *PMLA* contribution would, consequently, not be a piece by him but rather one by me, based on an interview with him (all in all, my work and interruption, not his). The editorial board of *PMLA* soon agreed in principle that it was very interested in the piece and would publish it if it passed the proper review.

Two months later I was back in García Márquez's home in Pedregal, tape recorder and the same book of nineteenth-century French drawings in hand. We spoke for well over an hour about the drawings. This was our most

---

[11] During this conversation about the requested article for *PMLA*, it was evident that García Márquez was well aware of the implications of his Nobel Laureate status. He told me that he could not write the piece unless he spent enough time on it to maintain his reputation, and that to do so would represent too much of an interruption.

substantive conversation; the translated and edited version of this dialogue appeared in print a few months later in *PMLA*.

One of my most stimulating and exciting conversations with García Márquez was one in which I was really an eavesdropper, not a direct interlocutor. It came about as an instance of serendipity with no effort on my part, but the fact that this conversation happened and that I was there to hear it had much to do with the brilliance and generosity of Carlos Fuentes. I happened to be in the final stages of a book on Fuentes and wanted to add an appendix consisting of an interview with the Mexican writer. Fuentes suggested we meet not in his home in Mexico City for this interview as originally planned but in Cartagena during the International Film Festival. The President of the International Film Festival was García Márquez and the invitees included the German film director Werner Herzog and the American writer William Styron.

On the first night of the festival, I sat in the lobby of the Hotel Caribe with García Márquez, exchanging small talk, now for the first time as if we were old friends, and he seemed more relaxed around me than he had ever been before. We were waiting for the other guests to join us for the trip over to the colonial city and the opening ceremonies of the film festival. After the ceremonies and the première of a Cuban film, we went to dinner inside the walls of the old colonial city, the setting for *El amor*. We went up to the second floor of the restaurant, García Márquez and Fuentes leading the way, accompanied by William Styron and two film people whose names I do not recall.

Fuentes immediately took control of the dinner discussion, posing two questions that would be the central topics for over an hour: what is the best novel you have ever read? and what is the one novel you wish you had written? The three writers, leisurely yet enthusiastically, joined in the debate of the pros and cons of different candidates. I do not remember the complete lists of novels discussed at that dinner, and I did not want to interrupt by taking out a notebook and pen. (But, after the discussion was over, while eating, I did discreetly jot down a few notes on a napkin while listening to Styron, who was sitting across from me and showing far more interest in cigars than novels.) For Fuentes, I remember, the matter of the best novel he had read revolved around discussions of *Don Quijote* and several novels by Faulkner. I believe Fuentes maintained that he would like to have written *Don Quijote* or one of Faulkner's novels. But when it came to the question of what novel García Márquez would like to have written, his response caught us by surprise with a novel not yet mentioned: Rulfo's *Pedro Páramo*.

In retrospect, García Márquez's choice of *Pedro Páramo* as the novel he wished he had written should not have been a surprise at all. This was exactly the kind of novel – minimalist, brief, and with mythological overtones – that García Márquez desired to write from the outset in the 1950s, and his first successful attempts at this type of work were *El coronel* and *La mala hora*. He also employed that same minimalist approach in the early story 'Un día de éstos'. After completing a very different kind of piece of work with *Cien años*, several of García Márquez's later works contain some of the elements he found so admirable in *Pedro Páramo*: *El otoño* has the quality of a stylistic tour de force; *Crónica* is brief and minimalist. García Márquez never did write, however, his own fully developed *Pedro Páramo*: no book of great depth (with mythological overtones) using a minimalist style to construct a brief story.

'I think ageing has made me realize that feelings and sentiments, what happens in the heart, are ultimately the most important', García Márquez said in an interview as he was approaching sixty years of age.[12] By then he had published *El amor*, his story of ageing and matters of the heart, and was also beginning to speculate that all of his books were really about love. This way of thinking distinguishes García Márquez clearly from writers who write theoretical speculations about culture and history (such as Fuentes and Carpentier), writers who speculate about theory and fiction in their novels (Cortázar and Sarduy), and writers who fictionalize human beings motivated mostly by impulses other than love (Vargas Llosa and Onettti). From the earliest books, García Márquez has told stories about humans either in love or suffering the solitude that is the absence of love.

In the early years, well before reaching the kind of wisdom that might be associated with García Márquez in his sixties, he thought of solitude as a lack of solidarity. On closer analysis, and with the maturity of his more advanced years, he has sounded progressively less like a neo-Marxist and more heart-oriented in his understanding of human beings as individuals and as social beings. The protagonist of *El otoño* suffers deeply from solitude, but this solitude is occasioned not by a lack of solidarity but by the absence of love. García Márquez is a political writer, but his primary work has been portraying the real human dimension – the hearts and bodies of individual human beings – of their social, economic and political circumstances.

---

[12] Marlise Simons, 'García Márquez on Love, Plagues and Politics', in *Conversations*, ed. Bell-Villada, 154–63 (155); reprinted from *The New York Times Book Review*, 21 February 1988, 1, 23–25.

The most intriguing adventure related to conversations with García Márquez was my meeting with him in Mexico City in the mid-1990s. The faculty and administration at the University of Chicago were at odds; the administrative leadership wanted to use the graduation ceremonies to honor the then Secretary of State with an annual award, but the faculty was in favor of honoring a quite different kind of figure: someone in opposition to that Secretary of State, someone like García Márquez. Professor John Coatsworth (then at the University of Chicago) contacted me with the following suggestion: if García Márquez were willing to appear at the University of Chicago in person to receive the award, President Hannah Gray would agree to give the award to the Nobel Laureate. Intrigued by the situation in Chicago, and figuring that García Márquez would also be at least intrigued (and perhaps willing to go), I called his home in Mexico City and asked to meet him there, and he agreed. I arrived Mexico City on a Saturday afternoon, and called him from the Hotel María Cristina near the Zona Rosa. He asked me if they served good *chilaquiles* (tortilla triangles with *mole*) at the Hotel María Cristina. I replied that I loved the *chilaquiles* at this hotel, and they had passed the palate test of José Emilio Pacheco, who had eaten breakfast there with great enthusiasm. In his typically self-assured manner, García Márquez did not hesitate to indicate that he would meet me at the Hotel María Cristina on Sunday morning for breakfast. That Sunday morning, as we devoured *chilaquiles*, I discovered that my intuition had been correct: García Márquez was indeed intrigued with the dilemma in Chicago. He carefully placed his glasses on the middle of his nose and read the letter from the University of Chicago, striking a pose that I will always remember for its appearance of erudition.

That morning, he carefully, slowly, and patiently explained, more clearly than I had ever understood it, his real situation and political position with respect to the Department of State of the United States of America. The common misconception among the general public (and among many academics in the United States and Europe) was that the Department of State had prohibited him from entering the United States. In reality, he was traveling frequently to the United States, and had been going often to New York City. Since he was placed on an informal 'blacklist' in 1961 because of his work with Cuba's Prensa Latina, however, he was never able to receive the standard tourist visa, allowing the bearer to make multiple entrances and exits. All his trips to the United States, which included regular visits to New York and occasional brief stopovers at Robert Redford's ranch in Utah, were only possible because for each trip he went to the U.S. Embassy and was given a discrete single-entrance and single-exit short-term tourist visa. García Márquez found this process, required of him because he had been blacklisted, both humiliating and unacceptable. His political response to the problem was to make public statements about his unwillingness to accept invitations to give public lectures in the United States (where he had received literally hundreds of invitations, including two from me) because of the unacceptable status of his visas as a visitor to the United States. His message to me at the Hotel María Cristina was that, in order to be consistent with the political position that he had established on this matter, he would not be able to accept this otherwise interesting invitation from the University of Chicago. Despite his stance, he did receive an honorary doctorate from Columbia University in 1971, and during the Clinton years he did appear on the campuses of both Princeton University and Georgetown University. I do not consider the later visits as political contradictions, but simply as changes of heart.

At that breakfast, I had him sign some copies of his books for friends, and finally handed him my own 1970 edition of *Cien años* (purchased in Cali in 1971) which he signed 'Para Raymond, el perseguidor' ('To Raymond, the pursuer').

There is a widespread tendency to perceive the Latin American novel as a sort of magic realist theme-park.[13] García Márquez is cast as the theme-park's founder, even though the discussions around magic realism began in Latin America in the 1940s, and different representations of the concept were under construction in the 1940s and 1950s, and can even be found in the 1930s in novels such as *Don Goyo* (1933) by the Ecuadorian Demetrio Aguilera Malta. That perception of the Latin American novel as a magic realist theme-park was widely promoted by the writings of Isabel Allende, whose first novel *La casa de los espíritus* (*The House of the Spirits*, 1984) probably did as much as the work of García Márquez to foster it. With the fiction of García Márquez, Allende, and a handful of others, nevertheless, the perception was created. The patently intellectualized and theoretical approach to the urban and cosmopolitan experience of Latin America, as it appeared in the work of Cortázar, was never as widely read as the work of Allende. Allende's first novel appeared in print in the year that Cortázar died. That year, 1984, was a watershed for Latin American literature, which was on the point of finding magic realism becoming its international hallmark, and the Latin American writer as public intellectual on the international stage entered a slow process of decline, being buried alongside the tomb of Cortázar.

---

[13] See Eduardo González, 'A Condo of One's Own', *Modern Language Notes*, 112/v (1997), 944–57 (954), a review of Franco Moretti, *Modern Epic: The World System from Goethe to García Márquez*, tr. Quentin Hoare (London: Verso, 1996).

What Latin American literature has really been since the publication of *Cien años*, however, could not be more distant from this theme-park perception. In the 1970s, the first generalized reaction against the Boom and its supposed magic realism came in the group of post-Boom writers headed by novelists such as Antonio Skármeta, Ariel Dorfman, Luisa Valenzuela, Gustavo Sainz, and Gustavo Álvarez Gardeazábal. None of these post-Boom writers, nor any of the thirty or forty of their generation, was easy to associate with magic realism (although a few journalists and editors attempted to do so), and critics such as Donald Shaw have demonstrated that the interests of the post-Boom writers were indeed far from anything remotely like magic realism.[14]

In the 1980s, more experimental and theoretically oriented novelists than the post-Boom writers, working under the influence of Borges, Cortázar, Sarduy, and the international postmoderns, wrote against the Boom and the post-Boom. For Ricardo Piglia, Diamela Eltit, R. H. Moreno-Durán, and a host of others, magic realism was a simplistic reduction of Latin American literary culture and unrelated to their diverse political and aesthetic agendas.[15]

In the 1990s, a less experimental and sometimes more literarily innocent group of young writers appeared on the scene, the most visible of whom was the Chilean Alberto Fuguet. His international group of 'McOndo' writers appeared in a volume edited by Fuguet.[16] Apparently unaware of the two generations of writers that had preceded him, Fuguet decided it was his task to write non-magic realist literature. He declared in 2001, fifty-four years after the publication of *Cien años* and seventeen years after the publication of *La casa de los espíritus*, that 'magic realism reduces a much too complex situation and just makes it cute. Latin America is not cute.'[17] Fuguet's generation also includes better informed and more sophisticated novelists (none of whom write anything even vaguely resembling magic realism either), who are well aware of their predecessors. The Mexican David Toscana creates

[14] For an informed introduction to the post-Boom, see Donald Shaw, *Antonio Skármeta and the post Boom*, Puertas 88 (Hanover NH: Norte, 1994), and *The Post-boom in Spanish American Fiction*, Latin American and Iberian Thought and Culture (Albany NY: New York State University Press, 1998).

[15] I have offered an introductory overview of these postmodern writers in *The Postmodern Novel in Latin America: Politics, Culture, and the Crisis of Truth* (New York: St Martin's, 1995).

[16] Alberto Fuguet and Sergio Gómez edited an anthology of short fiction by selected writers of their generation in a volume titled *McOndo* (Barcelona: Grijalbo Mondadori, 1996).

[17] See Alberto Fuguet, 'Magical Neoliberalism', *Foreign Policy*, 125 (July–August 2001), 63–68 (68).

masterful stories as a follower of Vargas Llosa, and the Bolivian Edmundo
Paz Soldán is an equally gifted intellectual presence who has published a
wide-ranging set of fictions and essays. The late Chilean writer Roberto
Bolaño is beginning to gather a large following and his writing is much
closer to the work of Cortázar and Donoso than to anything related to magic
realism.

The next García Márquez? Of course, many of us would like to believe that
García Márquez is unique and that no other genius of exactly his ilk has
yet to publish a book, or perhaps ever will. Several critics and writers have
made claims for this or that novelist being the 'next García Márquez', begin-
ning with the 1970s post-Boom writers Luisa Valenzuela in Argentina, Ariel
Dorfman and Antonio Skármeta in Chile, and Reynaldo Arenas and Severo
Sarduy in Cuba, among others. Two writers whose book sales have been
comparable to García Márquez have been Isabel Allende and Laura Esquivel.
Accomplished experimentalists with relatively little North American and
European readership outside academia are Ricardo Piglia and Diamela Eltit.
Young and more recent writers who have received critical acclaim in Latin
America, Europe, and the United States are the Mexicans David Toscana,
Jorge Volpi, Cristina Rivera Garza, and Carmen Boullosa, as well as the
Chilean who has promoted the McOndo group, Alberto Fuguet. Of these,
Carlos Fuentes has claimed that Cristina Rivera Garza is the best and most
talented novelist in Mexico today. García Márquez's compatriots Alvaro
Mutis, Fernando Vallejo, and Héctor Abad Facciolince have enjoyed well-
deserved critical acclaim, albeit on a scale not comparable to his.

   Among all these potential 'next García Márquez' figures, however, the
only one to catch the fancy of a widespread readership of writers and critics
on a scale comparable to García Márquez in the 1970s and 1980s is Roberto
Bolaño. His monumental novel *2666* (2003), like Borges's *Ficciones* and
García Márquez's *One Hundred Years*, is a significant reaffirmation of the
right of invention in Latin America and a reaffirmation of the viability of
literature in a world increasingly dominated by media and other non-literary
forms of expression.

Paradoxically, given the fact that García Márquez and others have viewed my
three decades of intermittent work on García Márquez as a sign that I have
indeed 'pursued' him, my experience of his work and circumstances is quite
the opposite. In 1970, as an undergraduate student pursuing a cultural adventure, I traveled by land from Concepción, in Chile, to Tacoma, Washington,
returning from a year's study at the University of Concepción. In Chile, and

along the way through Peru and Ecuador, I had heard anecdotally that García Márquez had published a very interesting novel entitled *Cien años de soledad*, and I intended to purchase it as soon as possible. Upon arriving in Cali in Colombia on a third-class bus, I walked with some fellow travelers to the Parque Caycedo (the central plaza of the city) and found a copy of *Cien años* at a bookstore, the Librería Nacional. I carried that book, the same copy that García Márquez signed over two decades later, to my hometown of Tacoma, Washington, and eventually read it in one weekend during the Thanksgiving holiday of 1971. The book was gripping, entertaining, and impossible to put down. My main interests at that time (my senior year as an undergraduate at Washington State University), however, were not the writings of García Márquez but the work of other novelists of the Boom, in this order: Julio Cortázar, Mario Vargas Llosa, and Carlos Fuentes. I had read *Cien años* over a weekend as entertainment, but I read Cortázar and Vargas Llosa obsessively under the mentorship of the German translator of Vargas Llosa and Cortázar at that time, the late Professor Wolfgang A. Luchting. (These readings were supplemented with heavy doses of Marcuse and other neo-Marxist thinkers in vogue in the early 1970s.) Paradoxically, when I reached the end of my senior year in the university's Honors Program, and presented myself for examination, the one question upon which I was required to write had nothing to do with my real intellectual interests at the time (Cortázar, Vargas Llosa, and theory), but García Márquez's *Cien años*. I wrote the exam on *Cien años*; this was the first time that the book seemed to pursue me.

My real intention, as I approached the advanced stages of my doctoral studies, was to write a dissertation on some aspect of the fiction of Vargas Llosa, preferably with *Conversación en la catedral* as the centerpiece (eventually, I did publish studies on Vargas Llosa). Coincidentally, however, my mentor at the time, Professor John S. Brushwood, returned from Colombia in 1974 with information about new young writers appearing in Colombia since the publication of *Cien años*. Brushwood had me setting aside Cortázar and Vargas Llosa once again. Instead, I began reading the likes of Héctor Rojas Herazo, Álvaro Cepeda Samudio, Gustavo Álvarez Gardeazábal, Albalucía Ángel, and Fanny Buitrago. These readings and a seminar Brushwood taught eventually led me to a dissertation not on Vargas Llosa, but on the Colombian novel from 1968 to 1975; it was an opportunity to take a careful look at a very specific set of novels written during a well defined, narrow, timespan. As it turned out, this post-García Márquez study also led me directly to García Márquez, for *Cien años* was the obligatory background to everything being written in Colombia at the time, and *El otoño* was the landmark novel of the year 1975 which closed the period that I was studying.

These anecdotes, as well as several coincidences in my subsequent professional career, make it clear, at least to me, that García Márquez's work has pursued me, rather than my having pursued it or him. I consider this worth noting in this epilogue primarily because, when compared with other modern and postmodern Latin American writers, García Márquez has always seemed to be one of the most entertaining and engaging to read, but the least inviting to engage critically, to write about. Alicia Borinsky has argued this point in her chapter on García Márquez in her *Theoretical Fables*.[18] The terrain of Cortázar, Vargas Llosa, and Fuentes, along with a host of other writers who followed them, are the academic's utopia, for their work is a self-conscious dialogue with the criticism and theory that have been at the center of most academic critical writing over the past three decades. García Márquez, on the other hand, warns us against the excesses of symbolic interpretation (correctly, I think), and offers little or no strictly theoretical speculation in his work. Paradoxically, I have found his work pursuing me and encouraging me to explain to others that the interpretative enterprise, as it applies to García Márquez at least, is not the typical interpretative process at all. The reader is well advised to proceed with caution.

[18] Alicia Borinsky, *Theoretical Fables: The Pedagogical Dream in Contemporary Latin American Fiction*, Penn Studies in Contemporary American Fiction (Philadelphia PA: University of Pennsylvania Press, 1993).

# GUIDE TO FURTHER READING

The non-specialist as well as the scholar of Latin American literature can easily locate and obtain a vast array of readings on the writing of García Márquez. For the general reader, two early interviews by informed interlocutors appear in the books *Into the Mainstream* by Luis Harss (1967) and *Seven Voices: Seven Latin American Writers Talk* by Rita Gilbert (1973). Both contain valuable interviews with García Márquez's Latin American contemporaries, as well as with the author himself. For a more complete set of many of the most insightful interviews with García Márquez, see the compilation edited by Gene Bell-Villada under the title *Conversations with Gabriel García Márquez* (2006). This contains translations into English of many of the most-cited and revealing interviews with the writer dating back to the early years of his career. In 1982, García Márquez published a lengthy conversation with Plinio Apuleyo Mendoza under the title *El olor de la guayaba: conversaciones con Plinio Apuleyo Mendoza* (translated as *The Fragrance of the Guava*). I have co-authored a book with Kevin Guerrieri, *Culture and Customs of Colombia* (1999), that offers a general introduction to the nation, including a chapter on García Márquez. In addition to these highly accessible books, García Márquez's autobiography, *Vivir para contarla* (*Living to Tell the Tale*, 2003), provides much insight for the non-specialist. In this first of two volumes (the second has yet to appear), García Márquez tells the story of his childhood and formative years; of, that is, the period before the publication of *Cien años*.

Full-length books on García Márquez range from the introductory to the specialized. Among the former, Gene Bell-Villada's *García Márquez: The Man and his Work* (1990) is among the more useful. Before Bell-Villada's overview, were Kathleen McNerny's *Understanding Gabriel García Márquez* (1989), Stephen Minta's *Gabriel García Márquez: Writer of Colombia* (1987), and George McMurray's *Gabriel García Márquez* (1987). A pioneer book that is still useful is Mario Vargas Llosa's *Gabriel García Márquez: historia de un deicidio* (1970). Isabel Rodríguez-Vergara studies satire in four novels after *Cien años* in *El mundo satírico de Gabriel García Márquez* (1991). A very well informed scholar with personal access to García Márquez, Gerald Martin, has written an exhaustive and lengthy biography, *Gabriel García Márquez: A Life* (2008). Martin's volume could well be considered the ideal complement to this one. He emphasizes the importance of the childhood home as the catalyst for the author's later writing.

Several compilations of studies on most of García Márquez's work provide convenient access to a variety of critical voices. One of the early volumes of this genre was Pedro Lastra's *Nueve asedios a García Márquez* (1969). Peter Earle compiled another of the early volumes to include the works published after *Cien años*, *García Márquez: el escritor y la crítica* (1981). This valuable set of short articles includes an early piece originally published in Colombia in 1963 by the Colombian critic Ernesto Volkening on the early fiction of the Macondo cycle, *Los funerales* and *El coronel*, as well as early commentaries by Ángel Rama, Pedro Lastra, and Emmanuel Carballo. It also includes the article Carlos Fuentes had written for *Mundo Nuevo* in 1967 immediately before the publication of *Cien años* and influential essays by José Miguel Oviedo and Julio Ortega. Bernard McGuirk and Richard Cardwell edited a volume titled *Gabriel García Márquez: New Readings* (1987), which offers incisive analyses of the author's work from the early stories to *El amor* in 1985, and includes scholars such as Carlos Alonso, Robin Fiddian, Aníbal González, Eduardo González, and Gerald Martin. At the end of this book is a translation of García Márquez's 1982 Nobel Prize address, a seminal piece of writing. George McMurray's volume *Critical Essays on Gabriel García Márquez* (1987) contains, as the title suggests, literary essays rather than strictly academic articles, covering the early work of García Márquez through to *El otoño*. Julio Ortega's volume, *Gabriel García Márquez and the Powers of Fiction*, contains five insightful pieces, followed. once again, by a translation of García Márquez's Nobel address. Ortega opens the volume with an article on the exchange system in *Cien años*, and the other essays are by Ricardo Gutiérrez Mouat, Michael Palencia-Roth, Aníbal González, and Gonzalo Díaz-Migoyo. In 1985, the *Latin American Literary Review* published a special issue on García Márquez, edited by Yvette Miller and Charles Rossman, that includes twelve valuable essays written in English by the scholars Vera M. Kutzinksi, Lois Parkinson Zamora, and Patricia Tobin, among others, as well as five 'meditations' by writers such as John Updike and Alastair Reed. Harold Bloom is the editor of a recent volume titled *Gabriel García Márquez* (2007) which contains a collection of some of the most high-quality scholarly writing on García Márquez to appear over the past three decades, including the early interview by Rita Guibert and essays by Gene Bell-Villada, Harley D. Oberhelman, Stephen Hart, Steven Boldy, Isabel Álvarez-Borland, and Robin Fiddian, among others.

Scholarly books that focus on particular works have been appearing since the early 1970s. In *El espejo hablado* (1975), Suzanne Jill Levine pioneered research on the literary sources of *Cien años*. Many of these early books are out of print, but are readily available in university libraries. In her book *Cien años de soledad: una interpretación* (1972), Josefina Ludmer offers one of the best early interpretative readings of the writer's masterpiece, and, in his *García Márquez: 'One Hundred Years of Solitude'* (1990), Michael Wood offers his own unique reading of the novel. For the teaching of *Cien años*, the best complement to the current study might well be *Approaches to Teaching García Márquez's 'One Hundred Years of Solitude'* (1990) edited by María Elena de Valdés and Mario J. Valdés, with an introduction by María Elena de Valdés and twelve contributions on 'course contexts' and 'interpretative approaches for the classroom'. The contributors include such renowned scholars as Isabel Álvarez-Borland, Walter Mignolo, and Lois Parkinson Zamora. Of the books dedicated to single books by García Márquez, two additional studies deserve mention: Robin Fiddian's *García Márquez: 'Los funerales de la mamá grande'* (2006) and J. B. H. Box's *García Márquez's 'El coronel no tiene quién le escriba'* (1984).

Specialized books with incisive and theoretically nuanced chapters that involve the fiction of García Márquez include Alicia Borinsky's *Theoretical Fables: The Pedagogical Dream in Contemporary Latin American Literature* (1993) and Roberto González Echevarría's *The Voice of the Masters: Writing and Authority in Modern Latin American Literature* (1985), as well as his *Myth and Archive: A Theory of Latin American Literature* (1990).

Studies of topics related to Latin American literature and including general studies on specific issues or themes related to García Márquez's work, include Gerald Martin's *Through the Labyrinth: Latin American Fiction in the Twentieth Century* (1989), John S. Brushwood's *The Spanish American Novel* (1975), Jean Franco's *An Introduction to Spanish American Literature* (1969), and Naomi Lindstrom's *The Social Conscience of Latin American Writing* (1998). These were all written with an understanding of the historical and political contexts of Latin America. My own *The Twentieth-century Spanish American Novel* (2003) is a more recent synthesis of some of the information offered in these studies. García Márquez's work can be found in discussions of broad literary and cultural contexts in these works.

Discussions have continued on the topic of magic realism. Stephen M. Hart and Wen-Chin Oouyang have compiled a volume of essays, *A Companion to Magical Realism*, assessing the movement often associated primarily with

García Márquez, but which, as these authors demonstrate, began in Germany, seemingly flourished in Latin America, and then spread to the rest of the world. Among the authors considered in this volume are García Márquez, Miguel Ángel Asturias, Isabel Allende, and Salman Rushdie. The quotations are translated into English and the style is jargon-free. The co-authors provide a broad introduction that contextualizes magical realism in discussions of globalization, the new politics of aesthetics, and the fantastic. Lois Parkinson Zamora and Wendy B. Faris have also edited a massive volume of studies on this matter under the title *Magical Realism: Theory, History, Community* (1995). As well as an introduction, the editors offer twenty-three essays on 'Foundations', 'Theory', 'History', and 'Community'. A broad range of disciplines is represented.

# SELECT BIBLIOGRAPHY

## Fiction

*La hojarasca.* Bogotá: Sipa, 1955; Buenos Aires: Sudamericana, 1969 etc. Tr. Gregory Rabassa, in *Leaf storm and Other Stories*, New York: Harper & Row, 1972; London: Cape, 1972; New York: Avon, 1973.

*El coronel no tiene quién le escriba.* Medellín: Aguirre, 1958; Buenos Aires: Sudamericana, 1969 etc. Tr. J.S. Bernstein, as *No One Writes to the Colonel and Other Stories*, New York: Harper & Row, 1968; London: Cape, 1971; Harmondsworth: Penguin, 1974.

*Los funerales de la mamá grande.* Xalapa: Universidad Veracruzana, 1962 (repr. Bogotá: La Oveja Negra, 1982); Buenos Aires: Sudamericana, 1967 etc. Tr. J.S. Bernstein, as *Big Mama's Funeral,* in *No One Writes to the Colonel and Other Stories*, New York: Harper & Row, 1968; London: Cape, 1971; Harmondsworth: Penguin, 1974.

*La mala hora.* Mexico City: Era, 1966 (An earlier edition, Madrid: Luis Pérez, 1962, is repudiated by the author); Buenos Aires: Sudamericana, 1967 etc. Tr. Gregory Rabassa, as *In Evil Hour.* New York: Harper & Row, 1979.

*Isabel viendo llover en Macondo.* Buenos Aires: Estuario, 1967 (subsequently included in *Ojos de perro azul*, below).

*Cien años de soledad.* Buenos Aires: Sudamericana, 1967 etc. Tr. Gregory Rabassa, as *One Hundred Years of Solitude*, New York: Harper & Row, 1970; London: Cape, 1970; Harmondsworth: Penguin, 1972.

*Relato de un náufrago . . .* Barcelona: Tusquets, 1970. Tr. Randolph Hogan, as *The Story of a Shipwrecked Sailor*, New York: Knopf, 1986.

*La increíble y triste historia de la cándida Eréndira y de su abuela desalmada.* Barcelona: Barral, 1972; Buenos Aires: Sudamericana, 1972 etc. The title story tr. Gregory Rabassa, together with two other pieces, *Death Constant Beyond Love* and *The Sea of the Lost Time*, in *The Incredible and Sad Tale of Innocent Eréndira and Her Heartless Grandmother, Innocent Eréndira and Other Stories,* London: Cape, 1977; New York: Harper & Row, 1978. The rest are included in *Leaf storm and Other Stories*, tr. Gregory Rabassa, New York: Harper & Row, 1972.

*Ojos de perro azul.* Rosario: Esquiseditorial, 1972; Buenos Aires: Sudamericana, 1975 etc. (tr. Gregory Rabassa, in *Innocent Eréndira and Other Stories,* New York: Harper & Row, 1978).

*El negro que hizo esperar a los ángeles.* Rosario: Alfil, 1972. (Many of the same stories as *Ojos de perro azul*, above).

*El otoño del patriarca*. Barcelona: Plaza & Janes, 1975; Buenos Aires: Sudamericana, 1975 etc. Tr. Gregory Rabassa, as *The Autumn of the Patriach*, New York: Harper & Row, 1976; London: Cape, 1977.

*Crónica de una muerte anunciada*. Bogotá: La Oveja Negra, 1981; Buenos Aires: Sudamericana, 1981 etc. Tr. Gregory Rabassa, as *Chronicle of a Death Foretold*, New York: Harper & Row, 1982; London: Cape, 1982; New York: Knopf, 1983.

*El rastro de tu sangre en la nieve; El verano feliz de la Señora Forbes*. Bogotá: Dampier, 1982.

*Collected Stories*, tr. J.S. Bernstein and Gregory Rabassa (gathering together the three previous English-language collections), New York: Harper & Row, 1984.

*El amor en los tiempos del cólera*. Bogotá: Oveja Negra, 1985; Buenos Aires: Sudamericana, 1985. Tr. Edith Grossman, as *Love in the Time of Cholera*, New York: Knopf, 1988.

*La aventura de Miguel Littín, clandestino en Chile*. Buenos Aires: Sudamericana, 1986. Tr. Asa Zatz, as *Clandestine in Chile: The Adventures of Miguel Littin*, New York: Holt, 1987.

*El general en su laberinto*. Buenos Aires: Sudamericana, 1989. Tr. Edith Grossman, as *The General in his Labyrinth*, New York: Knopf, 1990.

*Doce cuentos peregrinos*. Buenos Aires: Sudamericana, 1992. Tr. Edith Grossman, as *Strange Pilgrims: Twelve Stories*, New York: Knopf, 1993.

*Diatriba del amor contra un hombre sentado*. Barcelona: Grijalbo Mondadori, 1994. A one-act monologue, untranslated.

*Del amor y otros demonios*. Buenos Aires: Sudamericana, 1994. Tr. Edith Grossman, as *Of Love and Other Demons*, New York: Knopf, 1995.

*Noticia de un secuestro*. Buenos Aires: Sudamericana, 1996. Tr. Edith Grossman, as *News of a Kidnapping*, New York: Knopf, 1997.

*Memorias de mis putas tristes*. Buenos Aires: Sudamericana, 2004. Tr. Edith Grossman, as *Memories of My Melancholy Whores*, New York: Knopf, 2004.

## Essays and journalism

*Cuando era feliz e indocumentado*. Caracas: El Ojo del Camello, 1973; Bogotá: Oveja Negra, 1979. Untranslated.

*Vivir para contarla*. Bogota: Norma, 2002; Barcelona: Mondadori, 2002. Tr. Edith Grossman, as *Living to Tell the Tale*, New York: Knopf, 2003.

'Prologue', in *Strange Pilgrims* (above), vii–xiii.

'The Solitude of Latin America' (1982 Nobel Prize acceptance speech), *Granta* 9 (1983), 56–60. Tr. Marina Castañeda in Ortega and Elliott, *Gabriel García Márquez*, 88–91; and, tr. Richard Cardwell, in McGuirk and Cardwell, *Gabriel García Márquez*, 207–11.

## Interviews

Bell-Villada, Gene H. (ed.). *Conversations with Gabriel García Márquez* (Jackson MS: University of Mississippi Press, 2006).

Dreifus, Claudia. '*Playboy* Interview: Gabriel García Márquez', in Bell-Villada, *Conversations*, 93–132. Repr. from *Playboy* (February 1983), 65–77, 172–78.

García Márquez, Gabriel & Plinio Apuleyo Mendoza. *Conversaciones con Plinio Apuleyo Mendoza: el olor de la guayaba*. Bogotá: La Oveja Negra, 1982. Tr. Ann Wright, as *The Fragrance of the Guava*, London: Verso, 1983.

Gass, William H. Review of *Chronicle of a Death Foretold*, New York, 11 April 1983, 83.

Guibert, Rita. 'Gabriel García Márquez', tr. F. Partridge, in *Seven Voices: Seven Latin American Writers Talk to Rita Guibert*, New York: Knopf, 1973, 303–37.

González Bermejo, Ernesto. 'And Now, Two Hundred Years of Solitude', tr. Gene H. Bell-Villada, in Bell-Villada, *Conversations*, 3–30. Interview originally published in *Triunfo* (Madrid), 25/cdxli (1971), 12–18; repr. in González Bermejo, *Cosas de esritores,* Montevideo: Biblioteca de Marcha, 1971, 11–51; and in Rentería Mantilla, *García Márquez*, 49–64.

*Manifiesto*. Tr. Gene H. Bell-Villada, as *Journey Back to the Source*, in Bell-Villada, *Conversations*, 79–92. Interview originally published in *El Manifiesto* (Bogotá) in 1977; repr. in Rentería Mantilla, *García Márquez*, 159–67.

Simons, Marlise. 'Love and Age: A Talk with García Márquez', in Bell-Villada, *Conversations*, 141–47. Originally published in *The New York Times Book Review*, 7 April 1985, 1, 18–19.

——. 'García Márquez on Love, Plague, and Politics', in Bell-Villada, *Conversations*, 154–63. Originally published in *The New York Times Book Review*, 21 February 1988, 1, 23–25.

Williams, Raymond L., 'The Visual Arts, the Poetization of Space and Writing: An Interview with Gabriel García Márquez', *Publications of the Modern Language Association of America*, 104/ii (1989), 131–40.

## Studies

Acevedo Latorre, Eduardo (ed.). *Fabulous Colombia's Geography: the New Grenade as Seen by Two French Travelers of the XIX Century, Charles Saffray and Édouard André*. Bogotá: ARCO, 1984.

Álvarez Borland, Isabel. 'From Mystery to Parody: (Re)reading of García Márquez's *Crónica de una muerte anunciada*', *Symposium*, 38 (1984–85), 278–86. Repr. in Bloom, *Gabriel García Márquez*, 219–27.

——. 'History, Myth, and Metafiction in *One Hundred Years of Solitude*', in Valdés and Valdés, *Approaches*, 89–96.

——. 'Interior Texts in *El amor en los tiempos del colera*', *Hispanic Review*, 58 (1991), 175–86.

——. 'The Task of the Historian in *El general en su laberinto*', *Hispania*, 76 (1993),192–99.

Bell-Villada, Gene. *García Márquez: The Man and his Work*. Chapel Hill NC: University of North Carolina Press, 1990.

Bloom, Harold (ed.). *Gabriel García Márquez*. New York: Chelsea House, 2007.

Borinsky, Alicia. *Theoretical Fables: The Pedagogical Dream in Contemporary Latin American Fiction*, Penn Studies in Contemporary American Fiction (Philadelphia PA: University of Pennsylvania Press, 1993).

Box, Ben. *García Márquez, El coronel no tiene quién le escriba*. Critical Guides to Spanish Texts 38. London: Grant & Cutler, 1984.

Brushwood, John S. *The Spanish American Novel: A Twentieth-century Survey*. London & Austin TX: University of Texas Press, 1975.

Carrillo, Germán Darío. *La narrativa de Gabriel García Márquez*. Ediciones de Arte y Bibliografía. Madrid: Castalia, 1975.

Connor, Steven. *Postmodernist Culture: An Introduction to the Theories of the Contemporary*. Oxford: Basil Blackwell, 1989; 2nd edn 1997.

Corwin, Jay. *La transposición de fuentes indígenas en 'Cien años de soledad'*. Romance Monographs 52. University MS: University of Mississippi Department of Modern Languages, 1997.

Curcio Altamar, Antonio. *Evolución de la novela en Colombia*. Biblioteca Básica Colombiana 8. Bogotá: Instituto Colombiano de Cultura, 1975.

Earle, Peter G. (ed.). *Gabriel García Márquez*. Persiles 129. Madrid: Taurus, 1981.

Estrada Villa, Armando. *El poder político en la novelística de García Márquez*. Bogotá: Universidad Pontificia Boliviariana, Escuela de Derecho y Ciencias Políticas, 2006.

Fals Borda, Orlando. *Historia doble de la costa*. 4 vols. Bogotá: Carlos Valencia, 1979–86.

Farías, Víctor. *Los manuscritos de Melquíades: 'Cien años de soledad', burguesía latinoamericana y dialéctica de la reproducción ampliada de negación*. Editionen der Iberoamerica III/5. Frankfurt am Main: Vervuert, 1981.

Fernández-Braso, Miguel. *La soledad de Gabriel García Márquez (una conversación infinita)*. Mosaico 8. Barcelona: Planeta, 1972.

Fiddian, Robin. 'A Prospective Post-script: Apropos of *Love in the Time of Cholera*', in McGuirk & Cardwell, *Gabriel García Márquez*, 91–205.

—— (ed.). *García Márquez*. Modern Literatures in Perspective. London : Longman, 1995.

—— . *García Márquez, Los funerales de la mamá grande*. Critical Guides to Spanish Texts 70. London: Grant & Cutler, 2006.

Fluharty, Vernon Lee. *Dance of the Millions: Military Rule and the Social Revolution in Colombia, 1930–1956*. Pittsburgh PA: University of Pittsburgh Press, 1957.

Foster, David William. *Studies in the Contemporary Spanish American Short Story*. Columbia MO & London: University of Missouri Press, 1979.

—— . 'The Double Inscription of the *narrataire* in *Los funerales de la mamá grande*'. in McMurray, *Critical* Essays, 102–12. Study previously published in Foster, *Studies*, 51–62.

Franco, Jean. *An Introduction to Spanish American Literature*. London: Cambridge University Press, 1969.

—— . *Critical Passions: Selected Essays*, ed. Mary Louise Pratt and Kathleen Newman. Durham NC & London: Duke University Press, 1999.

Fuentes, Carlos. *La nueva novela hispanoamericana*. Mexico City: Joaquín Mortiz, 1969.

Fuguet, Alberto. 'Magical Neoliberalism', *Foreign Policy*, 125 (July–August 2001), 63–68.

—— and Sergio Gómez (eds). *McOndo*. Barcelona: Grijalbo Mondadori, 1996.

García Márquez, Gabriel & Mario Vargas Llosa. *La novela en América Latina.* Lima: Diálogo, 1968.

García Usta, Jorge. *García Márquez en Cartagena: Sus inicios literarios.* Los Tres Mundos. Bogotá: Planeta Colombiana, 2007.

Gilard, Jacques. 'García Márquez, le Groupe de Barranquilla, et Faulkner', *Caravelle* 27 (1976), 123–46.

Gómez Ocampo, Gilberto. *Entre 'María' y 'La vorágine': La literatura colombiana finisecular (1886–1903).* Bogotá: Fondo Cultural Cafetero, 1988.

González, Aníbal. 'The Ends of the Text: Journalism in the Fiction of Gabriel García Márquez', in Ortega and Elliott, *Gabriel García* Márquez, 61–73.

——. 'Translation and Genealogy: *One Hundred Years of Solitude*', in McGuirk and Cardwell, *Gabriel García Márquez*, 65–79.

——. *Killer Books: Writing, Violence and Ethics in Modern Spanish American Narrative.* Austin TX & London: University of Texas Press, 2001.

González, Eduardo. 'A Condo of One's Own', *Modern Language Notes*, 112/v (1997), 944–57. Review of Franco Moretti, *Modern Epic: The World System from Goethe to García Márquez*, tr. Quentin Hoare (London: Verso, 1996).

González Echevarría, Roberto. *Alejo Carpentier: The Pilgrim at Home.* Ithaca NY: Cornell University Press, 1977. Reissued, with updated introduction and bibliography, Austin TX: Texas University Press, 1990.

——. *Myth and Archive: A Theory of Latin American Literature.* Cambridge & New York: Cambridge University Press, 1990.

——. '*One Hundred Years of Solitude*: The Novel as Myth and Archive', in Fiddian, *García Márquez*, 79–99. Repr. from *Modern Language Notes*, 99 (1984), 358–80.

Gullón, Ricardo. *García Márquez, o el olvidado arte de contar.* Madrid: Taurus, 1970.

Gutiérrez Mouat, Ricardo. 'The Economy of the Narrative Sign in *No One Writes to the Colonel* and *In Evil hour*', in Ortega and Elliott, *Gabriel García* Márquez, 17–33.

Harss, Luis and Barbara Dohmann. *Into the Mainstream: Conversations with Latin-American Writers.* New York: Harper & Row, 1967. Tr. of *Los nuestros.*

Hart, Stephen M. and Wen-chin Ouyang (eds). *A Companion to Magical Realism.* London: Tamesis, 2005.

Hood, Edward Waters. *La ficción de Gabriel García Márquez.* American University Studies: Romance Languages and Literature. New York: Peter Lang, 1993.

Hutcheon, Linda. *A Poetics of Postmodernism: History, Theory, Fiction.* New York: Routledge, 1988.

——. *The Politics of Postmodernism.* New York: Routledge, 1989.

Joset, Jacques. *Gabriel García Márquez, coetáneo de la eternidad.* Biblioteca Hispanoamericana y Española de Amsterdam. Amsterdam: Rodopi, 1984.

Kermode, Frank. 'Novel and Narrative', in Most and Stowe, *Poetics*, 175–96.

Kutzinski, Vera. 'The Logic of Wings: Gabriel García Márquez and Afro-American Literature', in Fiddian, *García Márquez*, 214–28. Repr. from *Latin American Literary Review*, 13 (1985), 133–46.

Labanyi, Jo. 'Language and Power in *The Autumn of the Patriarch*', in McGuirk and Cardwell, *Gabriel García Márquez*, 135–49.

Lastra, Pedro (ed.). *Nueve asedios a Gabriel García Márquez*. Letras de América 19. Santiago de Chile: Universitaria, 1969.

Lawal, Nike S., Matthew N. Sadiku and P. Adelumo Dopamu (eds). *Understanding Yoruba Life and Culture*. Trenton NJ: Africa World Press, 2004.

Levine, Suzanne Jill. *El espejo hablado: Un estudio de 'Cien años de soledad'*. Continente. Caracas: Monte Ávila, 1975.

Lindstrom, Naomi. *The Social Conscience of Latin American Writing*. Pan American Series. Austin TX: University of Texas Press, 1998.

———. *Twentieth-century Spanish American Fiction*. Pan American Series. Austin TX: University of Texas Press, 1994.

Little, Christopher. '*Eréndira* in the Middle Ages: The Medievalness of Gabriel García Márquez'. in Fiddian, *García Márquez*, 204–13.

Ludmer, Josefina. *Cien años de soledad: una interpretación*. Trabajo Crítico. Buenos Aires: Tiempo Contemporáneo, 1972.

Martin, Gerald. *Journeys through the Labryinth: Latin American Fiction in the Twentieth Century*. Critical Studies in Latin American Culture. London: Verso, 1989.

———. *Gabriel García Márquez: A Life*. New York: Knopf, 2009.

McGuirk, Bernard and Richard Cardwell (eds). *Gabriel García Márquez: New Readings*. Cambridge Iberian and Latin American Studies. Cambridge: Cambridge University Press, 1987.

McHale, Brian. *Postmodernist Fiction*. New York & London: Methuen, 1987.

McMurray, George R. (ed.). *Critical Essays on Gabriel García Márquez*. Critical Essays on World Literature. Boston MA: G.K. Hall, 1987.

———. *Gabriel García Márquez*. Modern Literature Monographs. New York: Frederick Ungar, 1987.

McNerney, Kathleen. *Understanding Gabriel García Márquez*. Understanding Contemporary European and Latin American Literature. Columbia SC: University of South Carolina Press, 1989.

Mena, Lucila Inés. *La función de la historia en 'Cien años de soledad'*. Barcelona: Plaza & Janés, 1979.

Menton, Seymour. *La novela colombiana: Planetas y satélites*. Crítica Literaria. Bogotá: Plaza & Janés, 1978.

Minta, Stephen. *Gabriel García Márquez: Writer of Colombia*. London: Cape, 1987.

Most, Glenn W. & William Stowe (eds). *The Poetics of Murder: Detective Fiction and Literary Theory*. San Diego CA: Harcourt Brace Jovanovich, 1983.

Nichols, Theodore E. *Tres puertos de Colombia: estudio sobre el desarrollo de Cartagena, Santa Marta y Barranquilla*. Biblioteca Banco Popular. Bogotá: Banco Popular, 1973.

Oberhelman, Harley D. *Gabriel García Márquez: A Study of the Short Fiction*. Twayne's Studies in Short Fiction 24. Boston MA: Twayne, 1991.

Ong, Walter. *Orality and Literacy: The Technologizing of the Word*. New Accents. London: Methuen, 1982.

Ortega, Julio. 'Exchange System in *One Hundred Years of Solitude*', in Ortega and Elliott, *Gabriel García Márquez*, 1–16.

——. 'La primera página de *Cien años de soledad*', in Hernández, *En el punto*, 137–49.

——. '*The Autumn of the Patriarch*: Text and Culture', in McMurray, *Critical Essays*, 168–87.

——. *El principio radical de lo nuevo: Postmodernidad, identidad y novela en América Latina*. Tierra Firme. Mexico City: Fondo de Cultura Económica, 1997.

—— and Claudia Elliott (eds). *Gabriel García Márquez and the Powers of Fiction*. Austin TX & London: University of Texas Press, 1988.

Oviedo, José Miguel. 'García Márquez: la novela como taumaturgia', *American Hispanist*, 1/ii (October 1975), 7.

Palencia Roth, Michael. *Gabriel García Márquez: La línea, el círculo y la metamorfosis del mito*. Biblioteca Románica Hispánica: Estudios y Ensayos 333. Madrid: Gredos, 1983.

——. 'Intertextualities: Three Metamorphoses of Myth in *The Autumn of the Patriarch*', in Ortega and Elliott, *Gabriel García Márquez*, 34–60.

Parkinson Zamora, Lois and Wendy B. Faris (eds). *Magical Realism: Theory, History*. Durham NC: Duke University Press, 1995.

Penuel, Arnold M. *Intertextuality in García Márquez*. York SC: Spanish Literature Publications Co., 1984.

Ploetz, Dagmar. *Gabriel García Márquez*. Monografías. Madrid: Edaf, 2004.

Rama, Ángel. *Los dictadores latinoamericanos*. Testimonos del Fonod 42. Mexico City: Fondo de Cultura Económica, 1976.

Rentería Mantilla, Alfonso (ed.). *García Márquez habla de García Márquez*. Bogotá: Rentería, 1979.

Rodríguez-Vergara, Isabel. *El mundo satírico de Gabriel García Márquez*. Pliegos de Ensayo 64. Madrid: Pliegos, 1991.

Rojas Herazo, Héctor. *Respirando el verano*. La Universidad Popular. Bogotá: El Faro, 1962.

Shaw, Donald. *Antonio Skármeta and the post Boom*. Puertas 88. Hanover NH: Norte, 1994.

——. *The Post-boom in Spanish American Fiction*. Latin American and Iberian Thought and Culture. Albany NY: New York State University Press, 1998.

Sklodowska, Elzbieta. *Testimonio hispanoamericano: Historia, teoría, poética*. New York: Peter Lang, 1992.

——. *La parodia en la nueva novela hispanoamericana (1960–1985)*. Purdue University Monographs in Romance Languages 34. Amsterdam: John Benjamins, 1991.

Valdés, María Elena de and Mario J. Valdés (eds). *Approaches to Teaching García Márquez's 'One Hundred Years of Solitude'*. Approaches to Teaching World Literature 31. New York: Modern Language Association of America, 1990.

Vargas Llosa, Mario. *García Márquez: Historia de un deicidio*. Caracas: Monte Ávila, 1971.

Williams, Raymond. *The Politics of Modernism*. London: Verso, 1989.

Williams, Raymond L. 'The Dynamic Structure of *El otoño del patriarca*', *Symposium*, 32/i (1978), 56–73.

——. *The Colombian Novel, 1844–1987*. London & Austin TX: University of Texas Press, 1991.

——. *The Postmodern Novel in Latin America: Politics, Culture, and the Crisis of Truth*. New York: St Martin's, 1995.

——. *The Writings of Carlos Fuentes*. Pan American Series. London & Austin TX: University of Texas Press, 1996.

——. *The Twentieth-century Spanish American Novel*. London & Austin TX: University of Texas Press, 2003.

—— and Kevin Guerrieri, *Culture and Customs of Colombia*. Culture and Customs of Latin America and the Caribbean. Westport CT: Greenwood, 1999.

Yurkiévich, Saúl. *Suma crítica*. Tierra Firme. Mexico City: Fondo de Cultura Económica, 1997.

# Index